MW00529192

Advance Praise for *Deeper Than Money*

"*Deeper Than Money* is an honest but compassionate guide to learning more about yourself and how to best handle your money. It's for everyone who has ever glanced at the business or money section in a bookstore and thought, 'Nope, that stuff is not for me.' Yes, yes, this is for you!"

—Erin Lowry, author of the Broke Millennial series

"The money book we needed this whole time!"

—Simran Kaur, author and founder of Girls That Invest

"If you have ever told yourself you're 'bad with money,' *Deeper Than Money* is required reading. Chloe cuts through the shame and anxiety so many of us feel about money and arms you with an actionable strategy to get out of debt, build wealth, and be happier while you do it!"

—Jeremy Schneider, CEO and founder of Personal Finance Club

DEEPER *than* MONEY

Ditch Money Shame, Build Wealth, and Feel Confident AF

CHLOE ELISE

A TarcherPerigee Book

an imprint of Penguin Random House LLC
penguinrandomhouse.com

Most TarcherPerigee books are available at special quantity discounts for bulk purchase for sales promotions, premiums, fundraising, and educational needs. Special books or book excerpts also can be created to fit specific needs. For details, write SpecialMarkets@ penguinrandomhouse.com.

Library of Congress Cataloging-in-Publication Data

Names: Elise, Chloe, author.
Title: Deeper than money: ditch money shame, build wealth, and feel confident AF / Chloe Elise.
Description: [New York, NY]: TarcherPerigee, [2023]
Identifiers: LCCN 2023020844 (print) | LCCN 2023020845 (ebook) | ISBN 9780593541050 (hardcover) | ISBN 9780593541067 (epub)
Subjects: LCSH: Women—Finance, Personal.
Classification: LCC HG179.E444 2023 (print) | LCC HG179 (ebook) | DDC 332.024—dc23/eng/20230616
LC record available at https://lccn.loc.gov/2023020844
LC ebook record available at https://lccn.loc.gov/2023020845

Printed in the United States of America
1st Printing

Book design by Patrice Sheridan

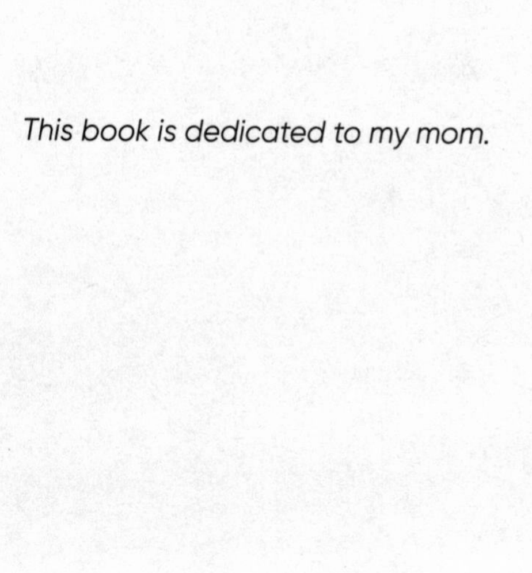

This book is dedicated to my mom.

Contents

Author's Note

In 2018, when I had the idea for my business, Deeper Than Money, and had just started planning it out, my mom helped me with editing some of the original documents used for clients. She then started to do some other administrative tasks for me (unpaid—just to help me out), and as my business grew, she picked up additional tasks. She was still working her ass off in her corporate job and working way more hours than she should have been, just like she had her whole life.

A few months into starting my business, we decided to visit a family friend's lake house (the same lake house I ended up buying five years later) for some relaxation. My mom and I were sitting on the deck drinking coffee when I told her one of my biggest dreams was to hire her full-time so we could hang out and she could finally relax. "Well, that sounds like a perfect dream for me, too," she responded. I had no idea that in July 2020, only two years later, I would make that dream a reality, and she would quit her job to come work for Deeper Than Money full-time.

My mom had been fearlessly battling cancer for four years at this point. In the fall of 2020, she was having more pain in her hands while doing certain tasks. I noticed with my business growing and many new tasks on my plate, we hadn't been talking on the phone or working together as frequently. I wanted to make sure her role focused on tasks she liked doing and was able to do comfortably. I asked what she wanted to be working on, and her response was "editing."

She'd always loved reading my blogs and editing them, but I wasn't writing much at the time. Shortly after our conversation, in August 2020, I sat down to write my list of 25 things I wanted to do while I was 25 years old (a tradition I have had since I was 13). It hit me: the perfect project for my mom and me to do together.

"Mom, I'm going to write a book. Are you in?" I could hear the pride in her voice on the other side of the phone. "Oh my gosh, that's so exciting—yes!" That night, I googled "how to get a book deal."

Ten months later, I had an agent and a book deal with a top publishing house. My mom and I spent hours upon hours making this dream come to life: I called her to brainstorm, she edited and sent the manuscript back, I rewrote, and more. Every single time she went to Target she would call me and say, "Someday I am going to walk into Target and yell to the whole store, 'This is MY daughter's book!'"

It still breaks my heart to write these words, but my mom passed away before seeing this book published or ever getting to walk into Target and pick it up off the shelves. Despite that, we worked so hard on this together, and she's here, on every page.

Moppy, you're the reason I wrote this book. You're the reason I am who I am today. Thank you for being the best mom in the world. Out of tens of thousands of words we've written together, I don't think I'll ever find ones powerful enough to describe how much I love you and how proud I am to be your daughter.

PART 1

Understanding Beliefs

CHAPTER 1

Deeper Than Money

Click. I hung up the phone with my travel agent. My head was spinning, but in the best kind of way. I had just dropped $10,000 in 15 minutes flat to book a last-minute trip to Europe. Being able to spend that money and have that amount of financial freedom was a monumental money win for me. I smiled as another, bigger win crossed my mind: silence. The two inner money dialogues that had plagued me my entire life were *silent*.

Money has always been represented by two voices in my head: The Bitch and The Hulk. At all times, with every swipe of my card, they were present.

Maybe these voices I'm talking about are familiar to you. The Bitch popped up every single time I spent money. She was constantly telling me I needed to justify every purchase I made. She would make me feel guilty for spending any money that could have gone toward paying off debt, or pass judgment on me when I bought anything "extra" for myself. She was the voice of

WTF are you doing? Who do you think you are, spending this money? You should be putting that money toward your student loans or your credit card debt. The Bitch was always nagging me and making me feel guilty for every purchase.

The other voice, The Hulk, would smash his way into my thoughts and convince me to forget all my previous goals, my commitments, or, let's be honest, my tax bracket and say, *Screw it. I deserve to treat myself,* or *I overspent anyway, so it doesn't matter if I splurge.* The Hulk was the voice that convinced me to completely shut down and give him ultimate control, resulting in me feeling like a completely different version of myself. These were times I'd disassociate from all the goals I originally had in place. I'd click on any buzzy social media advertisement and "add to cart" until I was able to hit the $150 mark to get free shipping. *I already spent $100, might as well spend $50 more to get free shipping.* The Hulk had an I-don't-care-I-want-it-now mentality with no regard for future outcomes and the second he got an inch, he took a mile, reminding me, *You already overspent, so why does it matter if you spend more?* The Hulk would turn a $7 coffee purchase into the start of the downward spiral of spending outrageous amounts of money because, as The Hulk would remind me, I was behind anyway, so I might as well impulsively spend until my paycheck was gone.

Those two voices would battle for ownership over every purchase I made. They both had me oozing with shame, and I was so out of whack with money that I felt at a complete loss. Even when I finally started making progress on my journey toward financial freedom, guilt and shame around money plagued me for years, negatively impacting my mental health and stopping me from achieving sustainable goals. Yes, I would make progress, but progress looked like taking one step forward and 20 steps back, and I felt like shit along the way.

But that's no longer my story. I've gone from being a broke 20-year-old college girl with more than $36,000 of debt to being on track to become a millionaire before I turn 28 years old.* I've learned not only how to quiet these voices, but also how to save, spend, and invest money without guilt, shame, and, most importantly, without giving up my lifestyle in my 20s.

If you're here, you probably know what it's like to feel a tinge of guilt no matter what it is you're spending money on. You're familiar with that overwhelming need to justify your spending. You, too, have this lurking sense that you're behind with money and a daunting feeling that it might always be that way. Couple those emotions with the low-key embarrassment from not totally understanding how to get ahead with money, and you've got yourself the perfect cocktail for staying stuck and struggling. The shame-filled approaches in the financial industry chew you up and spit you out, leaving you thinking there's something wrong with you, or that you're too dumb to be good with money, or maybe that you're just not working hard enough. This voice of financial instability is something that is so present in adults around the world that there have been numerous studies that show a link between mental health struggles and financial stress. The American Psychological Association's (APA) 2014 Stress in America survey says that 72% of American adults are stressed about money at least some of the time and 26% are stressed about it most or all of the time.[1] The financial approach of only looking at surface-level logistics leaves out huge parts of the conversation, like mental health.

Why does this old-school financial approach remind you of your toxic ex? They're both trash.

---

*I actually officially hit this goal of becoming a millionaire at 27 years old shortly after turning in my final manuscript, but the book was written prior to hitting this goal.

You're also likely feeling stuck with finances from a logistical standpoint. Maybe you're stuck in credit card debt and student loans, feeling like you're working way too hard to have as little as you do in savings. You agree that you have a lot of guilt or shame around money and know it's an issue, but you're thinking *I mean, sure, I'd love to just not feel guilty while spending, but how will that help me get ahead with money?*

It is time to introduce the new way of getting ahead with money: the Deeper Than Money approach.

The Deeper Than Money approach is an aligned approach—meaning I will teach you how to get ahead with money in a way that matches your goals and priorities—to help you implement a financial strategy while ditching shame so you can not only hit huge financial milestones, but also accomplish them guilt-free. This approach focuses on teaching you how to spend in alignment.

Spending in alignment is our holistic approach to using your money in a way that is emotionally, mentally, and logistically aligned with who you are today and who you want to become; it elevates your current and future life simultaneously. This approach will not only transform your day-to-day emotions around spending, freeing you from the two voices of The Bitch and The Hulk, but also will lead to you hitting more sustainable (and, therefore, faster) results like saving, paying off debt, or investing.

Older approaches rely on willpower to create an all-or-nothing mentality, a mindset that often creates vicious cycles of getting ahead and then falling behind. These approaches focus solely on restriction and shame-based principles, leading to frantic, all-over-the-place outcomes; strain on your mental health; and, frankly, super-inconsistent results that resemble this:

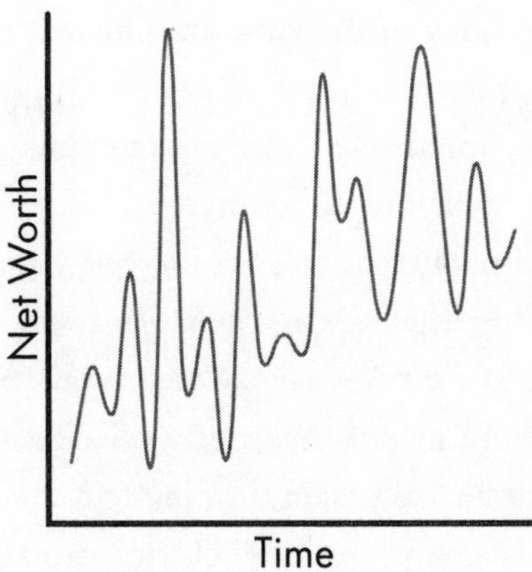

Instead of focusing on a restrictive, sacrifice-based curriculum, the Deeper Than Money approach focuses on getting sustainable results while still allowing you to enjoy life, complemented by strategies to make your money work hard for you. This approach leads to better, more maintainable results over time and still allows you to spend guilt-free, which looks something like this:

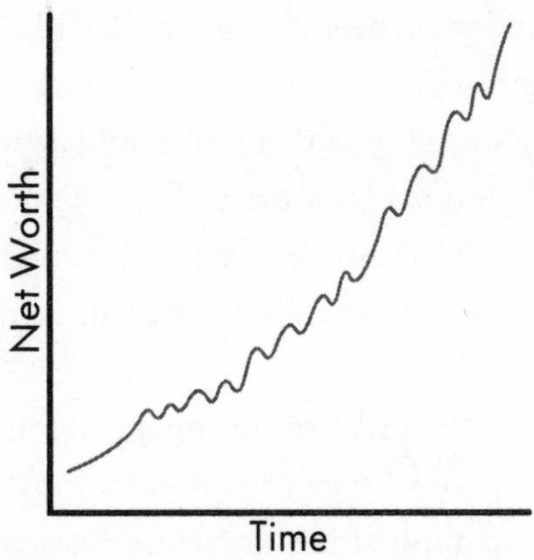

Instead of telling you to cut out your gym membership or your beloved $7 latte, I will give you the strategies you need to get ahead with money in the same amount of time without giving up things you love.

Let's say you are an iced coffee queen and love a fun little afternoon DCT (delicious coffee treat).

Traditional financial advice would tell you: skip your latte and give it up altogether. *Deprive yourself, asshole.*

But the truth is, for many people, depriving themselves doesn't lead to saving more money or paying off debt faster. In fact, it normally ends up hurting them, leading to a quick win and then huge setbacks. Have you ever tried cutting out all spending, only to say, "Screw it! I'll try again next month"? Restrictive spending techniques often lead to an all-or-nothing mentality that ends in a roller coaster of emotions and a lot of burnout. And even in the rare cases of deprivation leading to some money wins, the question becomes, at what cost? Skipping the coffee with friends? Missing the vacation? Not having clothes you feel confident in?

Deprivation actually hurts you: not only when it comes to your results, but also when it comes to the negative effects on your mental health and your overall mindset. It's likely to harm your quality of life, too.

I have an answer for you that is not only better than deprivation, it's also a hell of a better time.

For my skeptical babes out there, let me give you a quick example of a client who loved her coffee and didn't have to give it up to get ahead with money.

Meet Mackenzie, a real estate agent, dog mom, and vanilla sweet cream cold brew lover who wanted to pay off some debt without giving up a fun afternoon drink a couple times a week. She often went to coffee shops to work and get into a creative headspace, and she wanted to ensure she was supporting small businesses by purchasing coffee. Rather than me telling her, "Stop buying the cold brew, suck it up, and work from home instead," we implemented an aligned strategy to keep the cold brews coming while still allowing Mackenzie to save money, too. Right now, she's spending $7 per drink, 10 times a month, which was a $70 monthly expense. Once we understood her priorities, we sat down and looked at other areas of her life where we could implement some financial strategy. To give an example, *one* tiny piece of the strategy we implemented with Mackenzie was negotiating rent. We taught her how to successfully negotiate what she paid, which ended up saving her more than $150 a month. Now, instead of focusing on cutting out the things Mackenzie cared about, not only is she still getting her cold brews, but she has an extra $80 a month to put toward her goals. This is just one strategy I'll be teaching you in this book—how you can ditch deprivation and start spending in alignment. Yes, you can feel this good.

I won't tell you that you need to spend how I spend or dictate what you are allowed to spend your own hard-earned money on. I am going to teach you how to unlearn your *own* current self-sabotaging money patterns so you can create new patterns that aid in your wealth-building. This book will walk you through how to spend in alignment instead of purely trying to follow your restrictive budget that usually ends up in a *Screw it, I'll try next month* inner dialogue if you "mess it up."

When it comes to those inner dialogues of mine, I have worked to reach a place where, whether it's buying a decaf oat milk latte, paying rent, or booking a trip to Europe, my two toxic inner monologues are silent, and my feelings toward finances are more middle ground. When using the Deeper Than Money approach, money becomes more neutral in your life, allowing you to focus less on money itself and more on using it as a tool to focus on your priorities. The core mission is no longer a race to spend as little as possible but rather to align your spending with your goals while implementing financial strategies. That silence means no more stress, anxiety, or guilt around purchases, which allows you to spend money on enjoying your life now, while simultaneously building wealth for your future. Living and spending like this changed everything for me. Now it's time for you to create that same kind of confidence around money in your life.

DISCLAIMER: WE DO THINGS DIFFERENTLY AROUND HERE

This book is going to pick a fight with the finance industry and encourage you to test out a new way of living—one where spending isn't bad, shame isn't welcome, and each dollar that comes your way is used to elevate your life and get you closer to your goals and how you want to live. Believe it or not, the ticket to financial freedom doesn't have to come at the expense of giving up the things you love. I'm literally writing this chapter with a "forbidden" venti Starbucks vanilla latte in my hand, in my apartment that I rent instead of own. Oh, and I'm still going to be a millionaire before I turn 28.

And although you might be thinking, *Okay bitch, I get it. You have money and can spend it??? Cool????* I'm not telling you this because I want you to spend your money like I do. I'm telling you this because those examples are things that are big priorities for me in my life. It's perfectly okay if they aren't the same as your priorities.

This book isn't going to use a my-way-or-the-highway strategy to teach you how to spend your own hard-earned money.

This book is going to explain how to build financial confidence, understand the system, and use your *own* intuition and priorities to get ahead with money. This book is also not a fluff-filled mindset book preaching "Just spend a lot and trust that more money is coming to you." This book will give you proven strategies combined with deep inner work to create sustainable change so you leave with tangible, wealth-building, life-improving results.

This is the finance book that will finally make money feel fun and easy and prove to you that building wealth is, well . . . *Deeper Than Money.*

MONEY ISN'T ONE SIZE FITS ALL (OR EVEN ONE SIZE FITS MOST)

The standard advice that is supposedly the "right" way to manage money can bring about more confusion than clarity. That's because it doesn't honor the fact that we all have a unique set of circumstances. I get especially enraged when certain types of spending are praised while others are shamed, and generic metrics of "Save *X*% of your income" are used for people with completely different lives. Let me give an example.

Meet Katrina, a 28-year-old mom living in a city, raising two kids, and working a part-time job in addition to her full-time job. She spends pretty much every penny she makes on living expenses and is barely able to put anything into savings.

Meet Hallie, a 28-year-old single bachelorette living in the Midwest who makes the same amount as Katrina. Hallie, however, has super low expenses but loves to travel, shop, and go out with friends. She spends freely but still has extra money left over at the end of the month.

Let's say Katrina and Hallie both read an article telling them that in their 20s, they should be saving 20% of every paycheck.

Katrina might read the article and feel defeated based on her priorities, obligations, and current income.

Hallie might read the article and feel like she's already doing that, but even though she could do more, she only needs to do 20%.

The one-size-fits-all curriculum has got to go.

Furthermore, the way both Katrina and Hallie spend will likely be very different, and that's totally okay, too.

The reality is, when we stop making blanket statements about how money should be spent and instead focus on money being used in a way that supports two completely different people who have different priorities, we ditch the judgment and gain perspective on figuring out what we want.

This book is going to challenge your current morality policing around spending and money. It will encourage you to stop comparing your financial journey to what other people are doing and instead look inward to find your own alignment and priorities.

Finding alignment allows you to look past what you "should" and "shouldn't" do (as told by others) and instead look at your specific financial outcomes and decide what makes the most sense. As an example, I want you to think of things you classify as being "bad." Maybe it's drinking a bottle of wine alone on a Tuesday night, getting back with your musty ex, eating a package of Oreos for dinner, or scrolling on social media until 2 a.m.

I would argue that the things on this list are not inherently bad, although you might face undesirable outcomes based on those actions.

If you drink a bottle of wine on a Tuesday night, the outcome is likely a hangover.

If you get back with your crusty ex, the outcome might be more stress and frustration.

If you eat a package of Oreos for dinner, the outcome might be a stomachache.

If you scroll on social media until 2 a.m., the outcome might be eyestrain and being tired at work the next day.

What if you started looking at spending from a place of alignment and an outcome-based perspective instead of from a place of rules and restrictions?

Instead of saying, "I can't have Oreos," you instead say, "I absolutely can eat an entire package of Oreos for dinner. What is the outcome of eating them, and does that align with what I want or how I want to feel?"

Instead of saying, "I can't spend money on takeout," you say, "I absolutely can spend money on takeout. What is the outcome of spending that money, and does it align with what I want?" When you take shame out of the equation, you get to focus on the decision objectively and think about the outcome and how it aligns with you personally. Then you can dig deeper into what you'd need to shift in order to pay for takeout, how it might impact other goals, and whether you'd like to prioritize this purchase, so you're able to make a confident decision.

You can't truly change your financial outcomes until you stop relying on outdated, generalized advice and instead rebuild a solid foundation with money.

THE DEEPER THAN MONEY PROCESS

This book is going to walk you through six parts of holistically getting ahead with finances while knocking down the barriers standing in the way of you accomplishing your wildest financial goals. Here is the Deeper Than Money process:

1. Understanding beliefs

    Until you figure out what you believe to be true about money and dispel your outdated notions, the changes you make will only be at a habitual level—meaning a lot of solid money habits you implement will be short-lived, leading directly to self-sabotage. You will find yourself constantly frustrated that you've screwed up and feel stuck in a cycle of getting the same results with money. We are going to get to the root of these issues and help you decide what serves you and what doesn't.

2. Understanding yourself

    In order to understand how to spend money in alignment, you have to understand yourself: who you are and what you want for your life. We will discuss what spending in alignment looks like for you and your life.

3. Understanding money

    We will take a dive into what money truly is, the emotional charge behind it, and the role it has played in your life up to this point. We do this so you can change money's value in your life from a source of stress to a powerful tool to get you what you want.

4. Understanding spending

    Learning how to spend in alignment is far more important than learning how to stick to a budget. We will explore what this means, what it looks like, and how to implement it in your life. We also will discover what it means to lock in your "bajillionaire status," a term I use because it can represent whatever your money goals are rather than a specific number someone else assigns as a goal.

5. Understanding goals

   When you feel confident in your spending, it's time to make big strides toward what you want in life. By clearly defining your goals, you can craft a strategic plan for how you are going to get there.

6. Understanding boundaries

   Learning how to build wealth without also learning how to set boundaries to protect the wealth you're building can hinder your financial progress or lead to financial setbacks. We will not only talk through what personal and relational boundaries you can set in your life, but also discuss the super-sexy ways of tangibly protecting your wealth and advocating for yourself through negotiation, contracts (a prenup or a will, for example), and insurance.

We are going to get into all the juicy finance topics in this book, but the dilemma is that things are ever-changing and I am not allowed to reprint another copy and mail you an update every time there is a new type of account I would recommend or a new tutorial on how to open it. Because of this, I am giving you an incredible resource simply because you own this book. Go to deeperthanmoney.com/book to get a free resource guide with a ton of step-by-step trainings, tutorials, and updates. For example, in the book I will talk about a certain account to open and why it's so important, but in the resource guide, there's a specific video of me screensharing and showing you how to actually open it. Go and grab it now because it will be a superhelpful resource as we go along—and it's totally free for you with the purchase of this book!

Jeepers, am I happy you are here. Pull up a seat and join the party. This is the moment you draw a line in the sand and decide that you are going to get ahead with money. This is the moment you say to yourself, *Hmm, maybe I really should read this book. What if wealth building without guilt is possible for me?* No matter who you are, what's in your bank account, how much you know about money, or how old you are, I want to remind you that you are welcome here. You get to be the one who feels in control of her money, minus the guilt and stress in spending. And most importantly, you will use money as a tool to create financial freedom and build wealth without giving up the life you want now.

Buckle up, future bajillionaire. You're in for a wild ride.

CHAPTER 2

Broke Girl Problems

"Excuse me, miss. Your card was declined," the cashier at the local Hy-Vee grocery store said while she handed me my card back. "Do you have another card you'd like me to run?"

"Oh, shoot, this is my new card and I haven't activated it! My other card is in my car. I'll run out and grab it and be right back to pay for my groceries!" I responded kindly.

The only problem was that this was a fucking lie.

I walked out to my two-door, no-AC, no-radio Pontiac Sunfire that likely had the Check Engine light on and drove back to my college dorm, embarrassed and groceryless. I had zero intention of walking back into the store. I didn't have a second debit card, and I had no idea how to open a credit card. My debit card was declined because there was no money in my bank account. (Probably. I didn't have an online login set up to see how much was in it, so how the hell would I know?) When my card was declined, that would signal there was nothing left in my checking account. Or it meant I had already overspent and had at least one $35 overdraft fee. (Side note: the whole oh-she's-broke-let's-charge-her-for-that move from banks is dumb as hell.) The silliest part of this story is that this wasn't a onetime experience that changed my whole way of thinking. And this wasn't the moment when I decided to get ahead with money. This debit card roulette was kind of a regular thing. Oops.

Introducing Broke College Girl Chloe (BCG Chloe)!! She's a good time, but before I can tell you about her, let's back it up a hot minute. I want to demonstrate my "money story" for you so you can start thinking through your own money story. (We are going to get into why this is so important in the next chapter.) First, let's start with my childhood.

BABY CHLOE

I grew up in small-town Iowa. I was raised in a loving, two-parent household with an older sister and a younger brother. When it came to money, I knew three things for certain:

1. Money is something you do not talk about.
2. Money is something you have to work really, really hard for just to get by.
3. Money is extremely stressful.

When I understood what money was, I became super curious. I would ask my parents things like, "How much does that cost?" after they bought groceries, or, "How much money do you make?" to which my parents would respond by telling me that's rude to ask. (A super-common mentality for my parents' generation and still true for a lot of people today.) I knew money was stressful from the way my mom tensed when it was brought up in conversation. I knew money was tight when I'd ask why my friends would get money for things that I couldn't (like, if I asked for $20 to go to the mall) and how that often resulted in my parents instilling the important "You gotta work really, really hard" lesson.

I never received an allowance for doing chores or money for getting good grades, but I did run that town with lemonade stands, counting the money I earned by selling lemonade and cookies. This made me feel drunk with power. (Well, I was a kid, so maybe it was a sugar high?!) I realized I could take my lemonade-stand earnings and go buy the things I wanted: the things my parents wouldn't buy me. Let me tell you, I was shocked. Astonished. In awe. Up to this point, most things were out of my control. I mean, I was six years old. Now I could take my earnings and go buy the toy at Walmart I wanted without having to hear my parents tell me no. I was hooked.

And in that moment, the princess of hard work was born. It would have been cooler to become the princess of Genovia that day, but that unfortunately wasn't in the cards for me.

TEENAGER CHLOE

From there, working hard became a shining personality trait of mine. As I got older, it became clear that a 14-year-old selling lemonade on the curb was just kind of a thirsty move. (No pun intended.) Plus, it wasn't paying the bills (and by paying the bills, I mean buying the Hollister graphic tee I so desperately needed). So ya girl started working in more age-appropriate ways.

I used my earnings to look cool and buy things other people thought were cool. No longer would I be embarrassed by friends who called me out for having the off-brand notebook. I spent money to go see movies. I spent a lot on gas driving to my jobs and seeing friends. I spent money buying clothes at Plato's Closet. (They were secondhand, but to me, as long as they weren't my sister's hand-me-downs, they were gold.) I spent money at the mall on anything I thought could make me look cooler. However, over time I began to feel like a hamster on a running wheel. I was constantly working to "out-earn" my lack of financial literacy. I would run out of money, then I'd want to buy something, so I would pick up extra hours babysitting. I'd make enough to cover the thing I wanted and then the money would be gone. Then I'd work more. I was working my ass off for money, but money was not working hard for me.

I had learned how to make money. I just had no clue how to keep any of it.

Fast-forward to the spring before I left for college. I knew I wanted to go to college, in a because-that's-what-everyone-around-me-did sort of way. (We will talk about the privilege behind this in Chapter 9.) All my friends were going to college, and my parents had gone to college, so I figured that's just what I had to do. I went on zero college visits and kept procrastinating the impending decision until I visited my sister, who was a junior at a small liberal arts school in Iowa about three hours away from home. I figured if she liked it, then hopefully I would as well. I decided to go there, too. Just. Like. That.

I sealed the deal in the college admissions office, receiving a "decision made" shirt. Suddenly, I had committed to the biggest financial decision of my life up to that point. I knew absolutely *nothing* about debt. Honestly, I didn't even understand what debt was or how it worked, let alone the daunting world of student loans. I had just heard that it was something you had to have to go to college, so I said *~kewl~* and rolled along with it. When it was time to actually move in, I arrived on campus early because I was on the golf team and we had to practice before the school year started, allowing us summer housing. (No, you don't get scholarship money for playing Division III golf.) When we finished unpacking my dorm room, my mom and dad told me we needed to walk over to the admissions office and sign the financial aid paperwork. *Ewww.*

"Do I have to go?" I asked in a Mom-can-you-still-call-the-dentist-for-me type of way.

"Yes. These are *your* loans," she patiently replied.

Ugh, but what if I don't care? I thought to myself.

As we waited in the admissions office, I pleaded with my mom. "Please, do I have to go in there? I don't want to talk about my loans with them. That's embarrassing."

"I mean, you can wait out here while I talk to them but then you'll still have to sign it. The loans are in your name," she responded. I waited out in the hallway, and when the doors opened again, I reluctantly walked in. The financial aid officer showed me where to sign while explaining the parts of the loan to me. She seemed eager to get the paperwork done.

"So here are your loan totals," she said as I skimmed past any important info. I scribbled a half-assed signature and stood up.

Yes, the money expert who is about to teach you how to get ahead with money signed every single loan document without even knowing an estimation of how much debt she would be in after college. You still ready to party? Cool, let's keep rolling.

I had just borrowed tens of thousands of dollars as a 17-year-old, with *no* idea how much debt I would end up in. Honestly, I don't think I could've ballparked it for you. Legally, I was not allowed to buy a beer for four more years, but I could take out tens of thousands of dollars in debt without even understanding what that meant. Thank the good Lord I learned how to knit in my home economics class instead of learning basic finance!

I walked back to my college dorm. This is where we meet BCG Chloe again.

BROKE COLLEGE GIRL CHLOE

From a money perspective, my first three years of college looked incredibly similar to my high school experience, except now I had bills and had to pay for food and drinks.

I was this kind of broke:

- Joined any college club that offered free pizza night
- Borrowed my friend's car if I had to leave campus and would never put gas in it (sorry, Mickey)
- Drank Mad Dog (MD 20/20) alcohol, which I can only describe to you as flavored nail polish remover (I think if I smelled a bottle of it now, I would get a three-day hangover)
- Stuffed my backpack full of food from the dining hall because my meal plan only covered a few days a week
- Snuck alcohol into bars so I wouldn't have to buy a drink
- Donated plasma to pay some of my tuition

The week before finals in my second semester of junior year, my heart got ripped out. One morning, after a night out on a party bus, my boyfriend and I were nursing ungodly hangovers when I received a text from my best friend saying she needed to come over that instant. She arrived at my place and told me that my boyfriend, the boy who I genuinely believed was the one for me, had been consistently cheating on me. And honestly, it wrecked me. We had been dating a few years, which in puppy-love years is like a century. He was the center of my universe, and it felt like my entire identity had been shattered. I spent the next month drinking heavily, barely eating, and overall hating myself. I had thoroughly convinced myself that I was cheated on because I wasn't pretty enough, skinny enough, or cool enough. And on top of that, I felt unbelievably out of control. If I had convinced myself that this boy was my whole future, then what the hell did my future even look like?

After I had picked up the very last of the streamers from my monthlong pity party, I decided it was time to actually try to heal. I opened a journal, and on a whim, I started writing about the future I wanted and the girl I wanted to become. Not to get my ex-boyfriend back, not to prove a point, but to create a dream life that revolved around me and not around that boy, or any boy, for that matter. And although I've always been a dreamer, this might have been the first time I really envisioned who I wanted to become. It was the first time I started dreaming of the life I wanted to create for myself (boys optional). I wrote it all out: *I want to become confident. I want to feel strong. I want to stop feeling stressed. I want to feel peace. I want to feel hot. I want to be independent.* The list went on. I had no idea at the time that the next thing I wrote down would change the entire trajectory of my life.

I wrote on a second sheet of paper in my notebook:

What are things I have to do to become the girl I want to be?

And as the first thing on that list, I wrote:

Figure out money.

It was followed by a hefty list of other things like *Learn how to lift weights, Get a new wardrobe, Find a therapist*, etc.

Looking back, I truly believe it was God/the universe/energy laying His hands on me and saying, "Here's a nudge of intuition. Follow it." I believe that's what it was, because I have absolutely no clue what got into me. And boy, did something get into me.*

I woke up the following morning, and instead of crying all day, I worked on my list. After a loving nudge from God/the universe, I sat at my computer and googled "how to get ahead with money." As I scrolled, I kept seeing new words and financial jargon I didn't know. *Welp, that wasn't helpful.* On my next attempt, I headed off to the library and looked through every finance book I could find. I was determined to figure out money, get ahead, and create my happy dream life.

. . . Except for the fact that learning about finances was boring as hell—full of the boring voices of boring old men.

Immediately I thought, *Who in their right mind could read this archaic information, find it interesting, and actually have it help them?!*

Not to mention all the advice was directed toward 50-year-olds handling mortgages and life insurance, while I was just trying to figure out how to budget to buy something other than a Four Loko to drink that weekend.

Much of what I read was a snoozefest and largely irrelevant to me. All of it was rooted in restriction and shame—making me feel like I was even more behind when it came to money. The glaring message I got was, "You're an idiot. Just try harder and

---

*I'm not going to spend time making this PC. Some will get mad if I say "the universe"; others will get mad if I say "God." Whatever higher power you believe in, you can sub that in for yourself. To me, it's all one beautiful, powerful source, and I personally say "God."

spend less." I put my head down and tried to follow the rules in the books I read, because it was the only plan I had.

I went to work, started saving my moola, and eventually I started seeing results. I was taking BCG Chloe to a whole new level. Any "fun" I'd been allowing myself to have before (trips, going out, new clothes) was now scrutinized by my newly adopted lifestyle. Picture this: The Bitch and The Hulk on either shoulder, whispering in my ear. The Hulk would say, *C'mon Chloe, screw the budget and order a fun drink at dinner like the rest of your friends!* The Bitch would counter, *Twelve dollars for one cocktail?! When you could be putting that toward debt? Hell no.*

Most of the time, The Bitch won. I would say no and cancel plans just to avoid spending money.

So yeah, on paper I was starting to "get ahead." But at what cost?

I was miserable. I was saving money and getting results, but I was missing out on so much. I said no to everything and felt massive guilt when I did say yes. Even the $4 can of Four Loko was too expensive. According to the accepted advice, if I really wanted to get ahead with money, I should give it all up. So I would spend absolutely nothing . . . until I would eventually crack and go batshit crazy, buying anything and everything. Then I would feel terrible that I had messed up so badly and decide I now had to be even more restrictive to make up for falling behind.

After months of saving, I finally had enough money in a savings account to act as an emergency fund. And now that I had an emergency fund, it was time to pay off debt. I was bright-eyed, bushy-tailed, and ready to tackle my loans. The first step was figuring out how much debt I was actually in.

My car had broken down so I had bought a new car with a

$10,000 auto loan. And honestly, $10,000 didn't seem real to me. It sounded like such an insane amount of money that I couldn't totally wrap my head around it, so I tried to compartmentalize and ignore it.

I knew my student loans couldn't be nearly as much as my auto loan. There's no way. Going to school versus having an actual car? Not a chance. I was estimating $1,000 or less in student loans to add to my auto-loan debt.

Are you feeling the buildup toward an impending reckoning? Perfect.

One day, while working in the mailroom (my college work-study), I decided I needed to figure out how much student loan debt I actually had. I had some free time, so I called my mom to ask her where I would even find my loan information. She told me to log in to my online account. "Okay, but, like, what online account?" I barked back. She was shocked that I had never set up the online account. I was shocked that setting up an account was even a thing! She walked me through how to set up an account. (A boomer teaching *me* how to set up an online account??) I registered, created a login, and was on a roll. Then—*holy fuck.* "Mom, I gotta go." *Click.*

I hung up the phone, shut off the computer, and told the other student working in the mailroom that I had to go to the bathroom. I ran down the hall to the bathroom, looked under the stalls to be sure no one else was in there, and started sobbing. Just over $26,000. That brought my total debt to more than $36,000. I opened my phone calculator and typed in $36,000 ÷ $7.25 (how much I was making per hour at the mailroom). I would have to work 4,965 hours at minimum wage to pay off my debt (and that wasn't even factoring in taxes, either). I stared straight down at the ground so my tears wouldn't make my $7.99

mascara (which was a splurge) run down my face, knowing I had to quickly pull it together and walk back to the mailroom like nothing was wrong.

I had to be fine. Or at least act like it, right? Money wasn't something you talked about, remember? All that shame, fear, hopelessness, sadness, and embarrassment I felt looking at those numbers sat with me in silence, alone. And they convinced me I was the exception. I was the one who all the financial advice would never work for. I was the broke girl. That was my identity. It was what I believed. It was who I was.

To me (again, making minimum wage), that $36,000 of debt felt like an impossible feat. I felt stupid for even thinking I could try to pay it off. That number could have been $10,000 or $80,000, and it still would have destroyed me. It wasn't the number; it was what it represented: Getting ahead with money wasn't for me. I was the broke girl.

I'd be lying if I told you I didn't have another pity party for a few days. Hell, maybe even a week. But I eventually decided I was going to figure this out. There had to be another way.

I had already tried opening and learning from the crusty old books at the library, so now it was time for plan B. I needed to find financial education that wasn't just preaching and jargon. I spent the next 18 months absorbing everything about financial literacy I could find. I took courses, listened to podcasts, read books, and bought seminars. I even signed up for what eventually became my first financial coaching certification, solely because I wanted to take another program to be able to understand money for myself. In all my learning and digging in the financial-literacy world, I found that although there was endless information and advice, none of it was suited for a woman in her young adult life, wanting to get ahead without sacrificing the things she loves.

I couldn't find an ideology I could align with, so I decided to create one myself. By picking up this book, you're living proof that this ideology has come to fruition.

It took me 18 months to pay off my $36,000 of debt and officially become debt-free. (More on the actual strategy behind this to come.) There were bumps in this journey, like my car needing repairs or my boyfriend at the time stealing and draining my $8,000 emergency fund (more on how to protect yourself financially in Chapter 17), but nonetheless I paid off $36,000 in 18 months, and I was just warming up. I then saved eight months of expenses in an emergency fund, bought my parents a car for Christmas, started investing, and even bought my dream lake house. In addition to getting financial results, I truly began living my dream life. Other people saw this and wanted to learn how I was able to go from BCG Chloe to where I am now.

My current goal is to become a millionaire before I turn 28 years old. I went from a broke college girl at 20 years old to an almost-millionaire at 26 years old. And you can, too! If you just do this one tiny thing . . .

Psych. Hate to do it to you, but that one-liner fucking blows.

The truth is, you can become a millionaire. You can buy the dream house. You can do whatever the hell it is you want to do.

But it won't look like my story. It won't be that same path. It will be on an entirely different timeline. Maybe faster, maybe slower, but most definitely different. Each story is different. And that's a thousand percent okay. I told you my story so you know some of my background before we embark on this journey together. But the truth is, my story doesn't matter now. Yours does.

You don't need to know exactly how you're going to accomplish your goals or dreams yet, but you can start asking yourself the question, *What if I became the wealthy girl?*

The girl who not only always has enough money, but who always has extra. Who forgets when payday is because she never has to live paycheck to paycheck. The girl who takes the trip, buys the new outfit, and lives how she pleases, while also investing in her future self. The girl who never has to worry about money and who uses money as a tool to build her wealth and live her dream life. Go on. Write down what would happen if you became the wealthy girl:

____

____

____

____

I want you to start claiming "wealthy" as your new identity so you can look at the differences between old and new identities with money. Only then can you truly begin to embody claiming wealth.

What are your current feelings about money?

____

____

____

Now we are going to kick off the book with the first few tangible steps you can take toward becoming the wealthy girl.

THE STARTER KIT

The starter kit consists of the very first things you need to get ahead with money.

An FDIC-Insured Checking Account with a Linked Debit Card (with No Monthly Fees)

I don't care if you bank at a big corporate bank, a local community bank, or a credit union. I do, however, need you to be sure you have a checking account with a debit card for which you do not pay any monthly fees. Many online-only banks have been shifting to the fee-free side, but many of the bigger chain banks charge monthly account maintenance fees. A no-fee account is huge because those monthly fees add up. I have many clients who have two or three checking accounts, and prior to working with me, they paid a $15 monthly fee per account. That is $540 per year. Let's say you are 25 years old and plan to have a checking account until you are 70. That is 45 years. So 45 years × $540 per year in fees = $24,300 worth of fees in your lifetime. Phew. I don't know about you, but I'd rather have those dollars invested and making me money!

So if you have a bank account with fees, what can you do? Believe it or not, it may be as simple as calling or swinging by your local branch to request to switch to a basic account with no monthly fees, or finding a new bank that will provide that. (I promise they exist.) Many banks automatically give you their middle-of-the-road account that comes with fees, so always specifically ask for a no-fee checking account.

The same goes for insufficient funds and overdraft fees. (Yes, there are accounts that don't charge those.) If you are ever charged an overdraft fee, immediately call your bank, explain what happened, and ask politely if they would refund you.

You can research no-fee checking accounts through a simple Google search, but I recommend always calling or going in person and asking to double-check that you are opening a checking account with no fees. It's also important to check if there are any minimum deposits, transfers, or minimum balance requirements for the account that need to happen in order to not accrue fees. Banks are in the business of making money, so it's not uncommon for them to make you jump through quite a few hoops to get the "best deal." Do not be afraid to have your banker walk you through what this looks like. Websites like nerdwallet.com can be a helpful resource to look at all your available options.

A Debit Card

A debit card is a key part of the starter kit. Even if you're team credit card for everything, having a debit card is essential. First, plenty of places don't accept credit or may even charge an additional processing fee for credit purchases. If you don't have cash, your debit card could be a lifesaver! A debit card also can be a helpful tool for tracking your spending with no interest charges, which comes in handy, especially if you are trying to pay off credit card debt and want to be as efficient as possible. A debit card is a perfect starting point for mastering spending in alignment before adding a credit card to the mix.

A Regular FDIC-Insured Savings Account (with No Monthly Fees)

You can often set up a savings account at the same bank as your checking account. You won't be keeping a ton of money in here, because while your money sits in a normal basic savings account at your bank, it usually isn't paying you much money in interest. You might get a dime back every year in interest. The purpose of this savings account is for you to have an account separate from your checking to tap into if you need to get your hands on cash in a last-minute emergency scenario. I like to recommend keeping about $1,000 in your regular savings account. This is enough so that if your car broke down, for example, you'd be able to grab that cash and pay for it instantly—but not so much that you have a lot of money sitting in an account making you a measly dime per year.

However, there are some exceptions that would exclude you from needing a regular savings account:

- If your regular bank offers a high-yield savings account (HYSA; we will talk about that next), you can skip having a regular savings account and use your HYSA instead. If your bank doesn't offer a HYSA, or it doesn't have a great interest rate, I recommend you open a HYSA elsewhere. When your checking account and your HYSA aren't at the same bank, transaction delays from one bank to the other could mean you have to wait a few days before you can withdraw your money (if you transfer from your HYSA to your checking account). So if you think you'll need extra money in a pinch, having a little chunk waiting at your current bank in a regular savings account for an immediate transfer can provide some peace of mind. If the delay wouldn't impact you and you could still cover an emergency expense prior to the transfer hitting your checking account, then you could pass on a regular savings account.
- If you are a cash-flow queen and could easily cover a $1,000 or less emergency with the cash flow from your paycheck at a moment's notice.
- If you are a no-credit-card-debt-but-always-uses-credit-cards hunny and would prefer putting a $1,000 emergency

on your credit card to pay off after you transfer money from your HYSA.

A High-Yield Savings Account (HYSA)

Think of HYSAs like your fav Starbucks drink. Sometimes your latte might be hit or miss (too much almond milk, not enough white mocha), but it's always better than plain ol' coffee at home, right? Same goes for HYSAs. HYSAs are not where you are going to build long-term wealth. However, if you are saving up for something *or* deciding where to keep your emergency fund (more on this later), the HYSA is the way to go. Your HYSA is where you keep your wealth-*protecting* money, not your wealth-*building* money (also more on this later). The interest on a HYSA varies based on what is going on in the market (how the economy is doing, along with decisions from the Federal Reserve—the Queen Bee bank of the United States—which sets interest rates).

Even when rates are super low (less than 1%), they are still far better than what you'd see on your regular savings account, which is usually more like 0.01% or 0.05%. My rule of thumb is that anything over the $1,000 to $1,500 range should go into a HYSA.

Lots of different places offer HYSAs, so you can pick the one that works best for you. If you're nervous about opening one and need guidance, inside the free mini course you get with this book, I screenshare my computer and show you how to do it at deeperthanmoney.com/book. Even if you don't have $1,000 saved in your regular checking yet, you can still open a HYSA now just by putting $10 in it so it is ready for you when you have the moola.

Mobile Banking for All Accounts

This is a simple one, but be sure you have all the apps needed to log in to all your accounts: checking, savings, high-yield savings, and any other mobile banking accounts you may have. You want easy access to be able to see what is going on in your accounts. But take a page from your scheming ex's book, and be sure those apps and your phone stay password protected! In fact, ensure the passcodes are all different! You don't want a stranger to be able to swipe your phone and get into your bank accounts.

A Credit Karma Account

There are mixed reviews about creating a Credit Karma account, and although there are ways to check your credit outside of Credit Karma, I do like how user-friendly and educational it is. Many of my beginner clients love it and have used it to gain a deeper understanding of their credit and how it works. (We will talk more about credit in Chapter 9.) A big money myth is that checking your credit score or report will actually hurt your score. This is false. Keeping tabs on your *own* credit score and report never hurts you.

It's important to note that Credit Karma gives you an estimate and not an exact score. I still enjoy it for its user-friendly workflows and because it gives me a good idea of where my credit is. (Several credit card companies or online banks also will show you your FICO credit score online, as a free perk.) Even though Credit Karma is a business that gets paid for recommending cards and other financial products to you, it still is an educational platform that makes it easy to start understanding how your decisions are impacting your credit score.

Logins for All Accounts

Be sure you know about all your accounts and have the ability to log in and access them. When we dive into all that info, it'll be easier if you have it all in one place.

Recap of the Starter Kit

- ☐ A checking account with a linked debit card (with no monthly fees)
- ☐ A debit card
- ☐ A regular savings account (with no monthly fees)
- ☐ A high-yield savings account (HYSA)
- ☐ Mobile banking for all accounts
- ☐ A Credit Karma account
- ☐ Logins for all accounts

Now that you have your starter kit covered, you are equipped to dive deeper into your financial background.

CHAPTER 3

Ancestral Bullshit

I had been taking lukewarm showers for the past three years without complaint (and by "without complaint," I mean I brought it up and ranted about it anytime there was a casual segue in conversation). Whenever I had friends visit, I warned them that if we all need to shower, everyone has to shower quickly because the lukewarm water would turn to cold after 15 minutes. This may not bother some people, but if given the option, I prefer my shower water to err on the side of scalding. But for three years, I showered in just-above-room-temp water.

Fast-forward to present day, when recently my bathroom cabinet hinge snapped in half. You'd think that's kind of the point of hinges, but she must have bent and snapped a little too hard that fateful day and totally broke. Now, one of the lovely parts of renting versus buying is having less responsibility for the labor or cost of home repairs. When my cabinet hinge snapped, I immediately picked up my phone and submitted a work order on my apartment's app. Before I could say "cold showers," I heard a knock at my door and someone from the maintenance staff was already there to fix it. I happened to be working from home that morning and started chatting with him. He asked if there was anything else I needed fixed while he was there. I laughed and made the sarcastic comment, "If only you could fix the water temperature in my shower!!"

"Sure! No problem. I can take care of that in a second," he nonchalantly replied.

Come again, sir? What! I couldn't believe it.

Then it hit me.

I couldn't believe he could fix that for me because I had absolutely no idea that was possible. I had just accepted that it was something I had to live with. I didn't spend my time dreaming up ideas of how my shower water could get hotter. No! In fact, I spent my time complaining about a situation I believed was permanent and unfixable. In reality, the problem was both changeable and solvable, and now I take steamy showers every day.

The moral of the story: when you believe that something "is the way it is," your brain will naturally *not* look for ways to change it. Whether that belief or assumption is something as silly as how hot your shower is or as big as how much wealth you think you can build, it is that belief about what is impossible that limits growth. Understanding your beliefs around money *and where those beliefs came from* is a crucial first step in looking deeper to see how the things you have always "known to be true about money" might actually be keeping you stuck in your current financial situation.

Bear with me, because in this chapter, I am going to challenge you to question some of the most basic things you've been taught about money and have lived by because it's the only thing you've ever known.

Learning (or shall I say *unlearning*) the principles in this chapter has sent me into a few minor existential crises, so get ready to dive in and maybe learn a few things that might have you questioning your whole existence.

Pre-Existential Crisis Homework

1. Have you ever felt like there are cycles in your family that have been passed down and repeated that you don't want to repeat? What are they?

   ____
   ____
   ____
   ____
   ____

   Example: You always see your dad blowing up and getting angry at any inconvenience. You watch the same cycle repeat in your older brother, and you don't want it to repeat in you. (Did I just get this reference from binge-watching *One Tree Hill*? Maybe?)

2. Have you ever felt like there are things you know you *should* do but always procrastinate or keep yourself from doing? What are some examples?

   ____
   ____
   ____
   ____
   ____

   Example: You know that your credit card debt is growing and that on your next paycheck you want to use the money to pay it off. But when payday comes, you think of other things to spend it on instead. You tell yourself you want to wait in case something comes up and then end up having nothing left over to pay off the debt. Then you feel guilty and know the credit card debt is growing and wait for the following paycheck . . . only to repeat the cycle.

3. Have you ever had someone question the way you do things and been downright offended? What does that look like?

____

____

____

____

____

Example: One time I caught my roommate in college throwing away my stack of hundreds of plastic grocery bags that I had stashed under our kitchen sink.* I was furious at her. I needed to save those!!! *"For what?"* she immediately responded. This caught me so incredibly off guard because I had instinctively saved every one of my grocery bags after watching my mom do it for so many years as I was growing up. These were to be reused and even repurposed should the need arise. My roommate questioning the reason for my stash of hundreds of bags

*Yes, I was a naive little nonenvironmentalist in my early years. I promise that now my car and home are both fully stocked with reusable bags and totes to make up for my elephant foot of a carbon footprint from back in the day.

> had me spiraling because I really had no defense for this practice other than it was done out of habit. The anger I felt from her throwing them away hit upon a deep-seated scarcity issue I didn't even know I had at the time.

It can be eye-opening in a haha-I-didn't-realize-I-did-that-just-because-that's-how-I-grew-up sort of way, but as we dive into more emotionally charged categories, it can start to feel daunting. For example, maybe your parental figures passed on the belief of feeling constant guilt around money. Maybe they passed on the belief that you can use money to hold power over others. Maybe your parental figures passed on the belief that money ruins relationships or marriages.

It can start to feel a little heavy digging into the negative beliefs your parents passed down, but here's the good news: there's nothing wrong with you if you relate to any of this. And going forward: the buck stops here.

The bottom line is that you likely were taught rules about money that are the very obstacles (among other roadblocks) preventing you from changing your current financial situation.

So now, I want you to grab your favorite cocktail/mocktail glass and create the perfect concoction: Cycle Breaker Tonic.

Recipe for a Cycle Breaker Tonic

-1 cup of acceptance of where you are today, even if there were obstacles, oppression, curveballs, tragedy, tough times, or anything else in your way

-1 cup of forgiveness to the people who gave you your current set of beliefs—they did the best they could with what they had, and you agree to not hold grudges against them in this process

-1 cup of radical responsibility to acknowledge that, despite not having the same opportunities, privileges, or circumstances as others, and despite the external influences that have factored into where you are, you feel excited that you have the power to change where you are going

It can be hard to take a look back at your childhood or family dynamic through the eyes of a grown-ass adult instead of through the rose-colored glasses that you might have looked through in your childhood. It takes equal parts forgiveness, acceptance, and radical responsibility to believe that you're capable of changing where you are (while again, still knowing it's not your "fault" that you might have been dealt a tough hand).

Maybe you're in a cycle of living paycheck to paycheck.

Maybe you're in a cycle of overspending, feeling guilty, and overspending again.

Maybe you're in a cycle of feeling stress about money.

Whatever the cycle may be, know this:

You are going to be the cycle breaker. You are going to be the one who heals trauma, dreams bigger, opens your mind and your heart, and, therefore, changes the trajectory of what was statistically going to be your financial outcome. If it feels heavy, cool. It's heavy because it's fucking powerful work.

But anytime this gets heavy, I want you to place your hand over your heart and remember that when it comes to cycles running through your family, "It ran in my family until it ran into me."

The cycle stops here.

We want to be able to have grace for those who raised us and came before us, because they did the best they could with the resources they had, and just because they didn't heal *all* their passed-down trauma doesn't mean they didn't heal some of it. Changing their past cycles likely seemed difficult as well. In fact, it's actually human nature not to change.

Thousands of years ago, a caveman's brain had one main job: keeping him alive. And the easiest way his brain could keep him safe was to keep him doing the same tasks.[1] Similar means safe, because it's predictable. And if things were predictable, his brain knew from past experiences that he would be safe doing that thing. However, unfamiliarity could mean danger; a new climate, a new predator, a new cliff to fall off. So his brain was wired to send him fearful signals when in new places to warn him that the unknown was scary and that his brain didn't have enough data to know if it was safe.

Fast-forward to you sitting at brunch with a mimosa in your hand. Is the unknown of the server asking you on a date later that night the same level of danger as a caveman venturing out and falling off a cliff? Depends how hot the server is. Kidding. It's not the same type of danger, but our inner caveman brains are naturally wired to seek safety rather than explore new opportunities and push boundaries. When stress is added to the mix, we tend to double down on avoiding new experiences and stick to our comfort zone.[2]

You can thank your sweet baby caveman brain for working to keep you safe, but you can simultaneously work to distinguish real pings of fear from your brain not wanting you to take any risks or try something new. By doing so, you get to take radical responsibility for the choice to change your path, go outside your comfort zone, heal your past, and create a completely new future based on your own free will.*

It's about to get spicy. Let's ride.

In small-town Iowa, where I grew up, someone somewhere decided that children should get a driver's permit at 14 years old. Fourteen. Years. Old. Operating a vehicle. However, from 14 to 16 years old, you could only drive with a parent in the car, or to and from school by yourself. You could not drive alone with friends until 16. But whew, did I covet that day when I would be free and able to drive with my besties anywhere, no adults to be seen.

By the time I finally did get that real-life-drive-without-Mom-or-Dad license, I was ecstatic. It had been (in my dramatic teenage eyes) forever with my parents in the car and hearing them comment on every single little piece of my driving.

Finally, I was an expert in driving. Finally, I had my full license.

A few short days after turning 16, I picked up one of my best friends. It was 2011, and the only TikTok we had ever heard of was a hit Ke$ha song blaring through the aux cord that was connected to my iPod shuffle. (Ewww, I'm old.) Next up was "Ridin' Solo" by Jason Derulo, and we were sing-screaming it as I pulled up to a four-way stop. Pulling up simultaneously to my right was a police officer.

"Shit!!!!" I yanked the aux cord out of the radio, leaving

*It's important when we talk about radical responsibility that we also are acknowledging privilege and its impact on people's abilities to change their current outcomes. We will dive more into this in Chapter 9, but I want to continue to acknowledge that this will look different for everyone.

immediate silence in the car, threw my hands to 10 and 2 on the steering wheel, and waited at the stop sign for the cop to go through while I held my breath.

We drove through the intersection, and I kept turning my head back to see if the cop was going to whip a U-turn to come back for me, lights flashing.

My best friend looked over at me, confused. "You know listening to music isn't illegal, right?"

"Right," I said, dumbfounded.

Now, when she said that to me out loud, it sounded like the dumbest thing I had ever heard. But all I knew is that I had spent the last two years driving with my parents (especially my worry-prone mama), and anytime I tried to even touch the radio, my mom acted like I was running a red light into a busy intersection. I knew "real adults" could drive while listening to music, but without consciously realizing it, I had internalized the idea that listening to music while driving as a 16-year-old (never mind doing it at blow-the-speakers-out volumes) was a very, very, very bad thing. When I saw the police car, I impulsively reacted by shutting off the music so I wouldn't get in trouble.

My mom had never explicitly told me blasting music was illegal, but I had still made up an entire belief based on her body language, energy, and overall fearful reaction to it. My silly little underdeveloped brain looked to my mom's beliefs, actions, and words to help me decipher the truth of how to live. My parents' core beliefs, actions (or reactions), and words subconsciously melted into my sponge of a brain, leaving me trying to grasp what-the-literal-hell was going on at any given time and then using those same beliefs to live accordingly.

Moral of the story: our parents fucked us up.

Now, before you come at me saying that you have the best parents in the world and they couldn't have possibly screwed you up, hear me out:

First, I will argue with you all day that *my* parents are the best in the entire world.

Second, that's the fun little thing about money beliefs or limiting beliefs in general. It doesn't matter if your parents are the greatest of all time, and it doesn't matter if your parents do not do one thing right. Studies have found that our money beliefs are often solidified by seven years old, when our brains are not fully developed.[3] That means a lot of what we subconsciously believe to be true about money comes from things our parents said or did that we, as children, took as the truth (whether we took it out of context or not).

For example, my mom didn't mean to teach me that listening to music in the car was illegal; she was simply trying to be sure her 14-year-old was focused on the road.

Maybe at eight years old, you heard Mommy and Daddy (or whoever your parental figures were) talking about money and you heard Dad raise his voice. This could easily be an open discussion between two adults, but maybe subconsciously, you learned to believe that talking about money leads to fighting, so you should never talk about it. Your underdeveloped brain created your entire world and your entire belief system based on the things you heard and felt as a kid.

Enter: ancestral bullshit. To change your money actions, you need to first identify your money beliefs. Only then can you begin to make the kind of money moves that will get you where you want to be financially.

We will talk more in Chapter 4 about how to actually change these beliefs to be able to live according to your own rules with money, but it's absolutely vital that you first understand where they came from.

When it comes to passed-down beliefs, you are going to put those inherited beliefs into four categories:

1. The WTF Beliefs (beliefs you have that don't even apply to you)
2. The Ewww Beliefs (beliefs you have that you absolutely don't want)
3. The Core Beliefs: Stand by 'Em (beliefs you have that you're 100% keeping)
4. The Makeover Beliefs (beliefs you have that are a lil outdated but just need a refresh)

As we are going along, I want you to put any beliefs you can think of into these four categories, and we will work to break them all down.

TYPES OF PASSED-DOWN BELIEFS

Type 1: The WTF Beliefs (Beliefs You Have That Don't Even Apply to You)

The first type of passed-down beliefs can be the easiest to realize but often the hardest to let go of. Why is that, you ask? Generational trauma.

So it turns out that brown eyes or a crooked nose are not the only traits passed down from your parents—you also can inherit emotional responses based on hardships your ancestors endured. Child and adolescent psychiatrist Dr. Gayani DeSilva explains it best, saying, "Trauma affects genetic processes, leading to traumatic reactivity being heightened in populations who experience a great deal of trauma."[4]

My favorite way of thinking about this belief is through a story about rats. A pair of researchers, Brian Dias and Kerry Ressler, did a study on rats that will blow your mind when it comes to passed-down beliefs and generational trauma.[5] Of course, we can't make deductions based on the epigenetics of rats and immediately assume they apply to our lives as well, but I want you to think of the true impact of this study.

If you're a big research person, I highly recommend reading through the study. For everyone who definitely cheated in English Lit class by reading SparkNotes, I am going to give you my best ChloeNotes summary.

Dias and Ressler studied multiple generations of rats:

- Meet Grandma and Grandpa rat, who live together in a cage. As part of the experiment, periodically a burst of cherry scent is released into the air around them. Along with the smell, they are subsequently zapped with a small electric shock.
- This process continues, and Grandpa and Grandma rat continue to get shocked after the smell of cherries is released. Eventually they begin to shudder at the smell of cherries alone, simply out of anticipation of a shock.
- Next, Grandma and Grandpa rat have babies. Enter Mom and Dad rat.

- Mom and Dad rat are put into a cage, and the smell of cherries is released. Immediately, Mom and Dad rat shudder, despite having never actually been shocked. Woah.
- Then, Mom and Dad rat have babies. Let's now look at Baby rat.
- Baby rat gets put in a cage. Shockingly (no pun intended), Baby rat also shudders at the smell of cherries, even though Baby rat has never actually been zapped.
- This continues for seven generations.
- The fuq?!

I am absolutely not a scientist, and I want to reiterate that you can't necessarily look at this study with rats and make conclusions about your own life. However, this paints a picture of our own beliefs (among other things) that we might be holding on to that don't even apply to us. Did Baby rat need to be fearful of cherries even though nothing in its life had ever happened to cause it to fear cherries? Or was being fearful passed down as a survival mechanism from Grandma and Grandpa rat, who *did* have a reason to be fearful of the smell of cherries? So let me ask you: What beliefs are you holding on to that don't apply to you?

____

____

____

____

____

Here's an example that might be more helpful than the one about rats shuddering at the smell of cherries.

Meet Evan and Mileah. They have been dating for a while

now, and they decide to move in together. The day finally comes when they move into their adorable house, and it's time for the absolute worst part of moving: packing up boxes and boxes of stuff and taking them to the new place. Evan's things all fit nicely into one carload. But Mileah is a car and a half in, and she's barely finished clearing out her apartment closet. Evan starts calling her a hoarder. "I'm not a hoarder!!" she yells back. Evan points to her box of middle-school track jerseys. "What if I ever needed those for something!?" she responds defensively.

All of a sudden she thinks back to her grandma saying the exact same thing when she was downsizing to move into the nursing home. Mileah's grandma is 84 years old, meaning she was born in the last year of the Great Depression. During the Great Depression, the economy took a nosedive, and average wages fell by nearly 58% in the span of four years.[6] It was likely that Mileah's grandmother had a very real fear of needing to hold on to possessions in a time of great loss, growing up in the aftermath of the Great Depression. What were the beliefs passed down to Mileah's young parents, who hadn't experienced those hard times? Likely something along the lines of, "Keep everything in case something traumatic happens and you need it." That belief (which was a necessity during the Great Depression) likely was passed down generation to generation and now impacts Mileah, who is holding on to that seventh-grade track jersey. The question is, is the "hoarding" mentality of "keep everything just in case" a belief Mileah *still* needs in her life? No. Mileah is holding on to a belief from previous generations, but the world has changed and her beliefs need to catch up to the times. This is the perfect example of a belief she can put in the WTF category because she no longer needs to hold on to it or pass it down, because it doesn't apply to her.

What is a belief that was passed down to you that does not actually apply to your life?

____

____

____

Type 2: The Ewww Beliefs (Beliefs You Have That You Absolutely Don't Want)

The Ewww Beliefs might potentially apply to you, but they don't necessarily have to. These can be difficult to change because chances are they can apply to your current circumstances, which can lead you to feel comfortable with them. Let me explain with one of the biggest "aha moments" I had while trying to figure out my money beliefs.

I can remember very vividly going to the grocery store with my mom when I was young—maybe seven years old. As a seven-year-old, I very much had the same personality I do today—loud, fun-loving, and goofy—a wild-child persona my mom fully embraced. We would go down the aisles, and she would push me in the cart while I yelled "Weeeeeeeee!" or let me shoot a roll of paper towels into the shopping cart by passing it through my legs, yelling, "Hut, hut, hike!" We were playful throughout the whole store. That is, until we got to the checkout.

The second we would get to the checkout lane, I could feel my mom start to tense. Like any other seven-year-old, I would lean over and touch the toys or candy next to the register. However, now my mom's energy would completely change, and she would snap back, "Chloe, stop touching things." I can remember seeing her visibly stressed demeanor become more pronounced with each item scanned, as she watched the price on the register increase. I learned that at the checkout lane, the fun ended and the anxiety started.

Fast-forward to college. Every single time I approached the checkout counter, my Apple Watch would note my heart rate increase and tell me to take a deep breath or start a yoga workout. The stress around the checkout counter now plagued me as an adult.

But this was the key: it made sense for me, too. I was stressed at the checkout counter because as a 20-year-old broke college student, I was simply praying that my card wouldn't get declined at the register.

Fast-forward again. After some big money moves, I was no longer broke. But it didn't matter. That familiar feeling of stress still washed over me at the checkout. Maybe it was because I didn't have much in savings? Nope, not it. How do I know? Because even after growing eight months of savings in an emergency fund, every time I went to the checkout counter, I was *still* stressed.

That's when it hit me.

Yes, the belief made sense in my life, but that didn't mean I had to keep it. Even if you have debt, a less-than-ideal savings account balance, or whatever deficiencies you think you have, it is possible *not* to feel stress at the checkout (but only after you have attained a livable wage).* And on the flip side—even with a million dollars to your name, it *is* still possible to feel stress in the checkout lane.

Beliefs don't care what logic is behind them. They only care what you believe to be true.

---

*I want to be sure we talk about this in the context of understanding that it is possible not to feel stress at the grocery store checkout (or in any other example), assuming the person is making a livable wage that covers their basic needs.

Another type of Ewww Belief is one that may make sense to believe, but you can identify it as one you no longer want to feel.

For example, for me to change the belief that there was reason to feel stress about paying for the items in my cart, I had to be incredibly conscious while going to the checkout lane. I would prepare ahead of time to know that I had allocated that money for spending, and as I was walking up to the checkout counter, I would remind myself that I am safe and secure and grateful to buy these groceries. It took rewriting the experience time and time again to start to feel a true change. Think about going to the gym wanting to grow your biceps. It won't happen overnight, but the more you train those muscles, the stronger they get.

What is a belief that was passed down to you that might apply to your circumstances but that you don't want to keep anymore?

____

____

____

Type 3: The Core Beliefs: Stand by 'Em (Beliefs You Have That You're 100% Keeping)

These are the fun ones. What did your parental figures teach you that you absolutely want to keep believing? It can be as simple as your parents teaching you to be kind to people. That's a belief. It's one I absolutely will be sticking with and passing down. But what about with money? My parents taught me how to work hard and be grateful for the money coming in, and that's a belief I am giving a gold star to.

What are your core money beliefs that you want to hold on to?

___

___

___

Type 4: The Makeover Beliefs (Beliefs You Have That Are a Lil Outdated but Just Need a Refresh)

This is a catch-all category for beliefs that aren't necessarily beliefs you want to keep as they are but that need a little glow-up.

Let's take Cinnamon, for example. She can vividly remember her parents telling her that if she gets a tattoo, no employer will ever want to hire her because it's "unprofessional." A few years later, when she gets her first corporate job, the CEO walks into the meeting and has a visible wrist tat. Cinnamon then realizes that you're not doomed to lifelong unemployment if you choose to ink yourself. She decides to change her belief from "tattoos make you unemployable" to "I can choose what to do to my body and still be wildly successful in my career" (with a hot thigh tat to go along with her success). However, maybe she decides she wants to stay away from face tattoos because she wants her voice and career work to be the focal point, not dramatic face ink.

What's an outdated belief you have that needs a little makeover?

___

___

___

WRAPPING IT UP

So although you might be independent and living on your own, your beliefs might still be living under the roof of your parents' house. The good news is that when you can get to the bottom of the beliefs that are ruling your daily life, you can change them and ultimately change your outcomes. We will dive into this idea of changed beliefs leading to changed outcomes more in the next chapter, but for now, take a deep breath and remember that this shit is hard for a reason. You're a cycle breaker.

CHAPTER 4

Justin Bieber Is Hot . . . Isn't That the Truth?

Justin Bieber is the kind of hot that's really undeniable. Ya know that feeling when your friend is dating someone, and she shows you a pic because she wants to see if he's actually hot or if she's distracted by the fact that he has an adorable puppy? So she pulls up a pic of him, and you go, "I mean . . . he's not really my type, but he's cute!" In reality, we are all very aware that this is code for "I don't think he's cute."

I can confidently tell you no one on the planet has ever had that conversation about Justin Bieber, and I don't even care what era of Biebs we are talking about. Justin Bieber is an indisputable kind of hot.

I could go on and on about this man, but I'll stop here. Simply, Justin Bieber being hot is the GD truth.

Or is it?

The funny thing is that the line between beliefs and truths is as hazy as the decision to text your ex on a night out after a few too many vodka sodas. Your brain can have a hard time differentiating between beliefs and truths.

To me, Biebs being hot is the truth. But I know someone out there doesn't agree with me about his level of sex appeal. (They might need LASIK, but never mind that.) Who is right? Well, it turns out that if it's my truth but not someone else's, that actually means it's a belief of mine, not *the truth.*

Truth is something that is universal—like gravity. Even if someone were to "not believe" in gravity, that doesn't mean it isn't real. They wouldn't just start floating up into the atmosphere. Stating you don't believe in a truth doesn't make it less applicable to you. A truth is something nonnegotiable and indisputable. And to be honest with you, there are a lot of things that I saw as "truths" growing up that were actually beliefs. Anyone else's parents make them think it was illegal to turn on the light in the back seat of the car on a family road trip? Or that if you swallow gum it will stay in your stomach for 10 years?

TRUTHS VERSUS BELIEFS

The big difference between a "truth" and a "belief" is that you can change your beliefs, but you can't change a truth, like gravity.

Since a belief is something you can change, then if I believe that I can't start my own business, I will live according to that belief. If I wake up one day and decide to believe something different, perhaps that I am 100% capable of starting a business, I will view my opportunities differently, act differently, and, therefore, potentially change my results.

It can be wild to realize how subconsciously we consider "beliefs" to be "truths" (aka things we can't change). Let's test it out. Below is a list. Go through and write down "T" if you'd classify it as something that is a truth or "B" if you'd classify it as something that is a belief. Do *not* think too much about this. Just answer.

3 + 5 = 8 _____

Starbucks is a waste of money. _____

Debt is bad. _____

Abraham Lincoln is on the $5 bill. _____

Everyone has student loan debt. _____

The English alphabet has 26 letters. _____

College is a waste of money. _____

I will never make six figures. _____

There are seven days in the week. _____

Talking about money is inappropriate. _____

Justin Bieber is super hot. _____

There are 60 seconds in a minute. _____

You cannot go to Target without spending $100. _____

Earth is a planet. _____

I could never start a business. _____

I am not good with money. _____

You shouldn't invest while you have debt. _____

Now, the truths are in bold below:

3 + 5 = 8

Starbucks is a waste of money.

Debt is bad.

Abraham Lincoln is on the $5 bill.

Everyone has student loan debt.

The English alphabet has 26 letters.

College is a waste of money.

I will never make six figures.

There are seven days in the week.

Talking about money is inappropriate.

Justin Bieber is super hot. *(But I definitely wanted to bold this . . .)*

There are 60 seconds in a minute.

You cannot go to Target without spending $100.

Earth is a planet.

I could never start a business.

I am not good with money.

You shouldn't invest while you have debt.

Read that list again. Notice how "Debt is bad" and "I am not good with money" are not bold. That's because they aren't the ultimate truth. They can be true, but they can also be false, meaning they are both beliefs. For most of us, we will hear things like "debt is bad" and assume that is the truth. *The reality is that debt is neutral.* We are the ones who give meaning and assign morality to what debt is, and often the meaning we assign to it is a negative one. This is an example of a limiting belief that needs to be identified so you can begin to build your true, fact-based financial knowledge. Limiting beliefs hold you back from hitting goals or living the life you want to.

I've had multiple holy-shit-everything-I've-ever-learned-is-fake moments, but one in particular hit me harder than a ton of bricks. A few months into my financial journey, I was talking to a friend, and it somehow came up that he had quite a bit of credit card debt. My naive little brain was shocked at how casually he had mentioned it. "Ummmm . . . that's so stressful. You should be freaking out!" I said to him, projecting my own feelings about the situation.

"No. If it were you, you'd be freaking out," he said matter-of-factly. "But you also freak out no matter what is in your bank account."

If you could have seen my face after he said that! It was a mix of "WTF" and "OMG, wait . . . why is he so right?"

How was it possible that he had credit card debt and didn't feel stressed at all, but I had no credit card debt and I was constantly stressing about money? Didn't money (especially debt) result in stress for everyone?

CHALLENGING YOUR BELIEFS

It was one of those jaw-dropping moments—truly what personal-development dreams are made of. I realized that no matter what was in my friend's bank account, he wasn't going to be stressed. And no matter what was in my bank account, even if it was a lot of money, I was going to be stressed. The stress (or lack thereof) was the result of our individual beliefs around money, including our beliefs around the scarcity of money. They weren't universal truths. They were beliefs. And if they were beliefs, they were changeable.

I started questioning everything. I realized that I had beliefs that I absolutely did want to keep: the belief that everyone is equal, or the belief that Sunday is the absolute best day of the week. But there were also beliefs I wanted to update after realizing how detrimental they were to my results.

So at that moment, I opened my iPhone's notepad and wrote:

Chloe's List of Bullshit Old Beliefs

- Money is and always will be something inherently stressful.
- You have to work your ass off just to get by but never actually get ahead.
- Wanting more money is greedy, rude, and embarrassing.

And because I had the breakthrough of "OMG, what if I chose new beliefs," I followed that list with:

Chloe's List of Badass New Beliefs

- Money gets to be fun, easy, and stress-free.
- Money always flows to me with ease and is not solely dependent on my work ethic.
- When I build wealth, my overflow creates a massive impact on those I love and the people, places, and organizations I care about.

Now it's your turn. You're likely starting to think of some of these old beliefs you want to update from the previous chapter, so grab those identified beliefs so we can start revamping them. Fill in your own lists of bullshit old beliefs and badass new beliefs.

Bullshit:

____

____

Badass:

____

____

Bullshit:

____

____

Badass:

____

____

Don't be surprised if these beliefs change as your priorities and goals change. Just like Apple sends out iPhone iOS updates a few times per year, you can go back into your saved notes and continually add to or update your beliefs. Writing down your beliefs helps internalize them, almost like you're writing an instruction manual for your brain.

I know, we're taking a step into the "woo-woo" world of money and personal development now, but as a previous logic-only believer, I promise you this shit works. And not in a just-think-differently-and-everything-is-solved sort of way. Don't worry, young Padawan, I used to think mindset work was only fluff, too. I would laugh at anyone who gave solutions to money problems that didn't involve a spreadsheet. We will still get into all the actionable things you can do with money, but this part of it is equally important for sustainable results. I thought money was . . . well, literally *just* money. It wasn't until more than a year of trying to "strategize" my way out of self-sabotage that I realized: strategy is important, but to really untangle your money struggles, you have to accept that the solution is Deeper Than Money, and the journey toward healing your relationship with money includes looking at your beliefs. But how the heckenbob do your beliefs impact your day-to-day results? Let's break it down.

DECODING YOUR LIMITING BELIEFS

This process is called BTFAR (a commonly used concept in the personal-development realm). BTFAR stands for:

Beliefs >> Thoughts >> Feelings >> Actions >> Results

It is the breakdown of how our beliefs impact the tangible results we are experiencing in our lives. I was listening to a financial podcast about five years ago and the speaker said, "Tell me your results, and I'll tell you your thoughts." I was pissed. *Who are you to insinuate that my results are my responsibility? I didn't have a trust fund. I didn't grow up wealthy!* And while I do firmly believe that this phrase leaves vital things out of the equation for some people—like systemic oppression and inequality—it was a wake-up call for me that helped me realize that I had more power than I originally thought. My favorite way to do inner work is to take myself through the BTFAR process.

Beliefs

As we discussed earlier, we all have limiting beliefs. Here are a few of the common beliefs around money I see from clients:

- I'll never get ahead with money.
- Debt is bad.
- You have to work really, really hard to earn money. (As in, putting in many hours is the only way to make more money.)
- I'll always be stressed about money.
- I'm not good with finances.

Choose one of your money beliefs, write it in the blank below, and we will walk through BTFAR to see how this belief might show up in a tangible way for you.

One belief I have about money is:

____

Thoughts

Once you've established a belief in your subconscious, it comes through to your conscious mind via your thoughts. Perhaps your belief is "I'm going to be in debt forever." Then one day your student loan statement arrives in the mail. Maybe the thoughts that pop up in your head are along these lines: *OMG, how am I going to get rid of my student loans?* Or *I hate this.* Maybe *Crap, my payment is due soon.* Or *At this rate I'll never be able to pay them off.* You can see how your belief about being in debt forever is being reinforced by your thoughts.

The thoughts that come up (from the belief I chose above) are:

____

Feelings

Now that you have those thoughts spiraling around in your head, you likely will start to notice your emotions change, too. You've been thinking about your student loans all day, so you might realize a change in how you're feeling. Maybe you're aware of an increase in stress or feeling just a little on edge. Maybe you're frantic or overwhelmed. These feelings can lead to physical changes as well. For me, I always feel stress in my chest: my heart beats a little faster, my shoulders raise, my jaw clenches, and I get in a different physical state than before.

My feelings around money (surrounding the belief and thoughts I chose for this example) are:

____

Actions

As your feelings and physical state have shifted into a higher stress level, you're likely taking different actions than you would have otherwise. For me, actions used to show up like this: I would be at work thinking about how much I hate my student loans. I would start feeling stressed, overwhelmed, and physically tense. I would leave work and go to Target to shop my way back to feeling happy. Three hundred dollars later, I would feel guilty about spending that money (reinforcing the belief that I'll always be in debt). My actions likely would have been quite different if those initial thoughts (and subconscious beliefs) had not been triggered.

My actions around money (surrounding the belief, thoughts, and feelings I chose in this example) are:

____

Results

Your initial belief created thoughts, which brought feelings to the surface, which inspired a less-than-desirable action, which now leads to a result. My result being $300 of impulse spending that put me further away from my actual goals and filled my closet with things I didn't actually want. The guilt sinks in. Now I am even more behind on my goal. Now I am even more stressed about my student loan payment. And now, **alas**, I am further away from ever being debt-free—reaffirming my original belief that this cycle of debt will continue forever.

My results around money (surrounding the belief, thoughts, feelings, and actions I chose in this example) are:

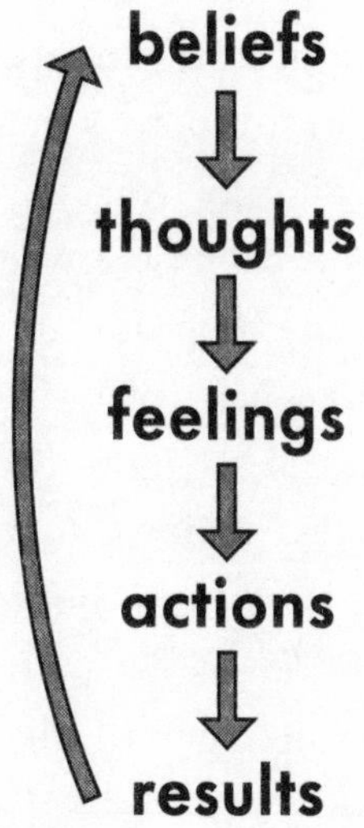

See the diagram to the left for a breakdown of our trusty new friend, BTFAR.

The first time I learned the idea of BTFAR, I was like *What is this sorcery, and how do I fix it?* From where I was standing, BTFAR was ruining my plans to be uber-successful and wealthy, because all my money beliefs that led me to self-sabotage felt like straight trash. How the heck do I stop BTFAR from happening?! The bad news: you don't. The good news: you don't. Even though BTFAR never stops cycling as fast as your fav cycling instructor, you can use it to your advantage.

TRACKING YOUR BELIEFS

The first step is to create a log of the most common beliefs you want to update. This is an ongoing process, but being intentional allows you to be always leveling up. So brain dump any limiting beliefs that have come up for you so far in this book:

____

____

____

Limiting Beliefs

This list you are creating of old beliefs or limiting beliefs will always be growing and updating. I recommend starting a note on your phone called "My Limiting Beliefs." (Of course, you're more than welcome to name it something a little more fun—one of my clients called it "Stank-Ass Beliefs.") In this note, whenever you realize a limiting belief is coming up for you, jot it down. That way you aren't trying to do this exercise a week from now and black out and can't think of anything. It can be hard to identify or list your limiting beliefs when you're in a positive headspace, which is why I recommend trying to take note of them in the moment. Then, when you sit down to do some of this deeper work, you already have your beliefs identified.

I often don't realize a limiting belief is occurring until, all of a sudden, I feel so stressed and overwhelmed and tense and my watch is beeping at me to "Take one minute to breathe." I do not like being told what to do, but my robot watch does know me well, so typically I slow down and take that minute not only to breathe but to check in with my current stream of thoughts. I can usually track down the problematic belief from there.

I will sit down with a piece of paper or my phone's notepad, or I'll verbalize out loud to myself (many women are verbal processors and this can be so helpful!) what I am thinking. Here's a peek into the Negative Nancy word vomit that happens in my brain if I let my negative beliefs run wild: *What if I don't hit my investing goal this month? And what if I don't finish my big project? OMG, and I still have that other thing I need to be doing. I am never going to get everything I need to get done today done.* Ah, there she is, in all her glory. Can you see her? Popping into my brain to mess with me: the belief that there is always something to stress about.

Those thoughts may seem different, but they all boil down to me believing that money is a stressful topic. But actually, when I really break it down, if literally *any one* of those things didn't get done or didn't happen, I would be fine. This realization means that the belief I want to adopt and live by is: nothing is an emergency except emergencies. Ah, just typing that gives me all the warm and cozy vibes, like taking that first big comforting drink of hot coffee on a cold morning. It just feels good, damn it.

Changing Beliefs

Now that you've written out your list of limiting beliefs, you want to call out the new beliefs that you want to adopt. Here are some examples of what that looks like:

- Debt is bad.
    - New: Debt is neutral. I am grateful debt allowed me to have an experience or make a purchase before I could pay in cash. Now I want to commit to paying that back.
- I'll never make a lot of money.
    - New: Money is an unlimited resource. I can make money in infinite ways. I simply need to make a plan and work toward it.
- I will never be good with money.
    - New: I trust my decisions about money. The decisions I've made and how I was taught to behave with money are in the past.
- Wanting more money is greedy.
    - New: When I want more money, I stay grounded in what that money will be used for, and when I get more money, I do more good in the world.
- It's rude to talk about money.
    - New: Talking about money builds my wealth and helps to collectively bridge wealth gaps by making money an accessible conversation to all.

Now that you've identified what those new beliefs are, it's time to catch the old beliefs in action so you can start to reinforce the new ones.

MAKING YOUR BELIEFS ACTIONABLE

As I type this, I can hear my two sweet mini Goldendoodles playing in the other room. They still play like puppies, but both have been potty-trained for a while. However, that wasn't the case when I first brought them home. How do you potty-train a dog? The easiest way is to take them outside and wait for them to pee (implementing the new rule) and then celebrate big time: "Yay! You peed in the right place!" However, if the inevitable occurs and your dog pees inside, you can't chastise them after the fact. If you wait 20 minutes to tell them, "Bad dog," you've waited 20 minutes too long and your dog is like, "What are you mad about, bruh?" But if you see your dog peeing, the best thing to do is to catch them in the act and say, "NO! No, no." Then take them outside and celebrate again when they pee outside. It might take a few times (or a lot of times, let's be real), but slowly, your lil pup gets the idea and starts only peeing outside. *Voilà.*

Now it's time to catch the dog peeing—but the dog is your brain, and the pee is your limiting beliefs.

So when a limiting belief pops up, catch yourself in the act. Verbalize it out loud. "Woah, girl. Right now I keep thinking ______________________________. I can change that belief. The new belief I choose is ______________________________."

You might catch yourself in any stage of BTFAR. Maybe you catch yourself feeling stressed and work backward:

> *I'm feeling overwhelmed* [feelings] >> *because I was thinking about things I could screw up* [thoughts] >> *because my belief is that there's always something to be stressed about* [belief].

When you've established the belief, catch the dog peeing and rewrite the new BTFAR cycle. Here's what this looks like for me:

- >> *New beliefs: Only emergencies are emergencies. Money is stress-free.*
- >> *New thoughts: I will get my top priorities done, do the best I can, and the rest can wait until tomorrow.*
- >> New feelings: Feeling more calm, less stressed, and less overwhelmed
- >> New actions: Being able to think through things intentionally and rationally
- >> New results: Less stress, more of top priorities completed, and healthy detachment from outcomes
- >> Now, the new results reinforce the new belief, and it's easier to continue with the new belief.

Let's look at a real-life example of this with Riley.

Riley perpetually tells himself he shouldn't be spending money online shopping. "I seriously need to cut myself off," he tells his friends after arriving home from a work trip to six new packages on his doorstep. He opens the packages and receives that **ahhhhhh** dopamine rush, only to immediately feel guilt over his spending.

Then, a week later, he finds himself back in a hotel room, alone in a new city on another work trip. Like clockwork, he is back on Lululemon's website, ordering that pair of joggers and justifying it by saying he had a long day of meetings, only to come home from that trip and get that sweet, sweet hit of dopamine from new packages, followed by guilt . . . again.

At the same time, Riley learns about BTFAR and how to catch yourself when you're in the midst of a limiting-beliefs spiral. He is determined to change this cycle and knows he has an upcoming business trip when he can put this into practice.

Cue Riley's 5 a.m. alarm to wake him for his 8 a.m. flight to

San Diego. He gets up, flies out, and puts in a long day of work. Exhausted, he Ubers back to the hotel room, DoorDashes dinner, and then gets the thought, *I'm bored. I want to online shop.* That is immediately followed by his belief, *No! I seriously need to knock it off.* Do you hear that? *Psssssssssssss* . . . the dog is peeing on the carpet. I repeat. The dog is pissing a loud stream all over the new HomeGoods rug.

Riley immediately pauses, opens the notepad app on his phone, and writes:

Old belief: It's bad to spend my money online shopping.
Old thought: I seriously need to knock it off.
Old feelings: Guilt and shame any time money is spent online shopping.
Old actions: A "screw it" mentality and needing to justify all purchases.
Old results: A constant cycle of spending out of alignment of my goals and then guilt and shame causing more spending out of alignment.

Damn, he thinks to himself. *That's not how I want to live with money.*

He then sits down and rewrites what he wants his BTFAR train of thought to action to look like:

New belief: I get to spend my money in alignment with my goals and priorities. And my priorities and goals include fun spending.
New thought: I can't wait to plan out and purchase in alignment.
New feelings: Freedom to spend money, security of

spending being planned out, and excitement of getting a new piece of clothing that I am glad I purchased.

New actions: Sitting down prior to a work trip or the new month and planning out how much I want to spend, and being able to spend it guilt-free. (Don't worry, we are going to walk through exactly how to do this later in the book.)

New results: Setting aside the amount of money I want to spend on my work trip, while knowing I can still allocate money for other things/priorities, too. (Again, bear with me if you are feeling like this seems impossible! We will get into the strategy soon.) Picking out my new piece of clothing that feels completely in alignment and exciting. Coming home to a package of intentional, planned shopping with zero guilt.

He sits on the hotel bed, staring at his phone, realizing how big of an impact it would make if he continued to catch the damn dog peeing and redirect it to this new belief. The new result would be so influential in his life and would lead to a better outcome than his original thought of *I seriously need to knock it off.* Riley continues practicing BTFAR by prepping before his trips and reminding himself that when negative thoughts or feelings pop up, he can open his phone's notepad and remember that his thoughts are still adjusting to the new cycle he is creating.

A few work trips go by, and now Riley always sits down prior to travel and preps his spending amount so he feels really good about the spending he does do and gets to arrive home to a guilt-free package. He no longer feels bad or shames himself into "needing to spend less," because his new belief is one that allows him to spend without guilt. Sometimes Riley doesn't even shop on his trips because he's no longer stuck in a toxic cycle of feeling guilt and then seeking the dopamine hit to feel better. He never has to justify his spending, because he knows he is an adult who works hard and gets to spend his money how he pleases. Changing to habits that allow guilt-free spending has actually resulted in him spending less per month on average (you actually eliminate overspending when you're in alignment), which has allowed him to put even more toward his current money goals than before. This shift improved Riley's tangible financial outcomes while also taking so much stress off his plate.

Now it's your turn. Was there something on that list of Truths Versus Beliefs that stumped you? Maybe it was that "Starbucks is a waste of money" or "I will never make six figures." Let's work through the BTFAR process here:

Old belief: ______________________________

Old thoughts: ______________________________

Old feelings: ______________________________

Old actions: ______________________________

Old results: ______________________________

New belief: ______________________________

New thoughts: ______________________________

New feelings: ______________________________

New actions: ______________________________

New results: ______________________________

It's time to practice, and more importantly, start recognizing the short- and long-term impact of getting a new result from these changes. Of course, at times the old beliefs will still get triggered and resurface. That's okay! You're a human with the baggage, trauma, and triggers to prove it. The goal isn't to rid yourself of doubt or every negative belief; the goal is to equip yourself with the tools to consistently love yourself into a new belief system that supports the results you crave in your life.

THE SCIENCE BEHIND BTFAR

If you're new to mindset work or personal-development work, this chapter might feel a little woo-woo for you, so let's wrap it up with some science talk about how working through your BTFAR thought stream actually works behind the scenes to create change in your life. To emotionally prepare, I want you to imagine you're in sixth-grade science class and the teacher is wheeling in a box TV on a cart and everyone starts chanting, "Bill Nye, the science guy! Bill Bill Bill Bill!" Hopefully that sets the mood, and you're ready to dive in and meet your RAS.

Your RAS, which stands for reticular activating system, is a network of neurons located in your brain stem.[1] Your RAS connects the subconscious part of your brain to the conscious part of your brain, basically choosing which information filters up to your conscious mind. Your old BTFAR thought stream (up to now) has existed solely in your subconscious, and pieces of it will continue to exist there. What I mean by that is, your old patterns with money are so ingrained into your subconscious that going forward, they will continue to pop up, even though you are working to update them with a new BTFAR stream. So instead of only relying on your own thoughts to catch an old pattern (to catch the dog peeing), you can also use your new secret weapon, your RAS.

Let's first test out your RAS and then I will explain how

you can use it to reinforce new beliefs and ultimately new outcomes:

The last time you drove, did you see a license plate that started with the letter *H*? Not just, "I probably saw one," but if you had to wager your entire life savings and every dollar you would make for the rest of your life on whether the last time you drove you saw a license plate that started with *H*, would you have a confident answer?

Unless you have a photographic memory, I am going to assume not. Why? Because license plate letters don't matter enough to get filtered through your RAS from your subconscious mind. See, the RAS is the stickler bouncer standing guard at the door to your conscious mind. Your mind is over capacity, but there's a huuuuuuuge line of subconscious information outside waiting to get in. According to behavioral and data scientist Pragya Agarwal, "The human brain can process 11 million bits of information every second, but our conscious mind can only handle 40 to 50 bits of information a second."[2] So the RAS steps in to decide which 40 to 50 bits out of 11 million get to enter the "club," or the conscious mind, every second. Your subconscious may be aware that you passed a license plate starting with *H*, but your RAS didn't think that piece of information was Hollywood elite enough to skip the line and enter your conscious mind.

Now, what if I told you that every time you texted me a picture of a license plate that started with the letter *H* I would Venmo you $5? You likely would intentionally start looking for *H* license plates because the *H* would become relevant to you. Your RAS is your conscious mind's bodyguard, so now that your conscious mind wants new people in the club, what is your RAS going to do? It's going to filter all license plates that start with *H* into your conscious mind so you can make some money off them. I bet you'll start to notice *H* license plates now since we are talking about them and making them relevant for your RAS to note for your conscious mind. All of a sudden, you're seeing *H* license plates everywhere! Did everyone in your area just go to the DMV and request to include *H* in their license plate? Obviously not. They were always there; you're just now noticing them.

Your RAS is your secret weapon for changing your beliefs and, therefore, also changing your actions and outcomes with finances. It's going to work its ass off to get people in the club who it thinks you want there. So if your current belief is "I am always stressed about money," your RAS is working overtime to only let info into your conscious mind that supports that belief. It's taking care to notice ways that money is hard, drawing your attention to things that are stressful, focusing on how you're behind other people, and obsessing over all the ways you feel unprotected with money. However, as you consistently begin to replace those old beliefs with new beliefs, your RAS is getting handed a new VIP list of what info is allowed into your conscious mind. If your new belief is "I am always secure with money," your RAS will start filtering and sending you pieces of information that support those beliefs. Maybe you will feel worthy of a raise at your job, finally be comfortable using your savings to pay off debt, or appreciate being able to pay for your groceries and not feel stressed. How cool, right? Science!!

Your RAS can be an important tool for creating long-term changes in your belief system, ultimately leading to new actions and new results around money. Even if you choose to disagree with me and believe that Justin Bieber is not hot (terrible taste, but whatever!), it's an unarguable fact that you get to choose your beliefs about money. Let this be the turning point where you choose new beliefs that allow you to get ahead.

PART 2

Understanding Yourself

CHAPTER 5

I'm Behind

It's 7 a.m. and your alarm clock goes off. You grab your phone and open your go-to social media app, starting your morning scroll. You watch the "behind the scenes" of the lives of everyone you care about, and a few people you don't (if you're being honest). You look at the trips they're taking, the new clothes they're buying, and the happy lives they're living. Your inner mean girl voice whispers, "She's so far ahead of you." You set your phone down and start your day feeling the insecurity linger as you look at the pieces of your life that you feel behind on: you have big debt payments, you don't have the relationship or family you thought you'd have by now, and, gosh, you don't even have your laundry folded and put away from the load you did last weekend. You are, in so many ways, behind.

You get to work and you can already feel the stress seeping into you slowly, starting in your brain as you think about your huge to-do list and the tasks falling through the cracks. The feeling continues to spread as your shoulders tense up and you feel that quick pulse of anxiousness beating in your chest. You have so much that you could be working on and so much that needs to get done. You know you'll leave work with that to-do list unfinished. You are, in so many ways, behind.

You look at what everyone else is doing and wonder how they are crushing it while you are just so . . . average.

These thoughts can consume you if you let them. In fact, studies have shown that more than 10% of our thoughts are comparisons.[1] We are constantly calculating if we're ahead or behind, above or below average. But what *is* average? And does it really matter?

Especially when it comes to something as measurable as money, it's easy to obsess over the balance in your savings account, your salary, the 401(k) your job offers but you haven't started investing in, or the huge sum of student loans you're barely chipping away at, wondering *Where would I be if I had just started earlier? If I would have learned about all these things five years ago? Would I be this far behind?* All these questions we ask ourselves—it's relentless.

When does it end?

You can be behind on bills, on your homework, or on the latest fashion trends, but let me tell you this: when it comes to where you are in life, there is no such thing as behind.

When I first started trying to figure out my finances, I googled "how to get ahead with money." Not only did I feel overwhelmed to see 998 million search results of things I "needed" to do, but I also immediately felt behind. Like if your friend invited you over to binge-watch a new TV series, but they're already on episode four, and you haven't even watched episode one. Ironically, those online sources in the financial industry were spouting countless ways of how to catch up and get ahead with money, but instead of feeling enlightened, I felt even more lost. Yeah, sure, a solution to my problem had been offered (many solutions, actually), but the further I got into my financial journey, the more I realized I didn't need those hacks on how to catch up, because I wasn't even "behind" in the first place. (Spoiler alert: you're not behind, either.)

I want you to rewind to your preteen years and think about your fashion sense back then. If you were like me, you begged your mom to let you stop at Limited Too at the mall so you could gawk at the "top fashion" that embodied everything you wanted to be. All the cool girls at school had the cutest, trendiest outfits. I can tell you, as the girl wearing her sister's hand-me-downs, I felt so behind them. I would finally get the glittery graphic tee, and the next week there was already a new trend. I was left playing catch-up once again.

Even now, it's so easy to look at people around you and experience that *Keeping Up with the Kardashians* effect, where everyone around you seems richer, happier, prettier, and trendier than you.

But have you ever looked back at old photos from when you were a kid and absolutely cringed at how atrocious you look? Even at that moment when you were finally rocking the in-style looks, just patiently waiting for Disney Channel to come recruit you. But now you wonder, *Who let me wear that?* It's all about perspective. You can feel like you're ahead, or idolize someone who is ahead, but when you look back, it was all just part of the cycle of feeling behind.

When was the last time you simultaneously had goals for where you wanted to go but felt perfectly at peace with where you were and enjoyed the journey you took to get there?

If you feel like you don't know when that was, have no fear. We are going to change that today.

Before you can do that, you need to ask yourself a pressing question: Who am I behind?

BEHIND "HER"

For years, I had a "her." In college, I had a boyfriend who was always making comments about this one girl, kind of comparing or sizing me up against her. (Let's forgive College Chloe for not seeing those huge red flags, okay?) Every time he did something that made me feel unwanted, I would cling to this idea that it was because I wasn't as ⋆*fill in the blank*⋆ (pretty, cool, fun, interesting, etc.) as her. I felt so far behind her. I just needed to become as successful and as fun as she was, but catching up to her felt completely unattainable. No matter what I did, I always felt like I was five steps behind her. I look back and want to hug that 19-year-old version of myself who felt so unworthy that she clung to who she thought she needed to become in order to feel loved. News flash: it not only did not work, but it also left me constantly comparing myself to an image of someone I wasn't.

Do you have a "her" in your life: that girl who just seems to be doing it all right? She might be the one effortlessly snagging that new job or promotion you've been wanting. Maybe she's got that social media–perfect relationship you're idolizing, or she jets across the world on a new adventure every week. She might be a specific person, but she could just as easily be an imagined benchmark you created based on seeing what all the other "hers" are doing around you.

If you're feeling behind "her," whoever your "her" is, I want you to imagine how freeing it would feel to no longer be running her race. How much of a relief it would be to no longer feel like you had to become more like her to feel worthy. How much stress it would release to stop feeling like someone was 10 steps ahead of you. When you want to be someone else, you'll always feel behind, because you can never be them.

Letting go of your "her" is hard to do, but it's a game-changer for your mental health. Unfollow her on socials, stop bringing her up when you're talking with your friends, and let her live her own life, without it influencing yours.

BEHIND OTHER PEOPLE'S EXPECTATIONS OF YOU

This is an easy one to relate to and a hard one to heal from. I want you to think of someone important to you in your life, who you feel has expectations of you that you aren't living up to. Maybe it's your parents, who want you to have a different career. Or a partner, wanting you to be someone you're not. Or a coach, wanting you to commit more to a sport than you want to. Whoever it is, I want you to picture who they want you to be and how it makes you feel when you are falling short of that image or are behind where they expect you to be.

In this scenario, you're fighting against someone else's idea of where you should be. And ultimately, you're falling short of a made-up expectation. They think you should be doing something else, living a different way. It is here where you have to recognize that when you are behind in someone else's expectations, it's because you are living differently than how they want you to live. And hey, I know it's easier said than done, but it's absolutely fine to stop letting other people's opinions, expectations, or even desires for you get in your way of living how you want. Here's the thing: someone's expectations of you could even be something you want. Maybe your parents are pressuring you to have a kid, and they keep reminding you that they had two kids by your age, so you feel behind even though you do want to have a kid but just not right now. It's okay to stop letting their ideas of how you should live impact you. Their ideas and timelines are theirs. You ultimately can't change anyone else's thoughts, but you can stop letting their thoughts affect you by remembering that feeling like you're not meeting other people's expectations of you is based on someone else's judgment of your life. Living a life that makes other people happy will never fulfill you, or them. Letting go of this desire to please others will be unbelievably impactful because you will no longer carry around the emotional weight of feeling like you aren't good enough. Furthermore, although this may seem unrelated to tactical financial advice, it's actually a core lesson. When you are so focused on someone else's expectations of you, you are much more likely to spend money how you think they want you to spend instead of spending in alignment with what you want for yourself.

BEHIND YOUR EXPECTATIONS OF WHERE YOU SHOULD BE

In fifth grade, we had to write a letter to put in a time capsule talking about where we thought we would be in 15 years. I wrote that I would be married, have multiple kids, two dogs, and live in the suburbs by now. Well, I absolutely nailed the dog part but totally shit the bed on the rest of it. Married? Consider that bullet dodged. Kidding, but for years I constantly thought, *OMG, I'm behind.* Pause. *Behind who??? The person 10-year-old me thought I should be? The person I dreamt up when my brain wasn't fully developed and I still thought if you kissed a boy you'd get cooties???* Who cares if I changed my mind and decided I wanted something different? If my fifth-grade self could see me now, *she* would definitely realize how cool my life is. If I'd had a female role model in movies or books or real life who was young and making money and doing whatever the hell she wanted to, I think my fifth-grade answer for what I wanted my life to look like would have been different. But here is the thing: even if my fifth-grade self *wouldn't* love the version of me now, that's still okay. Even if a past version of you exists who wouldn't love who you are today, it's because she hasn't experienced the same things you have (yet).

Today, we clear all the stuck or judgmental energy that is making you feel behind.

BEHIND "NORMAL"

We also often feel behind by comparing ourselves to what the "average person" is doing. One of the common questions I am asked in interviews is, "What percentage of your income should you be putting toward savings every month?"

I refuse to answer it. Giving someone a blanket statement and saying, "This is what people on average should be doing," can be incredibly damaging. Let's say I tell everyone, "You should be saving 20% of your income." (That is not a tip. I just made it up for this example.) Someone in suburban Illinois making $100k a year might have plenty more than 20% to save each month. But because I said 20% was fine, she doesn't end up putting away as much as she could and limits her potential. On the flip side, someone with the same income and a similar lifestyle but living in Los Angeles might be unable to save anywhere close to 20% right now and immediately think, *Wow, that's not even close to being attainable for me.* So instead, she just says, "Screw it," and doesn't save at all, limiting her potential. Let's take a step back. In both situations, this advice isn't helpful, because it's not aligned with each woman's lifestyle and income.

When I dove into the world of finance, I felt like there was too much "standard" advice that ended up doing more harm than good. Why? Because the standard of what is "normal" depends on so many factors, and salary alone cannot be what we base our standards on.

It's easy to feel behind when we see what is deemed "normal" and try to measure up to that. But you can't compare results without comparing resources, and that 20% example doesn't factor in financial backgrounds, privileges, and other impactful variables. (We will touch on this more in Chapter 9.)

GIVE UP BEING BEHIND

So the question is, are you really behind?

What if where you are right now is the exact spot in the whole universe, multiverse, or whateververse you are supposed to be? What if your current money situation is what leads to you taking the job that leads to meeting the love of your life? What if your current money situation helps you learn a lesson that allows you to make massive leaps and bounds in your career? What if this is, in fact, perfect?

What if instead of feeling like your student loans have put you behind because of debt, you saw them as a tool that paid for the college education that shaped you into the person you are today? What if you saw your credit card debt as you doing the best you could to cope with the stress of life using the tools and resources you had at the time?

Giving up feeling behind isn't as easy as saying, "Okay, now stop feeling that way." It's an active process of healing, loving, and rewriting the stories and perspectives of feeling behind. When you start believing you can't be behind "her," or your parents' expectations, or your own expectations, or societal norms, you stop putting pressure on yourself to run a never-ending rat race.

Today, I want you to practice feeling 100% on the right path, in the right place, at the right time. You have to train your brain to do this, though.

Challenge for today:

1. Write "I am present as f*ck" at the top of a note in your phone or on a piece of paper.
2. Throughout the day, anytime you tell yourself an old belief of how you're behind, write that lie in the note. Examples:
   - I am already behind on my to-do list.
   - If I would have just stopped using my credit card last year . . .
   - Why am I still renting when she has already bought a house?
3. Set an alarm for 12 p.m. (put your phone on silent and no vibrate in case you're in class or a meeting) that says "Check in: I am present." This will help hold you accountable and allow you space to reflect and write down these thoughts.
4. At the end of the day, go to your note. Rewrite the old beliefs, transforming them into what you want to believe instead.

The Old Beliefs

- I am already behind on my to-do list.
- If I would have just stopped using my credit card last year . . .
- Why am I still renting when she has already bought a house?

The New Beliefs

- Nothing is an emergency except emergencies. I will do what I can get done today and work on the rest tomorrow.
- I am so happy I got the clarity I needed to decide to pay off my credit card debt. There's no shame in having it, but I also feel excited to pay it off.
- I love renting because it creates so many options and conveniences for me, and I am so happy I am able to use my money in a way that best serves me. Seeing someone buy a house and feeling jealousy helps me find clarity that I might want to start thinking about something like that for myself in the future. (We will explore this idea more in Chapter 7.)

Repeat this tomorrow, but then, when the thought pops up in real time, "catch the dog peeing" (remember from Chapter 4) and say, "Hi there, limiting belief—GTFO." And then repeat your new truths to yourself.

Here's the deal: There is no such thing as catching up. You aren't behind anyone. You're right where you're supposed to be. You had to know the things you knew then to become the person you are today. If you knew these things 10 years ago, you wouldn't be the person you are now. Would you have gone to the same school? Made the same friends? Been in the same career? Give gratitude to your younger self for doing the best she could with what she had access to at the time.

That voice in your head telling you that you're not enough, that you're behind, that wealth is never possible for you: that is not you. You didn't come out of the womb into the world saying, "I suck. I'm full of shame." You were taught shame. That is not who you are. You're here to learn the truth about money and the truth about yourself. Your decisions, good or bad, are part of your story. That doesn't mean you can't change them and get a completely different result in the future. By starting today, you will have more money than you know what to do with at retirement. I hope that gives you chills, because it gives me chills every time. By showing up for yourself, reading this book, and taking action, you are putting yourself on a new trajectory.

The reason your brain is telling you that you are behind is that your brain doesn't know anything outside your own experience. It's telling you, "I know what the past six months looked like, so that's what the next six months will look like." Even if it's the smallest shift, you are changing your trajectory in so many ways. My goal for you is that you see the logistical result of your bank account transforming at the same time you shred your preconditioned money shame and the feeling of being behind. You're exactly where you're supposed to be right now.

CHAPTER 6

Main Character Energy

The first time I saw Disney's *Moana,* I bawled. Haven't seen it?! Before you continue, put a bookmark in this book, call in sick, cancel all plans, and watch *Moana.* Yes, order in your favorite takeout dish, drag your huge comforter into the living room, and have a movie day.

Okay, now that you've paused and watched it, let's talk about the scene where Moana is out on the water, discouraged as hell, and doubting everything about herself and what she's trying to do. She's like, "Screw this journey. I am going home." But she has a moment of hesitation. Her grandma comes back as a spirit guide and asks her why she is hesitating, and Moana basically asks back in a shaky voice, "OMG, Grandma, who am I?"

And then Moana starts with some low-hanging fruit, saying she loves her island and the sea. She reaffirms that she's her father's daughter and then she slowly starts to name more pieces of herself.

When someone asks you who you are, you might get that frozen, glossed-over look in your eyes, like when you're put on the spot and cannot for the life of you remember some of your favorite songs (or any music for that matter). You might respond like Moana did and start listing things you like and who you are in relation to other people: "I like going out with my friends and spending time at the lake. I'm a dog mom, a sister, a daughter, and an aunt." Or maybe you throw in your job title, too. But remember that *what you do isn't who you are.* Your job isn't who you are, despite how much your identity might be rooted in being a high achiever. Your relationships to others aren't who you are, even if they're important to you. You are the main character.

In the movie, Moana eventually goes beyond these surface-level descriptions; she takes a moment to identify who she truly is. You can hear her confidence grow as she remembers her identity and her purpose. She sings louder, and her voice isn't shaky anymore. By the end of the song, Moana remembers exactly who she is and what she wants, and she knows she can trust her intuition to find a way forward. And the funny thing is, intuition is what started it all anyway. Moana hesitated before she gave up on her quest and started to paddle home. That little hesitation was a ping of intuition. The thing about intuition is that it's fleeting. It is the little voice that whispers. You have to train yourself to come back to who you are and listen to that voice of intuition to keep in alignment and stay on the path to your goals. Anytime you're feeling lost, come back to a place of remembering who the F you are, and listen for that little whisper of intuition. You don't need to know the whole journey, but listen for that push to find your next step.

I cannot teach you how to spend in alignment (your new secret weapon) until you truly know who you are—otherwise, the outside voices of doubt will always sound louder than your own intuition. Another important aspect of Moana's journey is when she is experiencing these feelings of doubt, she is in a moment of failure: her boat is broken, she's lost, and she's struggling. Let this be a reminder that when you're feeling like you've failed or you're experiencing doubt, remembering who you are is always the best starting point for picking yourself back up. Moana remembers who she is, fixes her damn boat, puts her hair up, and sails across the MF ocean. And although your struggles or feelings of failure might be due to different circumstances than Moana's, you can use her as an example of looking inward for the answers you need to forge ahead.

Okay, so if you need to find out who you are (more than just your job title, your relation to others, or what you like to do), how do you figure this out?

There are two ways you do this:

1. Remember who you are at your source.
2. Choose who you are.

But wait, you're probably thinking, *WTF does this have to do with personal finance?*

No, this isn't just a feel-good chapter to help you believe in yourself so you can girlboss your way to the moon. This chapter is vital when it comes to learning how to get ahead with money using the Deeper Than Money approach because you can't spend intuitively when you don't know who you are and what you want.

See, as we've talked about, the financial industry loves telling you how to spend your money. Many financial experts teach you that the only way to get ahead is to listen to their advice on how to spend and to restrict yourself in order to hit your goals.

Yeah, screw that.

If you haven't already caught my vibe, the purpose of this book is to unlearn the advice that has been so ingrained into your head. I will teach you how to spend in alignment with who you are and what you want, and teach you how money can be an easy, flowy energy that supports all your life goals and dreams.

But here's the big problem: How are you supposed to learn how to spend, save, and invest in alignment, especially when you've been taught to ignore who you are and do what you've been told?

I can't teach you how to spend in alignment with *you* until you know who the F you are.

So today, we dive in.

STEP 1: REMEMBER WHO YOU ARE AT YOUR SOURCE

Remembering who you are means thinking back to who you are at your source, before outside voices told you to change yourself to fit in. It's likely hard to think back to a time when you weren't hyperaware of who other people wanted you to be. Maybe your parents wanted you to be obedient, your friends wanted you to be cool, and your teacher wanted you to be smart. Or maybe you wanted to be those things for them. But early on, you likely decided that there's something wrong with you, and you tried to be more like everyone else in order to be popular, skinny, cool, liked, etc. Not to mention how early on you likely learned how to people-please. The list of how you want to be perceived goes on and on.

At some point, you existed before that. And you just simply fucking existed. There were things you wanted to do just because you wanted to do them. Not to be cool, not because other people did them, but because that's what you wanted to do.

You had a whole personality that was just you. Regardless of whether you were goofy, shy, smart, inquisitive, playful, reserved, or whatever, it was who you were. That is what you want to remember.

If you really want to see who you are at the core, a great place to look is home videos. Recently, my family and I were watching old home videos from my childhood, and I came across a perfect representation of my personality from when I was three years old.

It was Christmas morning, post–gift opening, and my mom had whipped out the camera to pan the room and check in on my sister and me playing with our new presents. My mom zoomed in on my older sister, Chelsea, who was daintily playing around with her new doll. My mom asked, "Chelsea! What did Santa bring you?" She joyfully replied, "I got a new doll! Look, I just braided her hair!" Then, Mom pans the camera to me. I had just gotten a new play desk and my back was to her as I was busily scribbling away with Crayola markers in my notepad. My mom asked me the same question, "Chloe, what did you get for Christmas?" After a few seconds of silence, with the camera still pointed at my three-year-old self, I turned back, looked at her, let out a sigh, and sassily replied with a smile and, "Please, ma'am, I'm busy working." I giggled as I returned to my urgent work.

What I find so funny is that even that young, I still had the same sarcastic, low-key-asshole, goofy personality that I have today. *That* is who I really am. And what I find to be so sad is that in the years following that video, as I went to school, my personality changed. I started to ask the question, "Am I likable enough?" and I worried about whether or not other people (or my teachers) would like that spunky, goofy, loud attitude that was natural to me. When I realized I could be perceived as being bossy, too loud, or "too much," I worked so hard to be different. I tried being quieter and more reserved, and I mirrored how everyone was around me. Taking up as little space as possible became my priority. Then, in my 20s, I tapped into that goofy personality again, and as a result, I feel freer than ever.

So the moral of the story is: if you are lucky enough to have home videos, go check them out to remember who you were before people told you what was and wasn't likable. Of course, it's amazing to change and become a better version of yourself throughout the years, but I bet at some point, you were told to tone down who you really were. That's a bunch of BS.

Who are you at your source? You know, that "nature" piece of the nature versus nurture conversation? In a completely relaxed state, surrounded by no one or only someone incredibly close to you, who are you? What are you like when you're comfortable and feel safe—not in fight-or-flight mode and not worried about who you are supposed to be?

And that's not to say the childhood version of you is exactly the person you need to be today, which is why once you take a look at who you are at your source, you can then look at choosing the person you want to grow into.

When you are relaxed and have time to yourself, start listing it out:

I am ________________________________.
I like ________________________________.
I don't like ____________________________.
I feel ________________________________.

You need to recognize who you are at your core, so you can start tapping into what you actually want.

Your spending and your personality are more connected than you may think. In fact, there are studies that prove this connection. The Association for Psychological Science published a study that analyzed more than two million spending records from a surveyed group of people. They found that there was a connection between certain personality traits and spending habits.[1]

When they looked at specific correlations between spending categories and personality traits, they found that people who were . . .

- open to (and valued) experience and travel tended to spend more on flights.
- more extroverted tended to make more dining and drinking purchases.
- more agreeable tended to donate more to charity.
- more conscientious tended to put more money into savings.
- more materialistic tended to spend more money on jewelry and less on donations.

When you start remembering who you are and give yourself permission to truly be yourself, despite what societal norms may say, you'll find yourself able to fully recognize your own intuition.

Intuition is one of those things that is incredibly hard to articulate, but when you know it—oh, do you know it.

Intuition is that tiny little "yes" you feel when your best friend asks you if you want to go on an afternoon walk.

Intuition is that little "no" you feel when someone is walking behind you and you feel uncomfortable.

Intuition is the small whisper for you to speak up, pick up a book, apply for a job, or reach out to a friend you haven't talked to in a while.

Identifying your intuition can be pretty tough when you've likely been taught your whole life to look for external validation to make decisions. Intuition tells you whether or not an outfit looks good, or what to say back to that hottie at the bar, or what your next career decision is. We are so trained (especially as women) to poll our friendship circles, find the most popular option, and make that decision. And there's a big difference between getting some advice from people you trust and abandoning your own sense of intuition in order to do what other people want.

INTUITION CHALLENGE

This week, every time you have to make a decision, instead of immediately turning to ask your friends, family, or coworkers for help, take a couple deep breaths and think to yourself about each possible outcome of the decision. Which one truly feels like a little "yes" from your intuition? It might sound silly, but do this every time prior to reaching out for advice—yes, even on what to wear. This way, you are practicing trusting your intuition instead of using someone else's intuition to decide what's best for you.

STEP 2: CHOOSE WHO YOU ARE

The second part of finding who you are is choosing who you want to be. The first part of who you are is simply the traits and values you inherited upon birth, but there's another part: who you choose to become.

There will, of course, be things that are unchoosable. You can't choose to be 5'9" if you are 5'2". But there are a lot of things you can choose, despite who you might be naturally.

For example: I am not an organized girly. I wish I was, but damn it, I am not. A mess doesn't bother me, and I am oblivious to a lot of disorganization. By nature, I am a messy person. However, I enjoy my things being organized. I enjoy when things are decluttered, put together nicely, and easily accessible. I know it's natural for me to be messy, but I don't live that way. (Okay, sometimes after a vacation or a big laundry day, that shit will sit out for a hot minute.) I don't live that way because I have chosen to intentionally implement daily habits and set up guidelines in my life to ensure I don't default to being messy. I choose every day to be an organized girl.

Another attribute that I am less than thrilled to admit, but I will just own: I, by nature, am not incredibly thoughtful. I really am not. I am a 7 on the Enneagram (BTW, the Enneagram test is my favorite personality assessment), which basically means my core desire is having fun and making sure everyone else is having fun, too. However, sometimes I can be oblivious to ways I could be thoughtful when I am focused on being here for a good time.

But that doesn't mean I don't actually do thoughtful things. I do thoughtful things because I have decided that I want to be a thoughtful person. Although I am, by nature, bad about remembering people's birthdays or when they start a new job, I choose to be thoughtful and, therefore, have to be incredibly intentional about setting myself up for success. About six months ago, I made a spreadsheet of birthdays, anniversaries, and other big events for my friends and family, which I constantly add to. Once a month, I set aside time to see what's coming up that month and get a card ready or be sure I send a text, make a phone call, or whatever it might be. In particular, I'm working on going out of my way to celebrate my friends' career and personal milestones, like getting a new job, promotion, or apartment, or moving to a new city. This is after realizing how much emphasis our culture places on celebrating relationship milestones relating to marriage: engagement party, bridal shower, wedding dress shopping, bachelorette party, and wedding. There is absolutely nothing at all wrong with celebrating weddings, but I want to be intentional about making sure all my friends feel celebrated outside their relationship status, too. The outcome of choosing the value of thoughtfulness has been that I actually am more thoughtful, even though I had to set up systems in my life because these actions don't come that naturally to me.

When it comes to choosing who you want to be in addition to who you already are, you will likely need to choose your own path, especially when it comes to money. If you currently feel like a broke girl but want to become a wealthy girl, you will learn how to set up systems to support that. But the most important thing is becoming clear on who you are, so you can then decide what your dreams are and create a list of priorities for what you want to do with your money.

Is there a habit or personality trait you would like to adopt? For example, maybe it's "I want to be more patient" or "I want to be more generous" or even something like "I want to be the girl who always looks put together when I go to work."

I want to be ______________________________________.

Now, what is one action you can start doing today to bring you closer to that person you want to be? It may be as simple as doing a short mindfulness meditation when you are feeling impatient, setting aside money in your spending plan to generously treat your loved ones, or picking out an outfit the night before so you feel confident going into your workweek.

I am going to start ______________________________.

The great thing about habits and breaking down these goals into small actions is that it's easier to implement them over time. If you want to be healthier, immediately changing your whole diet, going to the gym seven times a week, drinking a gallon of water, getting eight hours of sleep, and stretching daily would be a huge shock to the system. Adding in new habits and systems over time (in addition to doing the inner work) allows you to identify with those habits and adopt them as your own because you get to choose who you want to become.

USING INTUITION FOR SPENDING IN ALIGNMENT

I've said it before, and I'll say it again: the biggest reason why you need to understand who you are and what your goals are is that this information will allow you to spend, save, and invest your money in alignment. You can't spend in alignment until you know what alignment looks and feels like to you. And you can't know what you need to do to align your choices with your goals until you know who you are.

Part of living a life you love is knowing what you love. Knowing what you love allows you to spend on what you love. If you're feeling lost about what you want in life right now, I want you to tap into your intuition and remember that it's safe to be who you are naturally while also being able to choose who you want to be, too.

In the next chapter, we will dive into your big dreams and learn how to use them to create aligned priorities so you can focus on spending your money in the way that is the most aligned for you, and not just saving to save or spending to spend.

CHAPTER 7

Your Dream Isn't Stupid

Getting ahead with money isn't the end goal. **Record scratch.** You might be wondering why I am saying that, or what a chapter on bringing your dream to fruition is doing in a money book—and I'm happy to answer that for you. It's because money is simply a tool. It might seem like money is the end goal when you're stressed about finances and just want to live your best life and spend how you want to, but the truth is: *freedom is the end goal.* Freedom is getting to a point where you use money to create more in your life: to buy what you want, live how you want, and create what you want.

After years of working with thousands of women, I've noticed that one of the coolest side effects of women getting ahead with money is watching them go out and chase a dream: start a business, travel more, change careers, start a family, etc. There might be things in your way right now, keeping you from pursuing a dream, and money might be a big barrier in that. But it won't for long.

Now, it's time to get clear on your dream life and figure out how to get there, so that when money starts helping you instead of holding you back, you're ready to press on the gas pedal and make that dream a reality. It's never too late to start dreaming. Why? Because it helps create the map to your dream life, and the goal is to always be using your money as a tool to create that dream life. And let me also be clear: this chapter does not need to be an all-hustle and all-grind situation. Your dream can be doing less in your life, relaxing more, and taking a step back from the hustle—and likely, money is needed for that dream to happen, too. But how can you use money as a tool to create your dream life when you don't know what that looks like?

MY PERFECT DAY

I started creating the map to my dream life back in 2017. Keep in mind that at the time, I was just out of college and living the average corporate 8 to 5. One day, I sat down and wrote out the following (and I still have this written in my journal):

My Perfect Day

7 a.m.	Wake up without an alarm
7:30 a.m.	Walk my dog and listen to a podcast
8 a.m.	Have breakfast and go to the gym
9 a.m.	Team meeting and admin work
11 a.m.	Content and course creation
1 p.m.	Lunch
2 p.m.	CEO work on the business
5 p.m.	Wrap up work and go do something fun with friends

At the time I wrote this, my day did not look like this at all. In fact, my normal day consisted of something more like this:

4 a.m.	Wake up and get ready for the gym
4:30 a.m.	Gym
5:30 a.m.	Work on my side hustle (this business!)
7:30 a.m.	Drive to work
8 a.m.	Work at corporate job
5 p.m.	Drive home
5:30 p.m.	Work on my side hustle
8 p.m.	Dinner
8:30 p.m.	Work on my side hustle
10:30 p.m.	Go to bed

I was a girl on a mission. (Even looking back, I wonder how I functioned on so little sleep!) It was a lot of work, on other people's clocks, and not a lot of freedom to flow through my day like I wanted to.

For some people, having the structure of a workday like that and the security of a stable paycheck sounds like a dream. However, I had always been the opposite. Remember little lemonade hustler Chloe from Chapter 2? I had always been a visionary and a daydreamer; therefore, I was very used to people telling me to be more realistic, especially when it came to entrepreneurship and starting the business I have built today. Listening to realistic Chloe was the reason I found myself at my 8 to 5 corporate job, but visionary Chloe was what fueled every extra second of my spare time.

People would laugh at me for the way I posted on social media about my side hustle. I would see screenshots of group messages making fun of me, and to be honest, there were times I wanted to give up. My family would remind me to keep taking my corporate job seriously because it was my "real" job. I constantly felt like the world, and everyone in it, was telling me that my dream was stupid.

However, the reality was that it wasn't *their* dream. Think about a time when you had a really scary nightmare or a really wild dream—one that felt so unbelievably real you woke up and looked around to be sure it was just a dream. When you try to tell someone else about it, they just don't get it. With dreams like that, other people won't ever feel the reality of it like you did, because it wasn't their dream. What if we applied that same logic to the dreams we have while we are awake? I once heard someone reframe this idea, and it has stuck with me for years. It goes like this:

> I want you to imagine our world and all the people in it. When every person goes to bed at night, they think about the things they need and want more than anything in the world, and they pray to God/the universe and ask for that thing.
>
> *God, please just help me find a new job.*
> *God, please just help me with my body image struggles.*
> *God, please just help me figure out how to get out of this debt.*
> *God, please just help me figure out my health struggles.*
>
> Then, God hears their prayers. Then He sits and looks down at the world and thinks, *Who can I give this mission to? Who will take it and love it and fulfill it and help all these people?*
>
> Then *woooooosh*. God sends down the dream to be smacked into your heart. For example, maybe one day you wake up and think, *I know this is crazy, but I feel like I really want to start*

a business that teaches teen girls how to work through body image struggles.

But then you think, *Well, that's probably a stupid dream.*

But it wasn't a stupid dream.

It was in your heart not only so you could fulfill a big dream of your own, but also because someone out there needed what you could give and you were the one appointed to help.

What if your dream wasn't just a silly little idea? What if it was placed in your heart as a way for you to help other people?

What if your dream of becoming a personal trainer results in helping a dad learn how to be healthy and take care of himself, and now he's able to teach his kids how to maintain their health?

What if your dream of buying a house turns into a huge blessing when you're able to offer your friend a place to stay when she needs it?

What if your dream of finally having enough money saved up to buy a dream car inspires a little girl who sees it one day, and she decides to start saving her money to hit her goals because of you?

We are often taught our dreams are selfish and that we should just ignore them. But what if working toward our dreams was not only beneficial for us, but for others as well? What if, instead, we listened to them? What would be possible for us?

Let's walk through what your dream life actually looks like.

EXPLORING DESIRE

The first step toward figuring out your dream life is exploring desire. This exercise might sound weird because you've probably not spent a lot of time thinking about it, but figuring out what you want can be powerful.

We are often taught through school, church, and old-school parenting that our desires are things to be hidden, swept under the rug, and kept to ourselves. Not only is it unusual to be asked our desires, but historically, laws were in place to deny our desires. White men were always afforded basic rights, like the right to an education and to vote, or the right to join the army. Women had to fight for those same rights. Voicing our desires can be seen as selfish, self-centered, and even self-righteous, and this has often resulted in associating desire with feeling ashamed. Our dreams have been frowned upon for generations.

Our culture has taught us that it's "right" to ignore our desires, but essentially, what is "right" has been defined by some other authority figure. Let's say your parents deem it "right" to grow up, go to college, get a good job, work there for 50 years, and then retire. If you're taught to ignore your own desires and follow along that assumed path, whose version of "right" are you following?

This mindset can result in a sacrificial mentality—one I struggled with for years. I had this impossibly strong subconscious belief that whoever suffers the most is the most valued. As a result, not only did I constantly ignore my desires, but I overworked myself, burning out in the pursuit of what others wanted. In the end, I had smothered so many of my own desires that if I was not praised for my sacrifice, I would become furious.

Remember, part of my belief was thinking that whoever suffered the most was valued the most. So if I suffered and wasn't valued, then what was all the suffering for?

You've likely seen someone in your life who's been negatively impacted by this sacrificial mentality. Maybe it's your friend who stuck it out in a degree program she *hated*, telling herself it would be worth it when she's making six figures, even though she will hate her job. Maybe you saw your coworker settle for being overworked and underpaid, all in hopes of getting that promotion. Maybe it's your sister who stuck it out in an unhealthy relationship, thinking it would all be worth it after her partner changed. In each example, these women are subconsciously looking at suffering as a long-term investment—all the struggle would be worth it someday. But what if there was no reward for the suffering? What if we decided to stop leaning into suffering and start following our desires instead?

In our nonstop hustle culture, we revere the idea of grinding through obstacles and enduring pain and sacrifice for our goals. Ignoring our desires and happiness in order to be "rewarded" with wealth, fame, or a fairy-tale relationship can really skew how we view our dreams.

Letting go of these damaging beliefs is a life-changing shift.

Today, let's start playing around with the idea of desires. It takes practice because we are often so out of touch with our wants and desires. So let's start now. If you get stuck on any of these, focus on solely describing how you would love to feel.

What is the job you desire?

____

How do you desire your partner (or if you're solo, a friend) to treat you?

____

What is the living situation you desire?

____

What is the amount of money or wealth you desire?

____

Start there and begin imagining these things. Daily.

How would it feel to get them?

Imagine looking into a crystal ball and seeing yourself receive the call that you just landed your dream job, or that the business you dreamed of starting is open and thriving.

How would that feel?

Listening to what you desire can help you get clear on exactly what you want and start moving it from a thought to a feeling, so you can start creating it as a reality. As we talked about with BTFAR in Chapter 4, when you listen to your thoughts of desire and start to imagine what it would feel like if you followed them, you start taking action to change your result.

WELCOMING JEALOUSY

Jealousy gets a bad rap, honestly. And there are outcomes of jealousy that should get a bad rap. Let's say you are jealous of your friend, Shaley, for the promotion she just got. Because you're feeling salty, you don't congratulate her, you don't go to dinner with her to celebrate, and you spend the next week feeling bitter and irritable. That's a negative jealous reaction. Not only did that emotion negatively impact you, but it also negatively impacted her because she felt like a close friend wasn't supportive of her big achievement.

We all want to be women who support women, but sometimes it's so damn hard when we see other women getting the thing *we* want, right?? So then we become bitter, secretly wanting her to fail and ultimately holding on to some really shitty energy.

If you're nodding your head along with me, you're probably confused why I titled this section "Welcoming Jealousy." Because it's bad vibes only, right?

Nope. Not when it's used as a tool for good.

Let's look at that scenario again where your friend Shaley gets a promotion. All of a sudden, you become so jealous. This time, however, you take a second, put your hand on your heart, and feel the fiery emotion of jealousy. You open your notebook or iPad and write: "I want ________________________________." And then the words start pouring out.

You start going to town, writing everything Shaley has that you want for yourself. You stay fired up, and you honor that inner child throwing a tantrum who initially thinks that Shaley getting a promotion means you are not going to get what you want. But you know that isn't true. You know that Shaley getting a promotion is stirring up *clarity* in you. And clarity is one of the best gifts you can ever get. Clarity helps you understand exactly what you want so you can go get it. You create the entire list of things that you are jealous about, that Shaley has, and you tell yourself, *Thank you for the jealousy because now I am so clear on what I want, and this experience of jealousy has lit a fire under my ass to create a plan to get after it.*

With this mindset, you can expand your thinking to see that Shaley getting the promotion is logistically a huge win for you, too. Not only has this shown you it's possible, but it's also provided an opportunity for you to take her to dinner and ask her for tips on what helped her get the promotion. You are genuinely excited to celebrate with her because you know your jealousy has nothing to do with her and everything to do with feeling like your desires aren't being met.

When you are triggered by jealousy, you can change the narrative instead of letting your unhealed reactions cause negative outcomes. Jealousy, when used for good, is a source of clarity.

Who is someone you are jealous of, or when was a time you experienced jealousy?

____

____

What clarity did it provide about what you desire?

____

____

Write the person a thank-you (no, you don't need to actually give it to them) for the clarity they provided you or for the example they set to show you what's possible.

CREATING THE DREAM

When you can understand your desire and use your jealousy to create more clarity around what you want, it's time to get specific about what the dream is and what you need to do to make it happen. Often, the problem with dreams is that we doubt ourselves and we let other people's feedback get in our way.

Reminders if anyone discourages your dream:

- It isn't their dream. It's yours. So of course they won't get it. Them shitting on it comes from them not being invested in your dream. That's okay if they aren't.

- It can hurt so deeply because they're speaking into that place of fear you have. If you already doubt yourself and someone says, "OMG, did you see her? Why is she doing that?" I get it. It can sting so badly because there is a tiny piece of you that is saying the same thing to yourself. That voice of doubt is there to keep you safe, but it's not the truth. Don't listen.

This reminder is here for you again because the moments of doubt will pop up . . . a lot. Learn to notice them without believing them. Let belief, excitement, and joy be louder than the voices of doubt.

Now it's time to create the dream. You can follow along by writing in here or grab a notebook for more space!

Step 1: What Is the Dream?

I recommend getting super specific, going all out, and pivoting as you go. It's easier to start something, be all in, and then make changes, instead of trying to do something really broad.

____

____

____

____

____

____

____

____

____

____

____

Step 2: Why Do You Want This? Why Was This Dream Placed in Your Heart?

Who can this dream help? Who can it impact? What joy will it bring to your life? To the lives of others?

Step 3: What Is Your Perfect Day?

Write it out like I did earlier in the chapter, hour by hour. I want you to imagine it. Every step of the way. How would having this day feel? What would it do for your life?

Hang this up somewhere you can see it. I want you to imagine how you currently feel every single morning when you wake up. How would it feel if this was the schedule you were waking up to instead?

Step 4: What Do You Need to Do to Practice Believing This Is Possible?

____
____
____
____
____
____
____
____
____
____
____

One year after starting my business, I was still working in corporate, but anytime someone asked me what I did for work, I would tell them about my corporate job and not even hint at my own business. I was embarrassed. I didn't want people to judge me, and honestly, I still had so many doubts that I would actually succeed. A huge shift came when I started believing that success in my business was possible for me. I would ask myself, *If I believed this would actually happen and that I'd be successful, how would I act now? What would I say? What would I do?* When I started doing those things, I started actually working toward creating the life I dreamed of and bringing my dream to fruition, and I proudly shared about being a business owner.

Step 5: What Is One Step You Can Take Today to Get Closer to Your Dream?

One of the weirdest parts of creating my dream schedule was how many of those items on my list I could actually start implementing immediately. I never went on walks in the morning, but in my dream schedule, I took my dog on a morning walk. So I started adding walks to my current morning schedule. The second change I made: I used to never, ever take a lunch break at work, but that was something I *could* implement, and when I did, I was so much happier. The more specific you get, the better. I wrote out my dream schedule, but I would also imagine the food I was eating, the clothes I was wearing, the appearance of the apartment I was living in, etc. In my perfect day, I had healthy snacks on deck, I had only clothes I truly loved, and my apartment wasn't cluttered. Those are things I could have started doing at the time, prior to my dream life ever coming to fruition. So I did. I started working on those other changes in my life that I did have control over at that point, and as I started changing and elevating my life, I noticed that I continued to believe in my dream even more.

STEPPING INTO YOUR DREAM DAY

The wild thing is that in my life today, my most average, normal day is almost exactly like that perfect day I had plotted out years ago. My current average schedule goes like this:

7:30 a.m.	Wake up without an alarm
8:30 a.m.	Take my dogs on a walk
9:30 a.m.	Eat breakfast, read, listen to a podcast
10:30 a.m.	Work out at the gorgeous downtown gym
11:30 a.m.	Shower, eat lunch
12 p.m.	Team meeting (in the summer, I often take this call from the rooftop pool)
1 p.m.	Walk to downtown office for CEO work
6:30 p.m.	Walk home and meet up with friends or have a chill night at home

My dream day I imagined a few years ago is my current baseline reality. Holy shit.

It's really crazy to reflect on that shift and how 16-year-old Chloe would be in shock if she knew what my life was like now. Hell, even 22-year-old Chloe would be in shock! I still do this exercise to create what I want my perfect day to look like a year from now.

I will talk more about our privilege trajectory in Chapter 9, but I am incredibly blessed and privileged for my baseline trajectory—basically where I would have ended up solely based on the opportunities I was born into. However, this life I live now wasn't where my trajectory was heading. I had to figure out the exact destination and then take small steps every single day to start creating this life and bringing this dream to fruition. Now it's your turn. The biggest part of starting to create your dream life is to start imagining it working, envisioning yourself living that life, and taking one step today to get closer to it becoming your reality.

Identifying your dream life is going to be vital as we talk about shifting from the mindset of "trying to spend as little as possible" to spending in alignment. But you have to understand your dreams in order to understand where you want your trajectory to lead. When you understand your dreams, you can start understanding your current priorities and how to use money to support them.

Your dream is in your heart for a reason, and it's time to start believing it is there not only to help you create your dream life but also because the lives of others are going to be positively impacted. Your dream is fucking powerful. And it sure isn't stupid.

PART 3

Understanding Money

CHAPTER 8

Money Thermostat

I was 23 when I first moved into my cool, new, big-girl apartment in Kansas City. It wasn't just new to me; it was new in general. The building had officially opened a few months prior, and they were offering two months' free rent. My previous apartment was in small-town Iowa, where I'd lived in a tiny one-bedroom unit with no central heat or air and a coin-operated washer and dryer in the basement. My rent was $600 a month. Now, my rent was tripled. Before I knew it, my two free months without rent were over, it was the 31st of the month, and my first rent payment was due.

Let's back up a little so I can tell you how I got here. My corporate job was headquartered in Kansas City, and I was offered a promotion to relocate from Iowa. I flew down the following week to meet the team I would be working with, get more information, and go apartment shopping if I decided to move.

I made the biggest spreadsheet of all time and pulled so much information from apartment shopping online, so I knew exactly where I was going to look, how much it was going to cost, and what amenities were included. I wanted to stay under a specific price point, but at the same time, I also wanted to be able to live my best life. At this point, I had spent my entire childhood in small-town Iowa, lived in a college town, and then moved to another small town in Iowa. I wanted a new experience and I wanted to play bigger.

When I set my mind on moving to a bigger city (a phrase my New York friends roll their eyes at), I wanted something different. This was likely the only time in my life I would be living downtown in a fun city, and I wanted to live it up in a high-rise instead of finding the cheapest option 25 minutes away.

I decided I would have the rest of my life to live in suburbia, and I wanted to spend a year living in the city. I did the math before I made that choice. I figured out the price difference for one year of living in one of the cheaper apartment options in the suburbs versus living in my dream apartment downtown. When I had that number, which was about a $3,000 difference, I decided that investing the $3,000 into experiencing the downtown life, atmosphere, and crowd was worth it. Spoiler: it was. I feel confident that the time I spent living downtown will truly go down as some of my favorite times ever. I met some of my best friends living there, and the memories we've made can make me laugh or cry on command. Making the investment to live downtown was, and still remains, one of my favorite decisions I have made to date.

However, going from spending $600 a month to $1,800 a month on rent shot my money thermostat through the roof.

My money thermostat? Let me explain.

Coming from college apartments, it was quite the experience moving into my new downtown apartment. I was amazed by the lights of the city and my newly built apartment complex, but something equally amazing to me was the smart thermostat hanging on the wall. I was in awe. I could set it *from my phone.* I could change it when I was in *another state.* I think I was most surprised at the fact that you could set a "range" of what was the coldest and warmest you wanted your apartment to be so it could fluctuate freely throughout the day, without ever dipping below or above your ideal temperatures. It was like magic compared to the old-fashioned thermostat my dad took pride in monitoring like a hawk.

I am not an Arctic polar bear, so I like to keep my apartment between 69 and 73 degrees Fahrenheit. Anyone who sleeps hotter or colder than that is likely a serial killer, in my opinion. My apartment faced the sunrise, and if I didn't close my blinds in the summer, the heat of the sun would warm my apartment incredibly fast. As soon as that happened, the air would kick on and bring my apartment's temperature back into the "comfort zone." On cool, overcast days, my air often wouldn't turn on at all. But on the super-hot or super-cold days, oh man, it had to work overtime.

YOUR MONEY THERMOSTAT

Your money thermostat is like the smart thermostat of your brain that dictates how you view and handle your money.

Just like a fancy thermostat that kicks on whenever it gets too hot or too cold for your liking, your money thermostat works similarly. It is initially programmed based on outside factors—how you were raised viewing money, beliefs you have about money, or experiences you've been through with money. All these things impact your money comfort zone. When something happens and you go outside that comfort zone, you will either subconsciously self-sabotage or get scrappy (depending on whether you're too hot or too cold, money-wise).

Your money thermostat is not bad; everybody has one, and its purpose is to keep you in the same place. Your money thermostat is basically where your nervous system feels calm. Remember back in Chapter 3 when we talked about our caveman brain solely wanting safety and security? Your nervous system is calm when it can predict what is going on—basically giving you a sense of control. If you know what it feels like to always have $0 in your bank account, then you will self-sabotage your way back to $0 because that allows you to have a sense of safety and control—you are used to operating there. You want to change your money thermostat. You want your nervous system to feel calm and relaxed with a massive savings account so it no longer subconsciously self-sabotages to get back to the predictable. Once you understand it, you can use your money thermostat to your advantage and understand why you might be feeling resistance around different situations involving your finances.

At one point or another, you likely have felt stuck in a money rut—never really making progress. Maybe you paid off some credit card debt but then you racked up the balance again. Maybe you have grown your savings but then there's always something that comes up and you dip back into it—resulting in you staying in the same place. Your money thermostat will keep kicking on to keep you there until you start to change its settings so your nervous system can feel safe in your new level of finances (amount in savings, for example).

Your goal is ultimately to not only raise the top of your money thermostat so you can start feeling worthy of receiving more money, but also raise the bottom of it, so you can start feeling more safety and security with money and not be so close to dipping into survival mode.

Let's explore your ideal thermostat settings.

What Does Your Money Comfort Zone Look Like?

We've talked about money beliefs—how they're passed down to you at a young age and how they help to create your money comfort zone. Along with those money beliefs, you learned as a kid what is "normal" and what is "comfortable." Unfortunately, if you learned that stress and anxiety are normal when it comes to money, those emotions are likely a part of your money comfort zone.

Let's use Jensen as an example. Jensen grew up in a household where money felt unstable. Her parents would often talk about not having the money to pay for things one minute and then buy a ton of things as soon as more money came into their account. Jensen became so used to money feeling unstable that this was her comfort zone. It didn't matter that the comfort zone felt scary and unsafe; that was her baseline. Years later, Jensen graduated college and started a corporate job, finally getting a steady paycheck. However, she always finds herself thrilled on payday—spending money like wild, only to be unable to buy groceries a week later because her account is empty until next payday. Although there can be financial-literacy barriers (or others!) at play here, we can recognize the comfort zone that Jensen's subconscious still craves: instability. As long as it is the same place she has been in time and time again, it gives her a false sense of control, because the outcome (instability) is familiar, and according to her caveman brain, familiarity means safety.

When we understand where our current comfort zone is, we can work to become comfortable with new financial outcomes and feelings.

Your Comfort Zone

How does money normally feel to you (stressful, calm, etc.)?

___

What is a normal amount of money in your checking account or savings account?

___

What is a normal amount of money for you to make or get in a year?

___

When you identify your comfort zone, you can identify how your money thermostat is currently supporting it.

What Is the Bottom Side of Your Money Thermostat?

On the bottom side of your money thermostat (pictured on the next page) is the money floor. The money floor is the lowest financial position you will allow yourself to be in before your money thermostat kicks in and you get back into your comfort zone. This is the line in the sand for you. When or if you get to

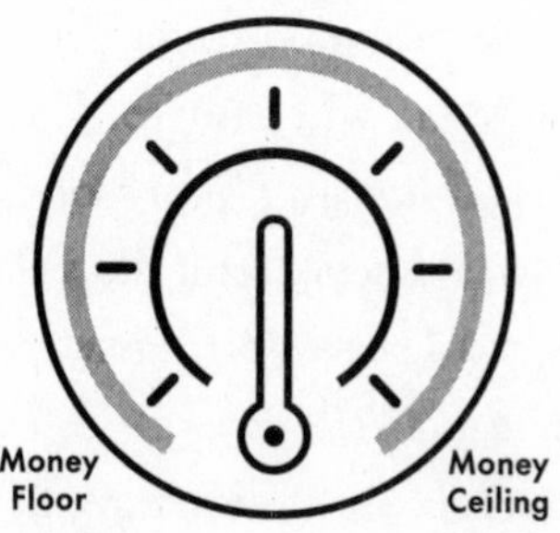

this spot, something inside you wakes the F up and gets scrappy to return to your comfort zone.

Everyone's money floor is different, but when it kicks in, our instincts get us in gear. For me, when I was a broke college girl, my money floor was –$50 in my bank account. (Yes, you read that right. Negative $50.) Once I had two overdraft fees and the total was –$50 in my checking account, I was low-key shitting myself. I would suddenly declare, "This will never happen again!" and I would pick up more hours and work my ass off to get back to where I had more than $100 in my checking. Then, whew. I would chill, not pay attention to my account for a while until I saw that –$50, and then start the cycle over again.

We all have a baseline, and it's different for everyone. There's no equation or percent of your income calculation; it's simply a feeling. For example, when my younger brother was home for the summer after college, he kept breaking my parents' rules that applied while "living under their roof," so they said he could sleep in his car in the driveway or pay for another place to stay. He chose the driveway in the front seat of his car. For an *entire* summer. To me? Wild. To him? His bottom limit. There's no judgment of what your bottom line is, but it's important that you raise it.

For me, when I increased my money floor, I raised my expectations of what I was willing to accept. I decided my new money floor was going to be $0. I would never get another overdraft fee again. What changed is that when my bank account used to get to $0, I wouldn't think much of it: *Oh, it's always like that.* But now that I had decided I would never let it dip below $0, I would start to get scrappy: *Shoot! I only have $60 in my checking. I need to be sure I plan out my expenses so it can't go down to $0.* I would start noticing my balance earlier and ensure it didn't get below $0. After a few months, I realized how easy it felt to keep my bank account above $0. So I raised my money floor again, to $100. It felt hella uncomfortable, but I kept working at it until that felt normal.

Now my money floor is anything below four figures, in any account I have. In my emergency fund, it's six figures. If the account dips below that, I get scrappy and raise it up.

What's cool is that because my money floor is so high, even when I need to dip into an account, there's no stress. I have raised my money floor to sit at such a comfortable level.

I want you to get to a place where you literally cannot fathom not having enough.

Then, I want you to get to a place where you get used to always having extra.

What's your current money floor? This can be specific to checking, savings, etc.

____

What is the new amount you're going to raise it to?

____

What do you need to do to hold yourself accountable to your new money floor?

____

If you can, set up alerts on your bank account to automatically notify you if your balance dips below a certain number; this is a great way to ensure you steer clear of hitting that money floor. To be sure your account stays at or above your desired level, set up monthly automatic transactions from your checking (or wherever your paycheck gets deposited) to your savings account so you automatically keep your account where it needs to be. Lastly, check in with yourself weekly. Maybe even set a reminder on your phone to check your balance or add money to your account to ensure it doesn't slip your mind.

Let's say your normal money floor is $100 and you want to raise it to $200. (Start with a small increase, hit that goal, and then move on to the next one.) The goal is to increase that account from $100 to $200 as fast as possible. Then, once it's in there, your ultimate goal is to never let it dip below $200. Start trying to think of $200 as $0. Keep this up and then raise it again until your new money floor provides you with the ultimate form of comfort, safety, and security.

What Is the Top Side of Your Money Thermostat?

We will call the top side of your money thermostat your money ceiling. Your money ceiling is the upper limit of what you believe is possible for yourself and what you're willing to receive. On a surface level, it's hard to imagine there would be such a thing as receiving "too much money" to your brain. But it's important to remember that these are subconscious beliefs that have been formed over years and years, many of which may be passed down generationally. For example, if it was normal for your parents to struggle with money, that will likely impact your money ceiling.

One thing I see often is that although people tell me they want to become wealthy, they have a subconscious reluctance to actually receive or move toward that goal. Ahh, this is their money ceiling kicking in. It tells them that if they start to earn more money, become debt-free, buy their dream home, or build wealth through investing, they are not being true to the person they believe they are. This is almost like imposter syndrome, but you're trying to convince yourself you are that broke girl, *not* the girl who actually achieves her biggest financial goals.

Maybe you've heard people tell you, "More money, more problems," or even seen riches destroy the lives and values of friends or family. And financial literacy plays a part in this, too. Big jumps out of your comfort zone with money can result in a dramatic swing back into your money comfort zone. I mean, you can often see it in lottery winners! According to the *New York Daily News*, 70% of winners end up broke within seven years.[1]

Believe it or not, when more money comes our way, we can sometimes resist accepting it.

We get a promotion but feel too guilty to tell our coworkers.

We get a gift but say, "I can't take this."

We feel bad when we raise prices or even say our prices (if you own your own business).

This apologetic behavior can be due to your money ceiling pressuring you to stay inside your comfort zone. Your brain is telling you that instead of celebrating your financial success, you should feel guilty and keep it to yourself. So instead, you self-sabotage back to your comfort level. We can recognize this in the common phrase, "Money is burning a hole in my pocket." Instead of feeling comfortable with the new level you've reached, whether it's paying off your credit card to a $0 balance or having $5,000 in an emergency fund, you can feel the need to spend it in a wasteful manner that's not in true alignment with your goals.

Maybe this is the first time you've ever thought about the fact that you might have an upper limit on your money thermostat. The money ceiling is often the reason why you self-sabotage if you ever start getting ahead with money or make more money.

This destructive pattern happened often for me in the early stages of opening a business. I so desperately said I wanted to make more money, but I was so unbelievably uncomfortable with the idea of actually having it that I would self-sabotage any opportunities that were outside my upper limit. I would work hard to get a client, and that felt good. But if I had multiple people reach out to work with me (which is the goal, right?!), I would keep putting off responding to them with information about working together. There also were several times when I was asked to speak at an event but found myself overthinking or procrastinating, so it never happened. I finally had to confront myself and come to the realization that I was subconsciously rejecting receiving more money. If you've ever noticed similar behavior when you try to go beyond "normal" and an unbelievable pull of gravity pulls you back to your comfort zone, that's your money ceiling saying, *Sup bitch.*

Once you figure out how to raise your money floor so your baseline is higher, you also need to raise your money ceiling so you can accept more than you're used to.

You raise your money ceiling by getting clear on what you want and how to get there, and believing that's what is possible for you. We will talk about steps for how to do this in the next chapter, but for now, we need to identify your money ceiling and start thinking about what you want to raise it to.

A good place to start is to think of the most you have ever had in your savings. I would guess there are some fluctuations, but you might feel there's an amount that you reach in your bank account where it seems like something always comes up and you can't get past it. Let's raise that.

What's your current money ceiling? Get specific on checking, savings, etc.

___

What is the new amount you're going to raise it to?

___

What do you need to do to hold yourself accountable to your new money ceiling (set reminders on your phone, save *X* amount this month, etc.)?

___

___

___

Let's take Megan, for example. She identifies that her money ceiling is $5,000 because that is the most her savings has ever gotten to. When she reaches that number, something always comes up that she needs to spend money on, and the total goes back down. Her goal is to raise it to $5,500. Then $6,000. Then $7,000 . . . all the way up to $10,000. Right now her savings is at $4,900, so she is going to raise that to $5,000 and work to keep it at $5,000 until that seems completely comfortable. Having her savings remain at $5,000 will take planning to ensure she is protected if any unexpected expenses come up. (We will dive into how to do this in Chapter 14.) Then, Megan will make the first jump from $5,000 to $5,500 and be sure she feels 100% comfortable with it. Again, she will continue to protect her new money ceiling by preparing for anything that might come up. She might feel the money ceiling start to stress her out when she looks at her bank account and whispers, "Oh, that won't stay there for long." She will then put her hand on her heart and remind herself that it's safe to have more money. She will imagine how good it feels to have that money in savings and notice if she has any mini freak-out moments when her subconscious wants to sabotage its way back.

How Do You Use Your Money Thermostat for Good?

At first it might seem like your money thermostat is working against you. It might feel a little defeating when you notice that subconscious desire to get back in your comfort zone. However, something magical will start to happen when you keep practicing raising both money ceiling and money floor. When you raise your money thermostat altogether, that range becomes your new comfort zone. And what happens when that becomes your comfort zone? Oh yeah, that's right—your money thermostat will now protect that range and ensure you stay within it if something happens. This new pattern is freaking exciting. I haven't had an overdraft fee in more than six years because I simply cannot fathom a world where that happens. The funny thing is that overdraft used to be my everyday reality. Yes, it does take logistical changes, and we will get to that, too, but understanding how your money thermostat works makes it possible to use it as a tool to keep you in a more elevated state. When you're in that new money thermostat range and feeling comfortable—well, friend, then you're free to raise it again, and that's the most exciting part.

CHAPTER 9

Shame in the Financial Industry

"If you actually wanted to be debt-free, you would never see the inside of a restaurant until you had all your debt paid off."

I will never forget reading something along those lines from a famous financial guru. *Seriously??* I thought as I looked up from the pages after an all-night cram for finals to see the milk-crusted bowl of cereal from my 11:45 p.m. craving. This was when I checked out a finance book from the library as a Hail Mary attempt to learn about money. I was looking for some shred of hope that it was possible to get ahead. Instead of hope, I was handed a family-sized serving of shame.

I read those words as a junior in college, having just found out how much student loan debt I had. It felt like reading a college girl's prison sentence: "No going out until you are debt-free." Which, let's be real, I could do basic math: (my $7 per hour job) × (how many hours I could possibly work) = not even close to becoming debt-free by graduation.

So really, the prison sentence was: "No going out until you're debt-free, which will be after college, so if you actually wanted to accomplish that feat, you'd give up your college experience." The moral of the story: if you have debt, you simply aren't working hard enough and don't deserve to enjoy life, let alone grab dinner at your favorite restaurant. Seems a little harsh, right?

I read that and decided I was going to go all in. I wanted to be debt-free, and this was the only way to do it, right? *You're either intense as a gazelle, or you're not trying hard enough.* So I went for it. Like I mentioned, it was finals week, but what came after that? The post–finals week celebration, which I skipped and stayed in my apartment alone. I remember it because it ended up being one of those nights where so many funny things happened and my friends still reference inside jokes to this day. The next night, I turned down any plans to go out. If you can think back to my mini life story from Chapter 2, this was also post-breakup, so needless to say, I was in my apartment scraping the last spoonfuls of ice cream from the container (because buying another pint of ice cream was no longer allowed with my new spending rules) and bawling my eyes out because I had found myself in a YouTube spiral of wedding videos.

Near the end of finals, I caved and told myself, "Screw it. What's the point? I'm never going to get ahead with money, and I need to treat myself." And ya girl was back out on the town. Granted, I was such a lightweight I probably spent $14 at the bar. But let's just say I made up for the nights of fun I had missed out on because of my new spending "diet."

The next morning, I woke up with both a minor hangover headache (the kind you get when you're 20 and your body still likes you) and a major case of shame. *How could I be so stupid and irresponsible? The financial book must only be for people who are better with money than me. I suck.* My internal dialogue, The Bitch, mixed with a splash of hangxiety was kicking my ass, and I hadn't even gotten out of bed yet.

A few days went by, I picked up the book again, and I reread that same first line. *Maybe I just didn't want it badly enough? Maybe I wasn't trying hard enough? I should be willing to sacrifice everything I care about if I want to get ahead with money . . . right?* The only thing I was sure about was that every time I picked up that book, I ended up feeling terrible.

Sure, restrictive advice had helped me save a little bit.

But at what cost?

How much are the memories I missed out on worth?

I declined going to a birthday dinner for my friends. I said no to getting coffee to catch up with a coworker. I even refused to pay for half of a birthday present for my mom that was from me and my sister, because she was older, so I thought she should have to pay for 75% of the gift.

After those few months of all-work-no-play mentality, I didn't feel proud for "sticking to it." I felt sad. I was closer to my "goal" but had missed out on parts of my college experience. What was the point of hitting that money goal when it decreased my quality of life?

The message in the financial industry was clear: implementing shame-based money principles is the only way to get ahead.

Fuck. That.

Looking back, I can see that when I was trying to Google search all my problems away, I was really searching for the book you're currently reading. (And truly nothing makes my inner child happier than providing the safety and security to others that I so desperately wanted and didn't get.)

The biggest problem with the shame-based money principles taught in the financial industry isn't the external shame from someone judging you for where you are. The biggest problem is that it teaches you to internalize shame. The voice of shame in the financial industry is so loud it will echo in your mind and make you question every purchase and financial decision you make, even after you put the financial guru's book down.

Why am I wasting money on new clothes when I could be paying off my student loans?

Why am I throwing away money renting when everyone else is buying a house?

Why am I so stupid with money?

When external shame is the norm, the internal dialogue of The Bitch will start to copy that same script. Now, not only do we need to say *fluff off* to the opinions and judgments of others, but we also have to set ourselves free from the cages we put ourselves in.

Shame-based money principles sell you the narrative that if you are broke, it's *your* fault. Radical responsibility can be empowering when seen through the lens of changing your life, but it needs to go hand in hand with releasing the narrative that "it's your fault."

To understand why we need to let go of this narrative, sit back and relax while we dive into a little history lesson. And don't worry, even if you slept through Mr. Lullman's history class (my bad), I doubt this was covered anyway.

YOU CAN'T SIT WITH US

A study completed by the Council for Economic Education found that as of 2021, students are required to take a personal finance class in high school in only five states.[1] In addition to that, a number of states offer a financial course but don't require it for graduation. Or they just require that financial concepts be integrated into other mandated curriculum. It is important to note that every year, more and more states are realizing the importance of including personal finance as a part of a well-rounded high school education, which is amazing. But in my opinion, it's something that should be as nonnegotiable as tenth-grade chemistry (as I can confidently say I have never had to recite the elements on the periodic table in the last 10 years).

If handling money or getting ahead with money is not taught (or not taught well) in school, then where is it taught?

At home.

Which means your financial teachers are now your parents. And a rule of thumb I like to go by is: you can't teach what you don't know. A study done by Chase Bank found that 83% of parents said they wish they learned more about money when they were growing up; 13% said their parents didn't speak to them about money at all.[2]

Regardless of your parents' financial status or what they know about money, that is a lot riding on their shoulders to teach you (in addition to about a million other things).

Now on top of the education piece, let's talk about the resources in this example. (Again, this is a super-basic example, and we will expand on it later.)

Coming from a family with wealth does not inherently mean you will learn to be wealthy or better off, but it can improve the chances for both. So in addition to financial education, what else could the wealthy family pass down to their kids?

They can pass down cold hard cash. Okay, not like a briefcase full of dollar bills, but more along the lines of being able to fund their kids' college educations, so their children start off their adult lives debt-free. Or maybe they can buy their child her first car so that when she is 16, she doesn't have to save up to buy one of her own or take on debt at a young age. Maybe they even have money passed down or some sort of inheritance.

Inherited wealth can come with a whole slew of its own problems, like never learning the value of a dollar, not understanding how money works, or using money as a tool for manipulation. Mo' money can often mean . . . well, mo' problems. You also can have grown up with wealth but not received a car at 16 or any sort of handout! We simply want to look at the different opportunities that having wealth can provide in some situations.

On the flip side, a family that is struggling financially likely wouldn't have the resources possible to pass down cold hard cash. Additionally, maybe the struggling family can't pay for college, so their kids end up taking out student loans. Or the kids need to get a job, which requires reliable transportation, so then they take out a loan for a car. Maybe they didn't learn about how credit cards work, so they open one and end up getting into the cycle of revolving credit card debt as well.

This is a basic example, but the point is that if you've ever felt like you weren't invited to sit at the table with the cool kids (or I guess the rich kids in this example??), you probably aren't off base. When finances are kept as private as they are in our culture, the opportunity to get ahead also stays private. So if you don't have the resources to learn how to open a Roth IRA or increase your credit score without negative financial outcomes, who are you supposed to turn to when your parents don't know, either?

Additionally, if you're reading this and you aren't a white male, you've likely had a historically late start when it comes to getting ahead with money.

In 1920, women got the right to vote in the United States.[3] When saying "women" here, I want to clarify that while the nineteenth amendment granted the vote to all women, many Black women in Southern states had the vote stripped from them until 1965, when the Voting Rights Act granted women of all races the full right to vote.[4] So it actually wasn't until 1965 that *all* women in the United States got the right to vote (and that still is not addressing many other barriers that BIPOC [Black, Indigenous, and people of color] women faced when it came to voting, including violence and other discrimination).[5] It then wasn't until the 1960s that women were first allowed to open a checking account.[6] And it wasn't until 1974 that white women were able to open a credit card separate from their husband or father (as a result of the Equal Credit Opportunity Act).[7] As a female business owner, it hurts my heart that it wasn't until 1988 that women were finally allowed to get a business loan without a male cosigner (thanks to the Women's Business Ownership Act).[8] Fast-forward to 2020, the U.S. Census found that families with a female head of household have more than twice the poverty rate as those with a male head of household (38% versus 18%).[9]

Women have dealt with their fair share of struggles in the past century, but when you look at the financial disadvantages that BIPOC have endured during an even greater span of time, it's astonishing. Laws like the Equal Credit Opportunity Act helped level the playing field so those applying for credit could not be evaluated based on race, color, religion, national origin, etc. However, despite these laws, marginalized groups still face challenges obtaining the same level of credit as their counterparts.[10] This, in turn, impacts their ability to access larger sources of purchasing power, such as mortgages or business loans, which are some of the most common ways for families to begin building generational wealth.

This might seem like a long time ago, but it's not at all. When I bought my first house in 2021, I was the first woman in my entire family lineage to ever buy a house by herself with only her name on it. The wild thing? I didn't have to trace back very far to confirm this information, because my grandmothers and great-grandmothers didn't have access to the same banking resources that I do. Your grandmother might not have been able to open a credit card separate from her husband at a point in her life.

Your. **Grandmother**.

It can feel frustrating to realize that despite the laws updating and changing, we haven't addressed the generations of damage done from a wealth-building perspective. Besides, even though the laws changed, there are still many ways financial institutions have implemented racist and sexist policies. One example is the practice of "redlining," which began in the 1930s. The federal government and lenders would classify certain (predominantly Black) neighborhoods as "hazardous" and draw a red line around them on government maps. This information was used to determine whether or not mortgages with competitive interest rates would be made available to someone who wanted to buy within that area. Buying in a redlined area usually meant getting into a fairly exploitative loan with unfavorable terms.[11] Redlining also impacted the value of homes in these areas, which affected people's ability to build generational wealth. Redlining was another way to reinforce segregation. Even when redlining became outlawed in 1977, these generational cycles continued to be reinforced by economic conditions instead of by law alone.[12]

Having roadblocks in your way, despite how unfair and unjust they are, does not mean you're screwed if you're anyone other than a white man. However, it's important to acknowledge that privilege exists, and whether you are someone who has privilege or someone who has been thrown all the obstacles in the world, financial freedom is still in the cards for you—the journey to get there just might look different. Therefore, you cannot compare results without comparing resources.

When I first started my business, and even now, I got messages like this (most often from men):

"Why do you even have a business? All this is literally common knowledge."

The problem with this kind of message is that this is common knowledge for *whom*?

The dickhead who sent the message is right, in a way. Financial literacy *is* common knowledge . . . for families who have certain resources (wealth, education, time) and also choose to and are able to pass them down to their children. Now, there's nothing to be ashamed of if you are fortunate enough to have had these resources shared with you both growing up and as you entered your adult life! But it's not fair to assume that "how to avoid debt" is common knowledge for people who don't have access to the same resources.

You might have been born into a wealthy family. You might not have been.

I'm not saying that being born into a wealthy family or a family that educated you on finances makes your life perfect. I'm pointing out that shaming people for not knowing something that you were lucky enough to learn from someone in your life is bullshit.

And while we are on the topic of privilege, pop on your swim cap because we are about to pencil-dive right into the deep end.

"I'M NOT PRIVILEGED. I WORKED HARD."

I hear this a lot in the online money space, especially when more controversial topics are brought up, like student loan forgiveness.

As a reminder, I grew up in a small town where being a hard worker was probably a bigger badge of honor than quite literally anything else. I remember being 14 years old and having my mom drive me to and from my three part-time summer jobs because I was old enough to work 8 hours a day, but still not old enough to drive a car. Ya girl was out there working hard (for like $5 an hour, but I didn't care).

I'm no stranger to the side-hustle game either, whether it was donating plasma, walking dogs, teaching online English classes, being a personal assistant, etc. You name it, I've done it—all on top of working full-time hours or being a full-time student.

I've failed at things, I've made mistakes, and I've cleaned them up myself. I've worked my ass off to be where I am today.

But hard work alone is not the only factor in my success.

In addition to my hard work, I've had **privilege**.

I grew up in a middle-class, loving, two-parent household. We lived in an amazing public school district that offered college course credits and free extracurricular activities. I grew up taking soccer, golf, and swim lessons, and I went to Sunday school.

I am also a white, straight, cis woman who has never experienced roadblocks, obstacles, or prejudices due to my skin color, sexual orientation, or spirituality.

I never had to contribute financially to ensure my parents could take care of household expenses or bills. I also was never responsible for providing childcare to my siblings.

I never had to worry about whether dinner would be on the table or if the water or electricity would be shut off.

I had (and still have) privilege. And quite a bit of it.

See, the biggest disconnect is that often people feel like acknowledging their privilege diminishes their hard work or means their hard work didn't contribute to their success. That's just not the case.

My hard work truly changed the trajectory of my life, but being born with my privilege means that even if I hadn't worked hard, my trajectory would still have been higher than that of others who don't have the same privilege I do.

As shown in the graphic, you can have two individuals both putting in the same effort, but with the advantage of privilege, one has a head start. Also, these are just two factors when talking about increasing our positive financial outcomes! It is not shameful to have privilege, but acknowledging it allows us to stop financial shame and stop condemning those who aren't following

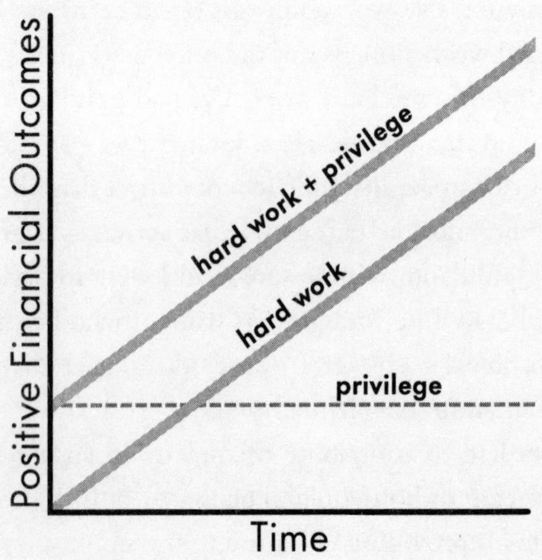

our same path. No journey is a perfectly straight line, so keep in mind that the person who is privileged isn't guaranteed to always achieve "more" than the person without privilege, and vice versa.

If I left privilege out of this conversation and made this chapter all hello-bitches-all-it-took-to-get-here-was-hard-work, what message would I be teaching you? I'd be teaching you that if you aren't where I am, it's because you aren't working hard enough.

What if you grew up with completely different circumstances than I've had? What if you've been working your ass off, but your baseline of resources looked different?

Now, don't let this idea of inequity demoralize you into thinking that you can't achieve the same as someone with more resources and privilege. It is important that we call out the different starting lines in life so there is zero shame if the journey looks different or requires different moves than other people.

Here's the cool thing: if you're reading this and you're like, *Holy shit. Wow. Now that I think about it, I've been hella privileged in ways I never realized*—then what?

USE YOUR PRIVILEGE FOR GOOD

- Talk about money at brunch. If you grew up understanding what a credit score is because you were taught how it works, and now at age 27 you have an "excellent" score, ask your girlfriends at brunch if they understand their credit score and explain how it works if anyone doesn't know. (And if you don't know, I am going to explain at the end of this chapter.)

- Have a good resource like GoodRx, which saves you money on prescriptions? Share it on social media, send it to some of your friends, or mention it at your church group.
- Low-key, take a higher percentage of splitting an expense on a bar tab with a friend you know has been thrown some curveballs.
- Speak up about inequalities when you see them. Your friends (or anyone!) should not have to fend for themselves when they experience prejudice, racism, judgment, or shame.

SHAME SUCKS. GHOST HIM.

Regardless of what has happened up to this point in your life, I would bet there are pieces of shame hidden in your relationship with money that have yet to be uncovered. Shame-based money rules like we talked about in the beginning of this chapter ("You can't spend extra while you're in debt" or "If you're not well-off enough, then you're not trying hard enough") reinforce this idea that shrinking yourself, shaming yourself, and putting yourself down are the only ways for you to get ahead. We are instead going to shift into a mindset of alignment-based principles. Here is the difference:

The ultimate driving factors of shame-based principles are sacrifice, discipline, and guilt to "do the right thing."

The ultimate driving factors of alignment-based principles are priorities, outcomes, and balance between where we are now and where we want to be (aka dreams, desires, and goals!).

That might sound all cupcake and fairy-tale right now prior to talking about implementation, but I promise you, this shit works. And I promise it's a million times more fun than letting shame rule your life, guilting you into doing what's "right" (based on other people's definition of *right*). Wanting to pay off your credit cards because you want that feeling of freedom, or building your emergency fund because you want security and safety is much different than paying off debt because you feel shamed into it or saving because you feel guilty for spending.

Let's look at some examples before we really break this down in the next chapter.

SHAME VERSUS ALIGNMENT

Example 1: You now have a job that is completely different from your college degree, and every time you go to make a student loan payment, you feel a deep twinge of shame for not needing that degree.

Shame-based belief: It's shameful and wasteful to work a job that's different from the degree for which you took out student loans.

Alignment-based belief: Going to college taught me so much about who I am today, and without that experience, I would never have figured out what I actually wanted to do. I wouldn't have become who I am today without going to school. I have the security of knowing that at any time, I can pursue a career that better aligns with my degree. But I chose a different career that is more fulfilling. That degree might not have been what I needed as a prerequisite to my current job, but it was a prerequisite to getting to where I am today, and for that, I am grateful for those loans.

Example 2: You're currently paying off past credit card debt.

Shame-based belief: Debt is bad. I got sucked into paying that high interest rate. I'm so dumb and irresponsible for getting myself into this situation.

Alignment-based belief: I did the best I could with the resources I had at the time. I now know differently, so I can do differently. Debt isn't bad or good. It's neutral. I chose to use debt, and now paying that debt off is what's most in sync with where I want to be going forward.

(If this is helping you come up with your own shame-based beliefs, make sure to take a second and add them to the list of old beliefs you want to update that you started creating in previous chapters.)

Adding shame to the equation doesn't make you pay off your debt faster; it only makes the process suck and creates an extra burden to carry along the way. And unfortunately, I cannot dismantle our broken financial systems tomorrow. Give me a few years, and that might be another story, but I can't snap my fingers and fix all systemic inequalities right now. But just because our credit system has major problems doesn't mean that ignoring it is in your best interest. And although I can't fix those problems today, I can show you how to beat the system right now.

As an example of our broken system in motion, and learning how to play the game and win, let's talk about the U.S. credit system. Our credit system is a huge barrier to financial freedom because there's such a lack of education around it. Furthermore, the rules are often incredibly misleading and outdated, causing many people to be stuck in one financial circumstance, without the opportunity to leverage a high credit score (for example) to get out of the tough circumstance. We are now going to talk about all things credit, so you can truly dive headfirst into a part of the financial world you might not have felt welcome in. You are welcome here. Let me teach you how to play the game and win.

YOUR CREDIT REPORT AND CREDIT SCORE

Think of your credit report like how that one high school English teacher (*I'm lookin' at you, Mrs. Grissom*) would read your essay, count every single one of your incorrectly used commas, and subtract them all from your grade to take your well-deserved A down to a B–, just for technicalities.

Your credit report is a report card of your past and present relationships with credit. Your credit report is often positioned either as the holy grail of financial health *or* as something you can 100% ignore. Both sides of that coin are BS. The truth is, yes, your credit report (and credit score) matter to you and likely will impact your financial life significantly. However, it also is not at all a crystal-clear overview of how you're doing financially or how well you will do.

There are people struggling financially with incredible credit scores, and there are wealthy people with not-so-great credit scores.

Let's first talk about what your credit score and report are *not*:

- They are NOT a measure of how financially successful you currently are.
- They are NOT a measure of how financially successful you will be.

What Is a Credit Report?

A credit report is the report card of credit. It reflects the who, what, where, when, and why of your borrowed money (debt) and how long it took you to pay it back. There are three companies referred to as "credit bureaus": TransUnion, Equifax, and Experian. These bureaus collect and send your data to a scoring agency (FICO or VantageScore are two common ones), which then creates your credit score.

The only accurate way of knowing what's on your credit report is to request a copy. You can get a free report once every 12 months from each of the three nationwide consumer credit-reporting companies (check out annualcreditreport.com). If you want to keep up on your score regularly and for free, the way to hack the system is to hit up a different credit bureau every four months.

On the next page you can see a breakdown of some of the basics of how our credit system works.

What Is a Credit Score?

A credit score is like the grade at the top of the report card, telling you at a glance how you are doing.

Imagine you are thinking about lending money to two friends.

Your friend Sidney is reliable as HELL. You've bought her a latte before because she didn't have her wallet, and she Venmoed you within two minutes. Her card gets stolen, she asks you for $100 to pay for rent, and she says she will pay you back in 3 days, as soon as her new card comes in.

The same day, your friend Naomi also asks you for $100.

Naomi still hasn't paid you back for the Beyoncé concert tickets you purchased for her in 2013. Naomi always has you buy her a drink, saying, "I'll get the next one," but never does. You know she owes other friends money, too.

If you had to choose, who would you rather loan your money to? And on a scale of 1 to 10, how would you rate each of them? The way you're judging Sidney's and Naomi's likelihood to pay you back is pretty much the premise behind a credit score.

Your credit score is a rating from lenders and financial institutions that tells other lenders and financial institutions how well you handle debt. It also can be impacted by bills you pay, like medical debts, utility payments, or your cell phone bill.

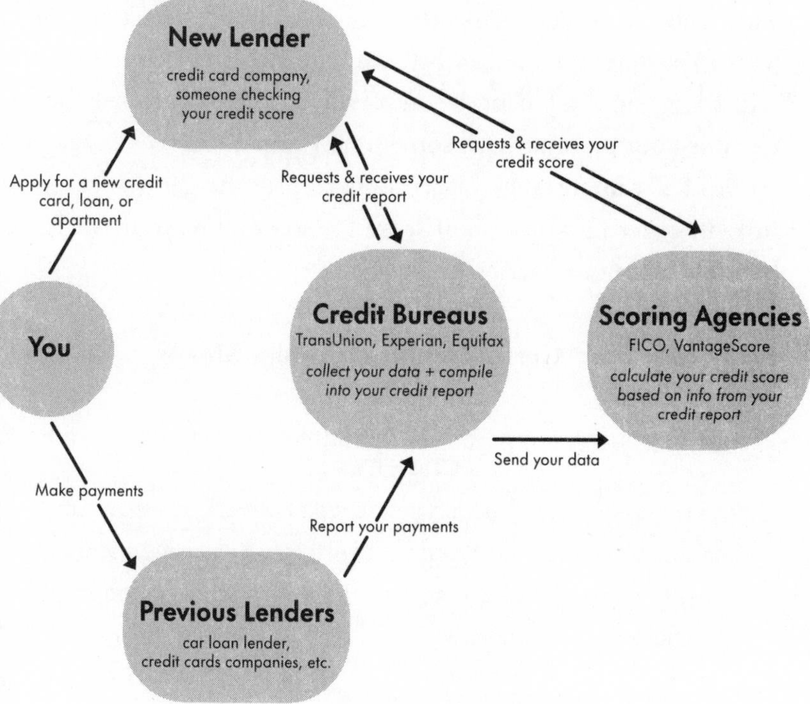

So Is a Credit Score Important?

Heck yes. It's a bullshit rating system, and, in my humble opinion, it is set up to make banks rich and keep many people in a cycle of poverty. However, you still need to understand the rules of the game you're playing.

A big example of how important credit score is and how it can impact your wealth building is its impact on what interest rate you can qualify for. Your credit score and report can be used by banks, lenders, and credit card companies to determine what interest rate you should be charged on a loan. In the case of buying a home, your credit score can be the difference between thousands or hundreds of thousands owed on your future mortgage. But it's not just banks that use your credit report and/or score. Your credit score can be used by a landlord to see if they will select you as a tenant, by an insurance company to help determine your premiums (in some states), and more!

It's hella important to learn how to play the game successfully in order for your credit score to be a tool in your wealth building and not a barrier.

What Do Your Credit Score Numbers Mean?

ACTION ITEM

Take a quick pit stop and log in to Credit Karma to check what your score is today. You can easily work to grow your credit score during the next six months, so don't worry if you are not happy with where you are right now.

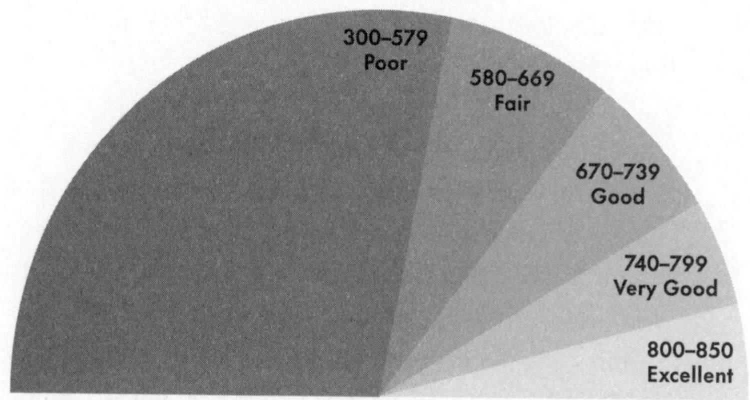

What Factors Make Up a Credit Score?

1. Payment history (35% of score)

   Payment history is the most straightforward: Have you made your payments on time? Because this is the most heavily weighted factor in your score, one missed payment could drop your score significantly. It makes sense, too, right? The number-one indicator of whether you'll pay on time in the future is if you have in the past. Track record matters, just like you trusted Sidney with your money because she paid you back in a timely manner, but Naomi had not.

   What can you do to raise your score?

   Mark all your payment dates on your calendar. If something comes up and you are going to have to miss a payment on your loan or electric bill or whatever, call the company and ask them to move your payment date back a week. This allows you to have time to pay it and also won't impact your credit score as a missed payment. Setting up automated monthly billing is also a game changer for people who have a hard time paying on time because they forget.

2. Credit utilization (30% of score)

   This category is a wee bit more complicated, but it all comes down to this: How much credit have you currently been offered, how much of that are you using, and what for?

   For example, if you have an available credit limit of $1,000 and spend $500, then you're 50% utilized. In the eyes of the credit-scoring models, they ideally want 30% or less. So for any amount you are above their "target" range, your score is negatively impacted. To make it more complicated, they also take into consideration what types of loans you are utilizing (e.g., student loans weigh differently on your score than credit card loans). If you have multiple credit cards, your utilization rate factors in your usage between all available lines of credit! You can find out what your credit limit is on each card, add those up, and then divide your current balances by that number to find your utilization ratio. If it's above 30%, you will want to work to use less of your limit, or increase your limit.

3. Length of credit history (15% of score)

   Although this one is super straightforward, it's not an easy one to fix by next week. The good news is that this only makes up 15% of your entire score. So although you can't hop in a time machine to open a credit card five years ago, you can ensure you're aware of checking how long an account has been open before closing it. That doesn't mean you don't close it or pay it off.

When I paid off my student loans (30 years earlier than the lender's timeline!) my credit score dropped by 32 points. At the time, I didn't care. I wasn't going to pay interest on my student loans just to keep them open. That's basically paying for my credit score to increase . . . and that is complete booty. The key here is to remember that the drop in my credit score was temporary.

I also knew I didn't need my credit score to be in tip-top shape at the moment because I wasn't planning to apply for a loan in the near future (such as a mortgage or an auto loan). That's really the only time you want to go into lockdown mode with your credit behaviors. As I continued to responsibly use my credit cards and never carry debt on them, I was able to bring the score back up without paying a penny for it. So don't be surprised if your credit score dips due to you making a big money move. It will go back up when we apply these overall tips. On your financial journey, you'll open new accounts and pay off other accounts, but as long as you are consistently making payments and playing the game, you'll be on your way to an excellent score in no time.

4. Credit mix (10% of score)

From a lender perspective, seeing that you can manage not only your student loan debt but also your credit card balance is a plus. This is where opening a basic credit card with no fees (after you know how to manage it) can be really beneficial if you only have installment loans like car, home, or student loans. You can build a strong credit score just by using a no-fee credit card and always paying it off on time and in full—without ever paying a dime of interest to the credit card companies.

5. New credit (10% of score)

   This is a measure of how many accounts you are opening or inquiring about (when a lender runs a hard credit check on you). A hard credit inquiry (aka hard check) occurs when you request a new line of credit. Typically, these occur with credit card applications, mortgages, car loans, apartment leases, etc., and the company must ask permission to run your credit check. It is great to shop around before opening a new loan, but be sure you are doing market research instead of having 10 different places run a hard credit check on you during the course of a few months. However, if you're shopping around for mortgage or auto lenders, make it a priority to do all your research within 14 to 45 days. The good thing is that during that time frame, multiple credit pulls only count as a single inquiry.

Your credit score is important because it will give you freedom and flexibility when it is strong. A good credit score can save you a sizable amount of money during the course of a loan, especially by landing you a lower interest rate. That score can also impact your being approved for a car or even how much you pay for your insurance. But at the same time, your credit score is not the only indicator of whether you are doing well or doing poorly.

Your Credit Score Starter Kit

- ☐ Open a Credit Karma account, check your credit score, and monitor your inquiries and any fluctuations. (You can set up email alerts.)
- ☐ Set reminders on your phone to be sure your bills are paid on time.
- ☐ Check to see how much of your available credit you are utilizing, and aim to lower this over time if it's more than 30%. (Lower than 10% is even better!)

WRAPPING IT UP

This chapter matters because, unfortunately, when inequalities are systemic, we can't talk about money without talking about the inequalities held in that construct. But at the same time, if you are privileged, you can use your privilege for good to create change in our world. And if you've faced inequalities and curveballs, it's important to acknowledge that while also knowing financial freedom is possible for you, despite external forces that have gotten in your way. Gaining financial independence is such an act of rebellion to a system of shame. No matter where you are right now financially or where you have come from, shame is not a necessary ingredient in finding financial success. It's time to say goodbye to shame, lean in to alignment, and take hold of empowerment.

CHAPTER 10

Idolizing Frugality

Let me set the stage for you. It's Sunday morning at 9:08 a.m. You've been snoozing your alarm for 38 minutes because you have a hangover that only an icy-blue Gatorade and Advil Liqui-Gels can fix. The thought of getting out of bed feels like the equivalent of climbing Mount Everest, and you wonder why the hell you've never invested in blackout curtains for your bedroom window. You're meeting two of your best friends in an hour for a classic brunch-rollover after a night out. You somehow pull yourself together with a baseball hat, big sunglasses, and a Liquid I.V. poured into your 40-ounce Stanley Cup full of room temperature water and make it out the door a casual 15 minutes late. You show up to brunch to find your two best friends in the booth with another girl you don't know. You are already on edge from the hangover and not in the mood for networking, but you slide into the booth and introduce yourself to the new girl and tell her you love her jacket. "Oh my gosh! Thanks. It's Gucci. It was $3,500," she replies.

This. Bitch.

You don't know whether it's the hangxiety or this terrible first impression, but you are instantly filled with internal rage. *Who does this girl think she is? Why is she rubbing her status in my face? Clearly she idolizes money, thinks she's better than me, and is over-the-top materialistic.*

Be honest with me. Given this scenario, what are the things you immediately assume about the new girl? Think of three assumptions you might have about her.

I assume she ______________________________.
I assume she ______________________________.
I assume she ______________________________.

There are no right or wrong answers, but we are going to dig into *why* we've assumed these things.

First, let me retell the same story.

9:08 a.m. Alarm goes off. Hangover headache. Need Gatorade. Roll out of bed. Make it to brunch. See friends. See new girl. "Hello, new girl. Your jacket is cool." New girl responds, "Oh my gosh! Thanks. It's from Target. I got it on sale for $20 yesterday!"

Cut scene. Now what do you think of the new girl?

Likely her comment didn't impact your thoughts about her more than, *Oh, sweet. I should go see if it's still in stock.*

Why?

In this example, she was modest and frugal, and in the previous example, she might have seemed flaunting or boastful. This is because in our culture, idolizing money is frowned upon, but idolizing frugality is accepted.

Growing up in church, I heard sermons that taught me to

believe money is the root of all evil and idolizing it will have you sent to the hot place. So I did what any hard-working teenager from a small, midwestern town would do. I idolized frugality instead. I pinched pennies. My obsession with spending as little as possible was more than a sense of pride when I bought things on sale—I started looking down on nice things and people who bought expensive items. This mindset became so toxic, but I never noticed how problematic it was, because it was socially acceptable.

The first step of figuring out how you might currently be idolizing frugality is doing a morality check on spending. Let's test out how you moralize money so you can free yourself from policing "good" versus "bad" spending and start spending in alignment.

Rate the scenarios below from 1 to 5 using this scale:

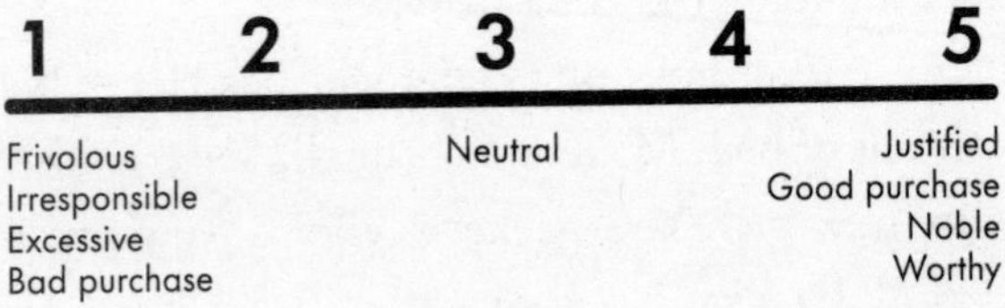

1	2	3	4	5
Frivolous Irresponsible Excessive Bad purchase		Neutral		Justified Good purchase Noble Worthy

You are rating these scenarios on the *act* of spending that money, not whether you'd *like* to spend money in these particular situations or not. These purchases aren't that deep. Don't overthink them; just rate them.

Scenarios to Rate

- Paying a parking ticket _____
- Paying for medication you need _____

- Buying a designer bag _____
- Spending $7 on a latte _____
- Buying food for your pet _____
- Paying rent _____
- Getting your nails done _____

Now that you've ranked them, let's compare spending $7 on a latte with paying rent. I am going to guess that even if you are a matcha latte princess, there is still a piece of you that ranks spending money on rent higher morally than spending money on a $7 latte.

Let's take the scenario a step further:

Scenario 1: You pay $1,500 a month on rent and spend $0 a month on lattes.

That piece of you that wants to be moral and noble is cheering. *Chef's kiss.*

Scenario 2: You negotiate rent to $1,360 a month and spend $140 a month on lattes (about 20 lattes).

Is this scenario somehow less noble because you're spending $140 a month on lattes? Even though if you hadn't negotiated, you'd still be paying that entire amount only on rent? Maybe part of you is so happy to finally have "permission" to spend $140 on lattes that you go ahead and spend it just because you can without even deciding if it's in alignment or not. Still, some guilt might creep in.

What thoughts come up for you in the second example?

____

____

____

Applying morality ("good" versus "bad") to your spending in scenario 2 might bring up thoughts like, *Well, yeah, but I could save that $140 and use it for something necessary instead of spending it all on lattes.*

What I want to point out here is the idea that spending the same amount of money, but on things we rank as morally good versus things we rank as morally bad or frivolous, can impact our internal dialogue of shame around spending. Let's call this the morality ranking system.

The biggest problems with the morality ranking system are that it comes from an authority figure's set of rules (for example, church, school, parents, society, government, a financial "guru"), it's highly generic, and it may not actually line up with what you value. When someone else is setting rules for your spending, you are not in an authority role with your finances; you are in a subordinate role. You are walking around with your own hard-earned money, but you're following what someone else is telling you is good or bad instead of choosing for yourself. And when you aren't choosing for yourself, that often feels like a massive restriction.

Now, that's not to say you can't fully agree with and take on certain sets of these "rules" that are passed down to you. You absolutely can, and if they align with your values and goals, you can keep them and integrate them into your approach to spending. Let's discuss what that actually looks like by considering the difference of morality ranking versus alignment ranking.

Here is the *alignment* ranking system:

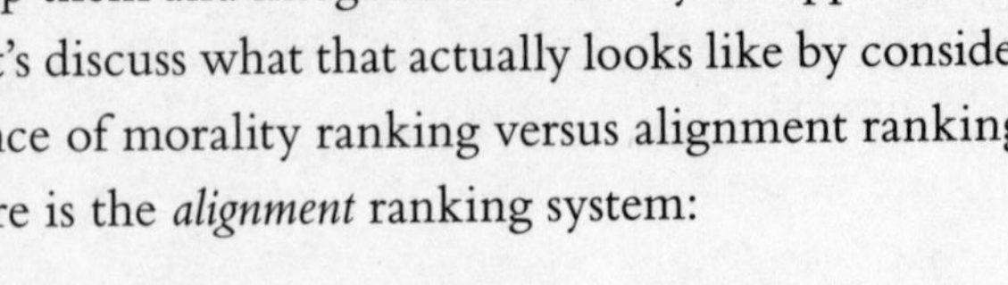

1	2	3	4	5
Regret purchase Don't value Not in alignment		Neutral		Love the purchase Works toward my goals In alignment

We will go deep into finding what alignment looks like for you in the next few chapters. But what happens when you switch to the alignment ranking system is that you stop using the morality of *good* and *bad* as generic terms and start looking at your spending for how it aligns with your goals and priorities.

Now, let's go back to our previous example about rent:

Scenario 1: You pay $1,500 a month on rent and spend $0 a month on lattes.

Let's say spending $1,500 on rent is in alignment with you because you aren't ready to buy a house and you enjoy the perks of renting. But you also absolutely love grabbing a latte, so $0 feels restrictive and a little out of alignment.

Scenario 2: You negotiate rent to $1,360 a month and now have $140 per month to allocate elsewhere.

If spending $1,500 on rent was already in alignment, this new $140 to your name every month feels so exciting and you're so proud you advocated for yourself. You ask yourself how many lattes per month would feel good to you, and your answer is 3 to 4 a week, or about 14 lattes a month. That number of lattes adds up to $98 per month, leaving you with an extra $42 to put toward something else that is also in alignment. Now you have rent, lattes, and $42 to put toward an extra expense or goal, and it feels like a win all around.

When you stop using the morality ranking system and start using the alignment ranking system, you're taking the first step toward freeing yourself from feeling any guilt when what is in alignment with you is not ranked "morally" best.

AN EXERCISE TO PRACTICE SWITCHING SYSTEMS

Open your mobile banking app, and scroll through your last 10 charges. First rank each charge on the morality ranking system from 1 to 5, like you did above.

How does it feel to use the morality ranking system?

____

Do you feel judgment for the charges that feel less moral?

____

Who created the morality ranking system you're currently using? Who chose the definition of "good" or "bad" spending?

____

Now go through these same charges and apply the alignment ranking system from 1 to 5.

How does it feel to use the alignment ranking system?

____

For the charges that aren't in alignment, what thoughts come up for you?

____

The goal of this exercise is to differentiate how the two systems make you feel. When using the morality ranking system, because you're using someone else's system, not only do you judge yourself, but also the only solution is to "just stop spending on that." On the flip side, when you're using the alignment ranking system and you find yourself ranking something as low and not in alignment, instead of judging or guilting yourself, you can ask yourself, "If this isn't in alignment, why would I want to spend like that? What is a way I could make a purchase like this be in alignment?" From there, you can take tangible steps to change out-of-alignment purchases going forward (which we will get into in following chapters).

IDOLIZING FRUGALITY VERSUS IDOLIZING MONEY

Idolizing frugality started to show up early on in my life, but it was accelerated when I started diving into the financial literacy world and was told that idolizing frugality was the only way of getting ahead.

To showcase my complete obsession with frugality, let me set the stage: I was 21, and it was time for me to get my own place. I was apartment shopping after college for the first time. Keep in mind, my standards were low because I had lived in dorms and rickety off-campus housing for the last four years, where rent each month was a couple hundred dollars. I had enlisted my older sister, Chelsea, to help me check out apartment options in the area. And I was filtering by the cheapest places I could find.

We rolled up to an apartment complex I had found online that looked promising from the website photos. But boy, was I about to get catfished. I walked in the door, and immediately the scent of cat flooded my nostrils. There was cat food on the hallway floor, and I don't even want to know how much cat piss was soaked into that carpet. It also reeked of cigarettes. Did I mention I am allergic to both cats and cigarettes?

When I asked about safety, I was informed that I should at minimum carry pepper spray if I wasn't going to own a gun. Gulp.

I politely thanked the landlord for showing us the apartment, and when we got into the car to debrief, I turned to Chelsea and said, "There has got to be a cheaper place. Maybe closer to $500 per month or something?!" She gave me that are-you-effing-serious look and said, "Chloe, this place *reeked* of cigarettes, was unsafe, and despite having the flexibility to spend more on rent, you want a *cheaper* apartment?" It hit me harder than the scent of cat pee. I had major guilt and shame around spending **that led to me idolizing frugality out of fear of idolizing money**. Despite having the financial ability to pay for an apartment that I would have felt safe in (and that my allergies would have approved of), I could not see past the fear and guilt of spending "extra" and it led to an obsession with spending as little as possible.

The problem with idolizing frugality is that the whole goal (whether consciously or subconsciously) revolves around spending the least amount of money possible, as if spending less is truly the more moral and noble thing to do.

What I didn't know on that memorable apartment-hunting trip is that there is a fine line between idolizing frugality (which I didn't see any problem with) and idolizing money (which gave me the major ick). Let's take a look at what the core focus of both idolizing frugality and idolizing money actually is.

Here's what idolizing money looks like:

- Valuing money or material possessions over meaningful things in life. Making money the center of your world, above friends, family, and things you love.

- Being driven by greed. The desire for more money, and getting it in a deceitful way, at the expense of others.
- Thinking and talking only about money. You are always trying to think about ways to make or keep money. You panic when you have to spend money and are constantly looking at your investments or bank portfolio.
- Feeling overwhelming jealousy when you see other people succeed financially and wishing for their failure. You can't stop thinking about how much more your friends are making, and you would do anything to live a lifestyle like theirs.

Idolizing money leads to your entire focus centering around—you guessed it—**money**.

So what does idolizing frugality look like?

- Spending money on things you don't actually like or need, solely because they were cheaper or on sale. This often shows up as guilt or shame in your day-to-day spending.
- Obsessing over spending as little as possible, potentially impacting your quality of life or your friends and family. (Have you ever driven 20 miles out of the way to use a 5¢ off/gallon coupon?) Believing the goal is to spend as little as possible (and idolize frugality) leads to shame and guilt for spending on any purchases.

The point is, we're taught that idolizing money, specifically wealth, ultimately dooms us to an unfulfilled or even criminal existence. Can idolizing money be problematic? Of course! But idolizing frugality can be problematic, too.

Although it's generally seen as more socially acceptable,

idolizing frugality still puts money at the center of a different kind of worship.

The reality is both idolizing money *and* idolizing frugality lead to an excessive focus on money.

Let's break down what idolizing frugality looks like by using Sarah as an example.

Sarah has a teaching job that feels incredibly demanding, and she gives her kids 100% every day. After a particularly stressful day, she runs to Target for shampoo, eggs, and a bottle of Rumple Minze for an upcoming weekend out with friends. (Poor taste in drinks in my opinion, but that's her thing.) While at Target, she takes a detour (as we do, right?) and finds herself browsing the women's clothing section. On the sale rack she finds a slouchy shirt that would probably fit her, and she could make it work for teaching. It's not the best quality, and she's by no means ecstatic about it, but it's only $12. Subconsciously, her goal is to spend as little as possible, so it satisfies that need and feels good enough to buy because she's getting a great deal. She wasn't looking for a shirt and isn't in love with it—and in fact keeps saying she wants to declutter her closet—but it was on sale, so she bought it.

Now, as Sarah's walking through the women's section, she stops in her tracks when she sees the perfect faux leather jacket she's been looking for . . . aaaaaand her heart sinks as she reads it's $52. She gets the ping from her inner voice, The Bitch, saying, *That's way too much. You can't buy that.* But Sarah immediately shuts up that voice with The Hulk, thinking, *You know what? Screw it. I work hard and never buy anything nice for myself. I deserve a treat.* She buys the jacket, too. When she goes home, guilt sinks in and she starts to shame herself even more for the purchase.

Sarah ended up back at her house with her shopping list

items plus two pieces of clothing: the $12 shirt she doesn't love but can make work and the $52 jacket she loves but feels guilty about. Six months pass, and the $12 shirt hasn't been worn once, costing her $12 per use (no usage yet) and taking up space in her closet, leaving it overcluttered with outfits she doesn't love. On the other hand, the $52 jacket has been worn more than 40 times. If she were paying for each usage of the jacket, it would be $1.30 each time—a steal compared to the $12 shirt that was never worn. However, she still has a ping of guilt when she grabs the jacket out of the closet, knowing she splurged instead of putting that $52 toward her credit card debt or finding something cheaper.

Sarah felt "allowed" to spend the $12 on a shirt that is now just clutter in her closet. She doesn't like it, she doesn't wear it, yet she felt allowed to buy it solely because it fulfilled her subconscious desire to spend "less." Sarah ended up buying the $52 jacket she is obsessed with and wears constantly, but she still feels bad because it was a purchase that didn't feel like spending as little as possible.

Because frugality is the underlying goal for her when it comes to money, Sarah's money is spent on a great jacket, a blah shirt, and an inability to find joy in either.

So if we aren't supposed to idolize money and we aren't supposed to idolize frugality, what are we supposed to do?

The goal is to see money as neutral.

When we can shift the focus to money being neutral, it becomes a tool. For example, you probably don't feel emotional about a hammer. You just use it when you need to hang up a picture or put together a piece of furniture. It's just a tool. Money can be seen in much the same way; it's a tool to bring you closer to the things you value.

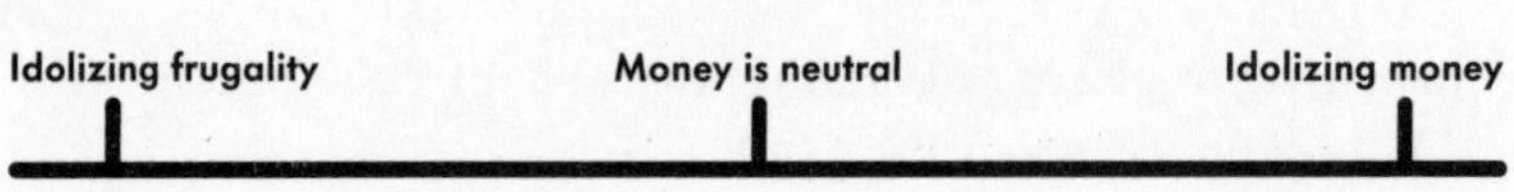

When money is neutral, it isn't ignored. The logistics of your financial situation matter, of course. But when money is neutral, you can focus on what each transaction looks like for you at that point in your life, not solely focusing on the money itself. You also can free yourself from morality-policing your every purchase and feeling the need to justify purchases above your necessary spending. Let's see what this freedom looks like in action.

Let's reframe Sarah's story, this time seeing what happens if she views money as a neutral tool to help her spend in alignment with her values and goals.

Sarah turns on some relaxing music in her Ford Escape as she leaves work and drives to Target. She takes a few deep breaths and works to calm her nervous system after a stressful day at work. She wants to decompress on the way there so when she's in Target she can be present and intentional with her spending, instead of buying from a place of Hulked-up impulse purchasing.

After grabbing the things on her list, Sarah decides to walk through the women's section. She sees the same $12 on-sale shirt, but knows she has plenty of shirts like that and doubts she would wear it that much, so she doesn't pick it up. She then spots the perfect faux leather jacket and sees that it's $52. She knows that she's allocated $200 for fun spending this month, and she definitely thinks this jacket is worth $52 of that. One of her top priorities has been to create a wardrobe that she truly loves so she feels more confident in how she shows up. Spending her money on this jacket fits with this priority. So she is in complete alignment. She puts it in her cart, guilt-free, and goes to check out.

What is Sarah's outcome now versus her previous outcome? Sarah's previous outcome was:

- Spent $12 on shirt + $52 on jacket = $64
- Feels guilty about the jacket
- Has an overcluttered closet of things she doesn't love

Sarah's *new* outcome:

- Spent $52 on jacket total
- Feels ecstatic about this new piece of clothing
- Adds it to her closet of only pieces she adores that's never overcluttered

In this new outcome, Sarah actually spent less, and she did it completely guilt-free and without overcluttering her closet. There are times when spending in alignment will mean spending less, and there are times when spending in alignment and seeing money as neutral will result in spending more. That's okay, too. The goal isn't to spend less; the goal is to spend in alignment with who you are and where you want your money to go.

So how do you master spending in alignment?

Put simply, you need to understand what alignment feels like so you can practice finding that feeling for yourself logistically and emotionally. (We are going to continue to dive into this in upcoming chapters.)

Here's the bottom line: just because guilt, shame, and strife are what money has felt like your whole life does not mean that is how it gets to feel going forward. Don't worry, I will teach you how to build wealth, but more money (after you have a livable wage) doesn't automatically fix stress. We want to work today to start enjoying and empowering ourselves with money, to spend in alignment, and to see money as a neutral tool that allows us to create a life of our dreams—instead of idolizing money or idolizing frugality.

PART 4

Understanding Spending

CHAPTER 11

Screw Your Budget

You know how you're either a Pepsi person or a Coke person and you likely have a strong opinion about what the best is? That's how I feel about the terms *budget* versus *spend plan*. I stopped using the word *budget* at the beginning of my financial journey because everything I had ever been exposed to surrounding budgets sounded restrictive and like zero fun was allowed. I wanted to use a new name to describe how I was going to allocate my spending based on my goals. So many of my clients have felt the same way, and even though it can look like a similar process at first, the first step of no longer calling it a "budget" allows my clients to disassociate from the restrictive nature of the word. A spend plan also allows you to feel more in control because you get to plan your spending rather than your limits. Creating a spend plan involves laying out what you plan to spend your income on and figuring out what (if anything) is left over after expenses and other purchases.

Before we dive in, I am going to teach you the biggest secret of live-laugh-loving your spend plan. This secret is one of the biggest reasons you have likely struggled with budgeting or a savings goal, or anything you've tried and fallen off the wagon with. The secret sauce of the spend plan is this: **you are allowed to change your mind.**

GASP. Shocking, right? You, the adult reading this book right now, are allowed to change your own damn mind.

In a culture of "You fail if you don't stick to this budget," you are taught that the second you change your mind, something comes up, or your desires change, you are screwed. So you either sacrifice those new needs and desires in order to "stick to your budget" or you say, "F that," and do what you want and the budget is left by the wayside.

When you create a spend plan, it's your *plan* to *spend.* Instead of thinking of it like the must-do, eye-roll-inducing chore list your mom would give you when you were growing up, I want you to think of it like driving to Target. Let's say you're on vacation in a new city, staying at an Airbnb with your friends. The group decides to pick up some groceries and snacks. So you and the girls pop into the rental car, and your bestie, Mikaela, is in the front seat with the aux cord because she has the best playlists. You're the driver, so you plug Target into Apple Maps on your phone, and you are on your way. (If you prefer Google Maps, I don't trust you.) Mikaela has her favorite hype playlist blaring through the speakers, and all of a sudden you look at your phone and realize you missed an exit. Initial panic ensues, but within seconds, Apple Maps reroutes you to your destination and you're back on your merry way. I mean, sure, you missed an exit. But it only added four minutes, and honestly, the vibes are immaculate; you're with your besties on vacation, and you're having such a fun time. Who cares if you have to take an alternative route, especially when you're enjoying the journey there so much?

Your spend plan is like your Apple Maps route to Target. You might miss an exit. You might add a stop at a gas station along the way. You might abandon your original plan altogether and instead go to a local store or a Target on a different side of town because it has something in stock that you want.

When your plans change, does that mean you've failed? When you miss an exit, should you stop the car, start crying and yelling at yourself, and say, "I failed, so I might as well just go home"? No. You say, "Oh, my original plans changed. How do I want to update my route?" Then you do it. You reroute.

Now, will there be times you accidentally miss an exit and it adds 20 minutes to your trip, so you end up stressed and running late? Yes, that's possible, too. And baby girl, sometimes that's showbiz. That's just how life can be. And even in those moments, it is 100% fine for the route to change and get you back on track to your original destination—or a new destination!

So as you create your spend plan, know that it is your guide, not a ball and chain keeping you to this one path. It's your road map that you will update and change to ebb and flow along with you as you ebb and flow. And that's how it's supposed to be. Welcome to a whole new world of looking at finances.

CREATING YOUR SPEND PLAN

Creating your spend plan will consist of a five-part deep dive into where you are right now, how to create a sustainable spend plan, and the implementation of what it all looks like. Let's break it down:

1. The Financial Audit
2. Skeleton Spend Plan
3. Calendar and Non-monthly Spend Plan
4. The Day-to-Day Spend Plan
5. Pulling It All Together

Without further ado, it's time to jump into your new spending BFF that will allow you to hit your goals flawlessly and sustainably while also giving you the grace to change your mind and the freedom to live your life without restriction.

STEP 1: THE FINANCIAL AUDIT

It is time for the financial audit. We're going to figure out where you currently stand in your financial journey. This part might sting a little bit. You might be tempted to keep telling yourself you will do it "tomorrow" but then you'll end up putting it off. Ya just gotta get this one done.

You need to figure out how much money is coming in and where your money is going.

You can do this manually and keep it simple, or you can use a budgeting app to help you. I'm going to help walk you through the most important steps of the process.

To start, download your bank statement(s) and credit card statement(s) from the previous calendar month.

Go from the first of the month to the last of the month. This time span will give you a clearly defined range of dates that we are going to dig into.

Next, it's time to create your buckets.

First things first, we're going to track down any money coming into your bank account. You might have money flowing into different accounts, in different forms (direct deposit, checks, electronic payments, etc.). I want you to find every dollar you earned that month and write it at the top of your notepad. This is the income you're working with.

If you and your partner combine finances, and all your income and expenses go into the same pot (I go more in-depth into how you can do this in Chapter 17), I would highly recommend you sit down and go through this financial audit process together. You might be working with double the income and expenses, so you want to be sure everything is accounted for.

Now it's time to dig into the expenses. You know how much money is coming in, but how much is coming out . . . and where is it going? Imagine you had a bunch of buckets in front of you and you were holding a water hose. Right now, it might feel like the hose is spraying everywhere and water is getting all over the floor, and when you look in all the buckets, there's no water (aka when you want to spend or put money toward debt, there's no money there). You want to create different buckets to hold your money so you can know where it is going. It's important to make your buckets realistic. You're trying to get rid of the gross, restrictive feeling of "normal budgets," where all you see is a list of allowed expenses that you have to try to fit into. Instead, your spend plan will include all the things you love and want to prioritize.

Next you're going to pull up your bank statement. Pretend it's your favorite social media app, and start scrolling. Write down the overall categories your money falls into—these are your buckets. Start with a few buckets; you can always add more. Do you buy coffee out a lot? Create a coffee bucket. Do you often spend money on makeup? Create a beauty bucket. Always buying your cats new toys or paying for vet bills? Create a pet bucket. When you have all the categories of where your money is being spent, you can go in and add the amounts for each of your buckets.

Below you will see an example of going through and doing a financial audit: taking each expense and putting it into the corresponding bucket.

Date	Description	Amount
12/07/2023	Debit Purchase - Visa 12/04 QuikTrip	$22.04
12/07/2023	Debit Purchase - Visa 12/04 Amazon Marketplace	$54.15
12/07/2023	Debit Purchase - Visa 12/04 Bar K	$10.93
12/07/2023	Debit Purchase - Visa 12/04 Made in KC	$43.27
12/07/2023	Debit Purchase - Visa 12/04 Downtown Market Kansas City	$27.52
12/07/2023	Debit Purchase - Visa 12/04 Venmo	$200.00

$22.04
Gas Bucket
$54.15 + $43.27 = $97.42
Shopping Bucket
$10.93
Drinks/Food Out Bucket
$27.52
Grocery Bucket
$200
Calendar Bucket

Each expense on your list will go into one of your buckets. The shopping bucket, for example, has $54.15 + $43.27 = $97.42 in it, because there are two expenses. Go through each expense, put it in a bucket, and add up all the expenses in that bucket so you end up with a list like this:

EXPENSE/BUCKET	MONTH 1			
Target	$123			
Amazon	$292			
Groceries	$403			
Online shopping	$608			
Dog expenses	$43			
Takeout	$199			
Travel	$350			
Gas	$60			
Miscellaneous	$190			

Now that you've completed Month 1, you are going to pull up the previous month and complete the same exercise, filling in Month 2 for each category/bucket. Then you will repeat it once more with Month 3.

When it's filled out, it will look similar to this:

EXPENSE/BUCKET	MONTH 1	MONTH 2	MONTH 3	
Target	$123	$150	$200	
Amazon	$292	$113	$319	
Groceries	$403	$340	$330	
Online shopping	$608	$902	$520	
Dog expenses	$43	$31	$27	
Takeout	$199	$372	$216	
Travel	$350	$370	$365	
Gas	$60	$55	$70	
Miscellaneous	$190	$200	$197	

Lastly, you are going to do a little math that can easily be done with your phone's calculator. You are going to find the average you've spent on each bucket/category in the last three months. To do this, you add the monthly totals and divide by 3: Month 1 + Month 2 + Month 3 = _______ ÷ 3.

For example:

EXPENSE/BUCKET	MONTH 1	MONTH 2	MONTH 3	AVERAGE
Target	$123	$150	$200	$123 + $150 + $200 = $473 $473 ÷ 3 = **$158**
Amazon	$292	$113	$319	$241
Groceries	$403	$340	$330	$358
Online shopping	$608	$902	$520	$677
Dog expenses	$43	$31	$27	$34
Takeout	$199	$372	$216	$262
Travel	$350	$370	$365	$362
Gas	$60	$55	$70	$62
Miscellaneous	$190	$200	$197	$196

Now that you have some real data, you have an idea of how much you're making every month and how much you are actually spending each month. I know it can suck to take time to write all that out, but most of the time when people tell me that budgeting or planning out their spending isn't working, it's because they're not planning accurately. "Yeah, I only spend $50 on eating at restaurants every month!" *PUHHHLEASE.* Not when you have been spending $500 on average in this category for the last 3 months. Getting an accurate look at what you're really spending right now is a vital piece of implementing the right strategy to start making big money moves.

And now, you did it! This compiled information is your current spend plan, or an accurate snapshot of how you are currently spending. In the next chapter, we are going to walk through how to take this spend plan and update it to reflect your goals. But first, we are going to practice utilizing a spend plan.

STEP 2: SKELETON SPEND PLAN

Now that you've done a real-life audit of where your money has been going, you're going to create a game plan for your future spending. Maybe after doing your audit you realized there were things missing that you want to better plan for. We're going to start framing out your new spending now. One of the biggest misconceptions about a spend plan (also the reason why budgets don't work long-term) is the belief that they should be the same every month. The idea that every month your expenses and savings will be the same amount is setting you up to feel like a failure. Your months don't look the same, so how is your spending supposed to stay the same? For example, your December spending might be higher due to expenses linked to celebrating Christmas, going out on New Year's Eve, paying your property taxes, and your electric bill going up due to the cold weather. It likely will look very different from May, when you are having a busy season of work, are not traveling much, don't have many additional expenses, and the electric bill is lower because you keep the windows open. You experience variety month to month, so similarly, you will experience variety in your spending month to month—and that is not a bad thing whatsoever.

So instead of creating one spend plan and trying to stick to it every month, you are going to build a progressive, up-to-date spend plan that changes with you, starting with the skeleton spend plan. Just like your skeleton is the framework for your body, your skeleton spend plan will serve as the framework for your larger spend plan. It's the part of your spend plan that is the same month to month with no changes. It includes things like rent or your gym membership that cost the same amount every month. Because these expenses don't fluctuate, you can start with the same skeleton spend plan each month.

If, as we start to create your skeleton spend plan, you think, *WTF. I feel like I'm missing stuff,* don't worry. Think of this like the first draft you would turn into Mrs. Grissom, your tenth-grade English teacher, just to get a completion grade, knowing you had a lot of work to do on it before your final paper was due. Don't overthink this. Just start creating it, and we will update it as we go.

When it comes to actually setting up and keeping your spend plan somewhere, I want you to ask yourself what truly is going to be the most sustainable and approachable plan for you. If you are terrified of spreadsheets, don't use one. If you prefer writing in a planner, do it. If you have a budget app you like, use it. (No, there isn't one budget app that is the GOAT, but if you prefer using an app, you can.) If you want to use your phone's notepad, you can. If you want to use a piece of paper and pencil, go for it. The simpler it is for you, the more sustainable it will be. On the other hand, the more complicated or the more of a chore it is, the more likely you are to say, "Screw it." Create this plan however works best for you, and remember that you can always change it as you get more comfortable.

I am going to put some basics in here that might be part of your skeleton spend plan, but remember that the only expenses that go here are ones that are the *exact same* month to month. The chart on the next page is only an example, so there might be some expenses you don't need on your list, and there may be others you'll need to add.

SAMPLE SKELETON SPEND PLAN

EXPENSE	AMOUNT	DUE DATE
Rent/mortgage	$1,704	1st
Wi-Fi	$55	1st
Car payment/car loan	$309	1st
Student loan payment	$503	1st
Trash	$12	9th
Gym membership	$42	13th
Electric	$79	15th
Car insurance	$92	22nd

YOUR SKELETON SPEND PLAN

EXPENSE	AMOUNT	DUE DATE

You might have fewer boxes, or you might have more. No worries whatsoever.

STEP 3: CALENDAR AND NON-MONTHLY SPEND PLAN

Now that you have your skeleton spend plan framed out, you can start building on it. Every month looks different, so you want to create a spend plan that flows with you. Every month, before the start of the month, you should set aside time to sit down and look at the month ahead. Begin by pulling up your skeleton spend plan (because it is the base of every month and doesn't change) and then add your calendar and non-monthly spend plan items to it. The calendar spend plan is exactly what it sounds like: a list of expenses specific to that month. Now you will create a calendar spend plan for the whole year. Think trips, birthdays, holidays, bills that happen in specific months, etc. The next page has an example of a calendar spend plan; now go to page 187 and create yours in the first four rows of the blank calendar grid.

Next, let's go through and add non-monthly expenses into the same chart. The goal is to add in all the expenses that aren't every month but also aren't annual. For example, oil changes. When I first started learning how to budget, I was so mother-effing thrown off by how every month it felt like something unexpected would always come up. I wouldn't plan for an oil change and then as months would go by, I would forget about it, until all of a sudden I needed one. Because I hadn't had to pay for one the last few months, I would forget to plan for it. Then, it would frustrate me to the point where The Hulk would say, "Screw it. I'll try to budget again next month instead." The goal of this spend plan is that it builds on itself so you cover all your bases. See page 186 for an example of a non-monthly spend plan. Now go back to page 187 and add any other expenses that are non-monthly but also not annual.

JAN	FEB	MAR	APR	MAY	JUNE	JULY	AUG	SEPT	OCT	NOV	DEC
Annual vet visit for dogs	Valentine's Day celebration trip	Spring break	Darby's bridal shower	Annual Memorial Day vacation	Annual dentist appt	Anniversary trip	Mom's birthday	Car registration	Halloween costume	Thanksgiving travel	Christmas
	Annual snowboarding trip for Bri's birthday	HOA fees due	Nick's birthday	Annual golf course dues	Father's Day	Taylor and Jordan's wedding	Dom's birthday	Kylea's birthday	Hallie's birthday	Dad's birthday	New Year's Eve outing
		Annual pest control fee	Pay to get taxes done		Dobber's Up golf tournament	TSA Pre-check/passport		My birthday trip			

JAN	FEB	MAR	APR	MAY	JUNE	JULY	AUG	SEPT	OCT	NOV	DEC
Annual vet visit for dogs	Valentine's Day celebration trip	Spring break	Darby's bridal shower	Annual Memorial Day vacation	Annual dentist appt	Anniversary trip	Mom's birthday	Car registration	Halloween costume	Thanksgiving travel	Christmas
	Annual snowboarding trip for Bri's birthday	HOA fees due	Nick's birthday	Annual golf course dues	Father's Day	Taylor and Jordan's wedding	Dom's birthday	Kylea's birthday	Hallie's birthday	Dad's birthday	New Year's Eve outing
		Annual pest control fee	Pay to get taxes done		Dobber's Up golf tournament	TSA Pre-check/passport		My birthday trip			
Oil change	Hair appointment	Car detail	Dogs groomed	Oil change	Massage and chiropractor	Dogs groomed	Car detail	Oil change	Facial	Dogs groomed	Massage and chiropractor
Facial	Massage and chiropractor		Facial	Hair appointment		Facial	Massage and chiropractor	Hair appointment	Massage and chiropractor		
			Massage and chiropractor								

JAN							
FEB							
MAR							
APR							
MAY							
JUNE							
JULY							
AUG							
SEPT							
OCT							
NOV							
DEC							

You're making great progress! The best part is that this is the hardest part, and when it's complete, you will just be making a few tweaks as you go. It's a one-and-done kinda thing, I promise.

Now, it's time to add all the other fun categories to round things out.

STEP 4: THE DAY-TO-DAY SPEND PLAN

Your day-to-day spend plan is exactly as it sounds: the things you spend money on day to day. This category encapsulates everything else, like the purchases and expenses that aren't monthly or annually the same but still happen consistently. This includes things like grocery shopping, online shopping, household items (think Amazon, Target, etc.), takeout, happy hour with friends, house projects, travel expenses, and all those other fun discretionary things.

First, concentrate on filling in the list as much as you can. You will essentially fact-check your work later, so no worries about being super accurate now.

It's totally fine to think of these expenses as it makes sense to you. For example, if you'd prefer to create a "Target" and an "Amazon" bucket instead of a "Household" bucket because that makes it simpler for you, that's totally okay! Remember to try to keep it as simple as possible. Don't worry about adding amounts yet; just add categories.

Let's use an example:

BUCKET
Target
Amazon
Groceries
Online shopping
Dog expenses
Takeout
Travel
Gas
Miscellaneous

Now it's your turn. I started it for you by adding a miscellaneous bucket. I always recommend you include this catchall bucket until you get used to your spend plan so it doesn't feel like there is always something that comes up for which you have not made a bucket.

BUCKET				
Miscellaneous				

Now we are going to pull it all together.

STEP 5: PULLING IT ALL TOGETHER

Okay, now that your spend plan is finished, you are going to practice actually using it. Think of it like you finally just put together the cutest new accent chair for your reading nook and now you get to sit in it for the first time.

We are going to pretend it's the end of the month and you are sitting down to create your spend plan for the upcoming month. For this example, let's say it is August and you are about to create September's spend plan.

First, decide how you'd like to do this—on a piece of paper, in an Excel spreadsheet, in a Word document, via an app, or whatever you prefer. Regardless, you're always starting with the skeleton spend plan and building on it.

Here's how to create September's spend plan:

1. Copy and paste all skeleton spend plan items into September's spend plan.
2. Copy everything from September's calendar and non-monthly spend plan.
3. Add in your day-to-day spend plan based on the amounts due, an estimate of what the amounts due will be, or what you are allocating to spend in that category.

Here's an example:

EXPENSE/BUCKET	PLANNED AMOUNT	DUE DATE/PLANNED DATE
Skeleton Plan		
Rent/mortgage	$1,704	1st
Wi-Fi	$55	1st
Car payment/car loan	$309	1st
Student loan payment	$503	1st
Trash	$12	9th
Gym membership	$42	13th
Electric	$79	15th
Car insurance	$92	22nd
Calendar Plan		
My birthday trip	$500	3rd
Kylea's birthday	$100	27th
Car registration	$290	30th
Non-Monthly Plan		
Oil change	$40	19th
Hair appointment	$120	23rd
Day-to-Day Plan		
Target	$158	
Amazon	$241	
Groceries	$358	
Online shopping	$677	
Dog expenses	$34	
Takeout	$262	
Travel	$362	
Gas	$62	
Miscellaneous	$196	

TOTAL	$6,196	
September income	$	
Leftover/under amount	$	

The last step is to add up the total amount spent, include your projected income for September (if it fluctuates, just guesstimate for now), and then subtract your total expenses from your September income to see what is left over or how much you're spending over your income.

HOLY CHEESE BALLS! You've made a freaking spend plan and practiced using it, too. Remember, the numbers I am using are made up and are absolutely no indication of what you should or shouldn't be spending. These are simply examples.

If this is your first time going through this process, you might feel a little panicked after seeing where you stand, especially if you find yourself in a place where you didn't realize how much you were spending or if you realize the total you spend per month is more than what you're making.

Refrain from shitting on yourself if you are feeling any of these ways. Remember, the entire goal of this chapter is to see where you are and create a plan going forward. And remember that we haven't added any strategy to this plan yet. Oh, buddy, we are just warming up.

Before we continue and learn not only how to update your spend plan to be in complete alignment but also the strategy to make your money work harder for you so you can see sustainable results *fast*, I want you to go through and note things that feel out of alignment for you. Maybe it's a bucket like "Takeout" and you had no idea that's how much you spent per month. Maybe seeing that bucket on paper (or on a spreadsheet or whatever) made you decide that you want to spend less on takeout because the amount you're currently spending is giving you major ick. That's no problem! You can absolutely update that category of your spend plan. But remember there's no shame in past spending. It is only data, giving you info that you can take and update going forward to be in alignment with your goals.

Your homework for this chapter, before we dive into spending in alignment and the logistics of applying it in Chapter 12, is to go through your list and create another category called "Most Aligned Amount." Here, note what, in a perfect world, you'd spend in each bucket. (See the chart on the next page for an example.) It can be more, less, or the same as what you have now.

Remember, the goal isn't to spend less in every category. In fact, the goal might be to give yourself more wiggle room. Maybe you always feel so much stress in the grocery store. Maybe you are trying to spend as little as possible and want to give yourself more leeway while buying food because you want to be able to prioritize eating organic for your health goals. Write a higher amount in the Most Aligned Amount bucket for groceries. Then, maybe in the Takeout bucket, you feel like the amount you have been spending is excessive and you'd rather put that money toward becoming debt-free (a goal of yours) or toward your vacation fund. In that scenario, you'd write a smaller amount in the Most Aligned Amount column. Many categories, such as rent, stay the same and are likely in alignment, so you can write the same number because it feels just right.

Setting a new goal for the most aligned amount is going to help you work strategically to make each dollar you spend be in complete alignment with you and your goals, in order to elevate your life today and in the future.

EXPENSE/BUCKET	PLANNED AMOUNT	MOST ALIGNED AMOUNT
Skeleton Plan		
Rent/mortgage	$1,704	
Wi-Fi	$55	
Car payment/car loan	$309	
Student loan payment	$503	
Trash	$12	
Gym membership	$42	
Electric	$79	
Car insurance	$92	
Calendar Plan		
My birthday trip	$500	
Kylea's birthday	$100	
Car registration	$290	
Non-Monthly Plan		
Oil change	$40	
Hair appointment	$120	
Day-to-Day Plan		
Target	$158	
Amazon	$241	
Groceries	$358	
Online shopping	$677	
Dog expenses	$34	
Takeout	$262	
Travel	$362	
Gas	$62	
Miscellaneous	$196	

TOTAL	$6,196	
September income	$	
Leftover/under amount	$	

Go through each item on the list and calculate the most aligned amount based on your same income. In the next chapter, we're going to help you figure out how to prioritize your goals while still spending in alignment. Keep this spend plan handy. In the next three chapters, you'll build on it, take it up a notch, and turn it into your secret weapon for getting ahead with money, without sacrifice.

CHAPTER 12

Future Me Formula

"May I please have two piña coladas, two gin and tonics, and four Scooby-Doo shots?" you ask the bartender at the swim-up bar at your favorite all-inclusive resort in Cabo. Your best friend, Brenna, walks over to help you carry the drinks back to your table with your circle of friends waiting to play the finger game. (No, that's not sexual. It's your favorite drinking game from college.) Brenna laughs at you and says, "Nothing like free drinks all day long," and you smirk back at her, knowing that because it's an all-inclusive resort, you've technically already paid for the drinks with the cost of booking your stay . . . but damn, they feel free, right? Shout out to "past you" from five months ago, who paid in full and booked this Cabo trip. Now that it's here, every time you order anything off the menu without having to pay for it, or drinks at the bar with no charge, it feels so freaking amazing. Honestly, it does feel free. That feeling is everything. So now, we are going to bring that all-inclusive vibe to your spend plan and update it from its current state to a freedom-based plan that elevates your life now, while also setting up "future you" for the time of her life, too.

In the previous chapter, you created your spend plan based on how you've been spending up to this point. However, if you're here, it's likely because you want to make some changes to what your spending looked like in the past. Maybe you want to shift some things around to not only get ahead with money faster but also to stop feeling so much stress around finances. In this chapter, we are going to explore how to add strategy to your spend plan so you can free up more of your income to spend in alignment with your lifestyle while also putting money toward your goals.

First up, we want to use the info you mapped out at the end of the last chapter as a starting point. So grab that data, and let's jump in:

What is your income for next month? ______________

(If your income fluctuates, use the low end of what it could be.)

What is your total spending projection for next month?

____

Now subtract your spending from your income. What is the total left over?

Income – total spending = ______________

It is time to perform a beautiful balancing act. You are going to find the sweet spot of putting a good amount toward your goals (the leftover amount) while still allowing yourself to spend in alignment in your life right now. It truly is an art, and although it takes time to master this part of the process, it's the most freeing feeling when you do. Why? Because it allows you to look at your "leftover" money as a goal amount instead of an "extra" amount.

Let me show you what that looks like.

Current formula:

Income – spending = leftover to goal

This equation is likely what you've been doing. Your income rolls in, you spend it, and if there happens to be anything left over, maybe you throw a little at your savings account or credit card debt. Maybe you blow it on who knows what, or maybe you don't have any left over at all. The bottom line is: the current formula isn't working for you. What you want to do instead is get so clear on your spending that you know exactly how much you have left over to put toward your goals. Then, because you've got that part nailed down, you can change the equation to what I like to call the "Future Me Formula."

Future Me Formula:

Income – amount to put toward goal = spending

If you noticed, it's the same as the current formula, but the "amount to put toward goal" and "spending" have flip-flopped. This swap of the goal and spending amounts allows you to be more intentional about the amount you put toward your goals. You are now prioritizing your goals, not just putting what is "left over" toward them. I call it the Future Me Formula because you are prioritizing the goals of future you. However, you have to get super clear on your spending and create a buffer to be able to do this equation successfully.

Let's break down how we can do that.

CREATE (MORE) LEFTOVER

Step 1 is creating leftover (or more leftover) income after spending.

If you are currently in the position where you don't have any left over, or if you've realized you are spending more than you are bringing in, finding a way to optimize what you *do* have to work with is the first and most important step prior to setting up the Future Me Formula, so you can create money to have toward your goal amount (income left over). On the other hand, if you are in a place where you do have income left over, don't stop reading—this step of using the Future Me Formula is a great way to ensure you don't have any leaks in your spend plan.

Creating (more) leftover can come from so many different areas. I am going to give you some options to pursue in this book, but I also will include more examples for you to check out and explore on our website at deeperthanmoney.com/book.

So, here are some ways to create more leftover money.

Stop Any Leaks

Leaks are expenses you literally do not use or fees you're accruing: things that are not at all adding to your life and are easy to get rid of without missing them.

If you thought, *WTF is that charge?* as you went through your financial audit and looked at all your purchases, that means you're currently the captain of a leaking ship. You are working your ass off to bring in money, and it is leaking out of your account through charges that aren't intentional. Leaky ships can't sail through the ocean. Leaky ships slow down or, well, sink. It's time to patch up the leaks in your bank account.

Make a list of any leaks you might have:

- Any mysterious charges you can't figure out
- Old subscriptions you don't use or even know about (Hulu, Netflix, SiriusXM, unused gym memberships, recurring app store purchases, etc.)

Also think through ways you might be spending that would be easy to change and improve your life at the same time:

- Bring your favorite water bottle on road trips instead of buying a plastic water bottle at gas stations. (Saves money and saves the planet—yay!)
- Bring reusable bags to the grocery store so you don't have to buy bags at the checkout. (If you are an Aldi girl, you know what I am talking about, and you are contributing to another sustainability win, too!)
- Set a weekly reminder to put any veggies or fruits that are going to go bad soon in a container in the freezer for smoothies instead of throwing them out a few days later. (Saves money on groceries + less food waste.)

Brainstorm other ways you currently might have money leaks. The key here is that money leaks are things that are easy to eliminate. This is not me telling you to get rid of expenses you care about or subscriptions you love. I want you to begin by focusing on getting rid of the things you are paying for that are not elevating your life.

Now this is the fun part:

- Call and cancel all the subscriptions you don't use. (Holla!) Add up how much that will save you. You will soon be creating your ultimate plan of where to put all that "extra" moola you now have. One of my favorite hacks is to set up cancellation alerts when you sign up for that free two-week trial of a subscription service!
- Call your bank and ask about charges that surprised you and then call the specific business and cancel the charge or subscription (assuming it's a subscription you don't use)..
- Think about how you can change the "leaky charges" that have to do with your habits. Maybe it's setting an alarm in the morning before you leave for work to brew yourself a mug of green tea instead of stopping by the gas station and buying an energy drink for your morning pick-me-up. Or even better, if you love that energy drink and know you're going to stop and get it anyway, swing by Costco (or another wholesale store) and see if you can buy it in bulk. Even if it costs you a little more up front, paying $20 for a 24 pack once a month is much more cost-effective than spending $2.99 per day. It's all about being realistic and planning for the little things. Again, I must note that if your absolute favorite thing is having your morning routine where you swing by the gas station and grab that drink, and you want to prioritize paying for it, then it isn't a leak. Leaks are all things you can stop paying for while simultaneously elevating your life.

Remember that your beloved gym membership or your weekly coffee on Friday mornings are not leaks just because you've heard a financial guru say to "cut it out." Leaks are truly expenses that you can ditch or swap without impacting your lifestyle or priorities.

Time to Negotiate

Call and negotiate your credit card interest rate if you have credit card debt. (I give you a script in Chapter 16.)

Call and ask current companies you use (cell phone, car insurance, Wi-Fi, etc.) if there is anything they can do to lower your bill.

For things like car insurance, there are likely so many options that can lower your bill, like using an app or monitor on your car for speeding, or letting them know if you work from home instead of driving daily.

Bring in More Money

I am a huge proponent of making more money by doing things that you like and care about. You would be surprised how many special skills you have that you can monetize.

For example, if you take a long walk every day, start walking dogs for people in your neighborhood. I have seen people make \$15 per dog walk—plus you get to hang out with dogs and get exercise, and that's a win-win! If you do the math, \$15 per walk × 30 days a month = an extra \$450 per month you're now making without spending any extra time truly "working."

Another example you can look into is donating plasma. Hey, don't knock it until you try it. I donated all through college, and boy, you sure can bring in some cash from this at a fast pace. Plus you're technically saving lives at the same time. Another win-win!

There are hundreds and thousands of ways to bring in extra money online, but the key here is to find ways that align with you and your goals. This also does not mean you need to monetize your hobbies, as you might want to keep them as sacred ways for you to unwind and enjoy life. However, I do highly suggest finding ways to bring in money that you don't heavily dislike. The opportunities are endless, anything from taking online surveys to starting a business as another stream of income.

If you want to increase your income, set a goal amount per month to bring in, and then do some research on what ways make the most sense for your life. (We offer a list of side hustle recommendations at deeperthanmoney.com/book.)

Side hustles are absolutely not necessary to getting ahead, but they can be helpful and even fun when you find options that are the best fit for you.

Spend Less Money Without Sacrifice

There are ways you can lower your expenses without giving up your favorite experiences.

- See if you can find a job working at your gym (cleaning, folding towels, etc.) a few times a week, not only to get paid but also to get a free gym membership.
- Spend 15 minutes a day doing online surveys that will pay you in Starbucks gift cards, so you can get your coffee without breaking into your paycheck.

- Cancel your audiobook subscription or stop renting movies on Amazon, and start renting audiobooks and movies from your local library for free.
- Swap grocery stores. Going to a more affordable grocery store can save you hundreds of dollars a year buying the exact same foods you do at your normal grocery store.
- Switch to annual plans. This may take some saving up, but a lot of subscriptions cost less if you sign up for an annual plan instead of paying monthly. Look into what subscriptions you know you will keep for the next year that offer annual payment discounts.

UPDATE BUCKET AMOUNTS

Now that you've audited your original spend plan, updated it, and ideally found some more money left over, it is time to take your current spend plan bucket amounts and sustainably shift them to your goal spend plan amounts you determined earlier.

You likely have a particular bucket (or category) about which you feel the most out of control or the most stressed. Let's use the category of ordering takeout as an example. Say you discovered during the financial audit that you've been spending $400 a month on takeout (and spit out your matcha latte in shock at that discovery). I want to reiterate that spending $400 a month on takeout is not inherently bad (again, just an example!), but if it's out of alignment for you, then it's a good thing to shift until you land on an amount that does feel good for you.

Let's say you want your new goal to be about $300 a month, or $100 less. You feel like that shift will be totally achievable and sustainable. You ultimately want to bring it down to $200, which feels even more in alignment, but you don't want to restrict yourself and end up frustrated. So you land on $300 a month for now. Great! So how do you actually implement spending $300 a month on takeout (your new goal) instead of the $400 you've been spending?

The first step is all logistics: set your goal amount spent for that bucket (in your spend plan) to $300.

The next step is adding all the lazy-girl-finance vibes and keeping it super simple. We're all about what's realistic and sustainable here. Can you really picture yourself being one second away from pressing "confirm" on your DoorDash order but then stopping to pull up your spreadsheet, notebook, or budgeting app and checking how much is left of the $300 you allocated for takeout? Or are you more likely to just order and deal with it later? Yes, there are many ways you can implement your new goal by using a budget app, but sometimes that still means categorizing everything manually and in the heat of the moment. And when that is a task standing in between you and medium-spicy chicken pad thai, the chances of you taking the time to categorize past takeout expenses to see what you have left is slim.

So instead, this is what I recommend when you are first starting out and practicing hitting your new goal amount, especially in a struggle category: treat it like a gift card. I suggest only doing this with one or two categories that feel like the biggest stressors or where you feel you struggle with "overspending." You can implement this method by either getting a secondary checking account with a linked debit card, or getting a free debit card linked to your PayPal or Cash App account. You can also use a credit card, but that requires having a credit card for a specific bucket only and no other purchases. I would absolutely *not* use a credit card for this if you are in any form of credit card debt.

Let's walk through how to use this approach. You open a second checking account (or PayPal/Cash App) with a debit card attached to it. Once a month, you transfer the $300 (the goal amount) from your main checking account to this card. Then, when you go to order takeout, you unlink your primary debit card from any saved payment methods—we're not using that for this category. Instead, you'll add your new takeout-specific debit card. When you go to order DoorDash, instead of having to do any math or calculations, you open your bank account and see how exactly how much is left to spend on takeout for the rest of the month. $125 remaining? Great, go ahead and order the spring rolls, too. With very little effort on your part, you can keep track of any hard-to-keep-track-of spending categories and make it easier to stay on target.

You can implement this same process with other apps you use on a regular basis. For example, if you're a Starbucks queen and you want to spend $50 a month on Starbucks, load $50 onto your Starbucks card each month. Every time you go, you know exactly how much money you have left.

Two big things to keep in mind while implementing your new goal category amounts.

1. This will take practice.

   Switching from the "I have to spend as little as possible and stick to a budget or I've failed" mentality to an "I have freedom to choose and spend how I want and spend only in alignment" mindset will take practice. It's okay if it feels a little weird in the beginning. The cool thing about this new way of spending is that it becomes easier the more you practice.

2. It's okay to change your mind.

   There will be times you go to order that medium-spicy chicken pad thai and realize you don't have enough allocated money left to buy the meal. You are always allowed to change your mind and dip into other categories to cover it. Just remember that you are the one who set the goal, and you're also allowed to update the goal. When you feel that you would like to change your mind about the amount of spending allocated to a specific category, come back to the reason why you wanted to spend that much and decide if it's in alignment to add more money to that category.

That is the magic of spending in alignment: it is based on complete choice and freedom, and not on the willpower to stick to a stationary budget. It actually is one of the biggest secret weapons to getting ahead with money faster, too.

But how do you actually practice spending in alignment? Stay tuned to find out.

CHAPTER 13

The Holy Grail

I want you to imagine that you are eight years old, and you're in the magical kingdom that is Walmart. You are walking through the toy department with your mom because she needs to buy something for your cousin's birthday party next week. The second you step into your favorite aisle, your entire world lights up because you spot the toy you've seen on Nickelodeon commercials for weeks now, and you squeal, "MOM, CAN I PLEASE HAVE THIS TOY??!" You are elated. Inspired. Thrilled. "No. You can't have that," your mother, the apparent tyrant, responds.

How did it feel to be eight years old and see something so freaking amazing, to feel so freaking excited, and to be lit up by something you'd so desperately love to add to your life? And then to hear, "No. You can't have that." What was eight-year-old you feeling in that moment?

Sadness, disappointment, and anger?

I can remember so desperately thinking, *I cannot wait to be a grownup so I can buy whatever I want with my own money.*

Now I want you to think of the last time you were at Target.

You're walking along, you see something you absolutely love, and you think . . . *What? No, you can't buy that.* Ah. Bingo.

Isn't it weird how the same things we wanted to change ended up becoming a part of who we are? Hello, passed-down beliefs. We meet again.

If you were anything like me and grew up being told you couldn't have the things you so desperately wanted, did you also become the adult who now walks through the store telling yourself those same things? If so, welcome to the team. Text me your T-shirt size, and I'll mail you your jersey.

Now, I'm not saying that parents should buy their kids every toy they want. I also remember appreciating the toy I wanted so much more if I was told I had to wait until Christmas. I am, however, saying that even when I was a college grad with a full-time salary and low expenses, that same voice of The Bitch would tell me I still couldn't spend. And instead of telling myself I have to wait until Christmas or my birthday, I would wait until I had a bad day at work, listen to The Hulk say, *Screw it,* buy the things I had been depriving myself of to try to get that boost of dopamine, feel guilty, and then go back to saying, "Shit, now I REALLY can't buy things." The cycle continued and normally looked something like this:

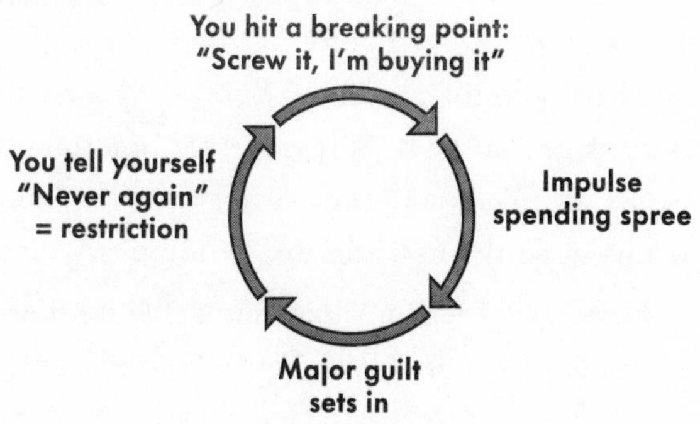

But why was I stuck in this cycle? Yes, because of beliefs, but because of *which* belief?

Ahh, yes, that age-old belief that spending is bad and the ultimate goal is to spend as little as possible.

We're finally ready to talk about the Holy Grail: spending in alignment. We have been walking through all the pieces that you need in order to learn what alignment means for you, and now we are going to spend time working on logistically implementing this new framework.

Spending in alignment is the holistic approach to using your money in a way that is emotionally, mentally, and logistically aligned with who you are today and who you want to become in the future. It's used to elevate your current life and future life simultaneously.

Spending in alignment is like finding the perfect shade of nude lipstick. Have you ever grabbed the NARS shade your bestie loves, or the Dior color your favorite influencer swears by, and it just doesn't look quite the same on you? Spending in alignment works the same way. Just like you have to match the perfect nude lipstick to *your* skin tone and lip color, your spending should match *your* goals and priorities, not someone else's. You need to figure out what alignment looks like for you.

Because alignment and intuition are so closely linked, we have to be in tune with our bodies in order to spend in alignment. In order to be in tune with our bodies, we have to be in a state of calm instead of stress. When we are in a state of stress, our judgment is clouded and we can't tell what the best choices are for our goals. So the first step of spending in alignment is making sure that you are in a neutral state before making any purchases, not in an emotional high or an emotional low. An easy way to calm yourself is to take three deep breaths and stimulate your vagus nerve, which helps you tap into your intuition.[1] Intuition is one of the most magical superpowers we have, but when we are stressed (and our nervous system is in fight-or-flight mode), we can't tap into it.

Holistic hormone health expert Katrina Rae Swanson says:

> The vagus nerve originates in the brain and runs all the way down to the abdomen. It plays a role in some of our major organs' functions in our bodies. It impacts everything from hormone functions, to gut functions, to cardiovascular functions. The vagus nerve is also associated with the parasympathetic nervous system, or rest and digest. If you are making important decisions from a place of chaos, and your nervous system is working in a place of fight or flight, it can potentially impact the decision you are making. When you are making decisions from a state of rest and digest, your mind is calm, your body is calm, and you are able to look at things logically. Deep breathing techniques are some of the most effective yet simple ways to bring your nervous system into a place of balance.[2]

To clear the way to make financially aligned decisions, you must first deal with all the stress that could be clouding your judgment.

Even Spider-Man (Tobey Maguire will always be my Spider-Man) can't shoot his web when he is super stressed out. Let that nervous system cool down and get to a neutral state. Stress on the body when making spending decisions is like tequila in your bloodstream when you see an elevated surface to dance on: sounds like a great decision in the moment, but when the hangover sets in and you see the video from the night before, you realize you weren't thinking clearly. The more stress you feel when making a purchase decision, the more likely you are to look back on that decision with regret.

Then, your next step when using this holistic approach to spending is factoring in three questions to every purchase—what I like to call the Big 3:

1. Is what I am purchasing in complete alignment with me, my current life, and my future goals?
2. Is the price of what I am purchasing in complete alignment with me, my current life, and my future goals?
3. Is the outcome of this purchase in complete alignment with me, my current life, and my future goals?

QUESTION 1: IS WHAT I AM PURCHASING IN COMPLETE ALIGNMENT WITH ME, MY CURRENT LIFE, AND MY FUTURE GOALS?

Here we are looking at an item that you are considering purchasing, and ignoring the price tag. As you are walking through the store or shopping online, things always look sexier when we can't have them. (Is this why Justin Bieber became hotter after he got married?) Although this might seem counterintuitive, allow yourself to forget about the price tag. At first (if you're anything like me) you might be thinking, *You dumb bitch. I will just want everything.* Yeah, I thought the same thing. But when you continue to allow yourself that freedom, you will realize how many things you don't actually want.

Let's take coffee mugs, for example. I used to *always* want more mugs. If you would have told me I could buy whatever I wanted without looking at the price tag, I would have told you every mug on the shelf was in alignment. But then, once I actually thought about it for a second, I would realize that if I bought every single coffee mug in the store, my kitchen cabinet would get cluttered, and that would negatively impact my life. I didn't actually want that. I was just so used to living in a mindset of "I could never have that," I felt like I wanted it even more.

Your immediate reaction to this strategy might have been, "Chloe, I literally *can't* have anything I want, though. I don't have the money."

Now, this may be an extreme example, but let's challenge that mindset. (No, this isn't a tone-deaf, just-believe-you-can-buy-anything-and-it-will-come-true bit of advice, so bear with me.)

Let's say we are talking about a $2,000 Louis Vuitton purse, and you have $90 in your checking account. You feel like all your favorite influencers have nice purses, and you recently became really self-aware that you have never made a luxury purchase like this, and you want to. You might think that you have to tell yourself you can't have the coveted LV. However, I would argue you *can* have it. Why? Because with every purchase, there are outcomes. You could open and pay with a credit card. You could sell a kidney. You could rob a bank. Are those potentially smart options for you to do? Likely not (especially the last one). But the point is that you hypothetically could, and I genuinely believe that if it were a life-or-death situation, you'd become resourceful enough to come up with that $2,000. We want to reteach ourselves what to believe about money so we can stop living from a place of restriction and start living from a place of natural consequences—allowing ourselves all the freedom in the world, while understanding that all our decisions have outcomes and we get to choose what outcomes we want.

So the Louis Vuitton purse itself might be in alignment (you're obsessed, and it lights you up), but when you think of the outcome (going into credit card debt or selling a kidney—is that even legal?), it isn't in alignment right now. That's okay! We will talk about what to do then in the next step. But first, let's look at an example.

Meet Maria. She has $4,000 in her checking account that she won hitting a half-court shot at halftime of a Lakers game. When she tells herself she can have the $2,000 Louis Vuitton purse, yes, of course her outcomes are different. She thinks over the outcomes: she has the cash to spend, but this would mean she doesn't have that money to put toward her student loans. Different outcomes, but no matter your financial situation, giving yourself the option to choose allows you to learn how to spend in alignment based on the purchase and outcomes of the purchase.

To Maria, putting money toward her student loans feels like it would elevate her life more than the purse would, and that's how she makes her decision. Because when she digs a little deeper, she realizes that in telling herself she can buy the bag, she is now able to approach the decision with an abundance mindset rather than a scarcity mindset. It's like if you were to tell yourself you have to cut out all sugar and snacks for a month. I would bet that as soon as you tell yourself that, you'd begin craving sweets even more than you previously did. Why? Because you couldn't have them. And a week in, if you're tired of depriving yourself, when your grandma Lillian offers you her homemade chocolate-chip cookies, you finally crack, take a bite, and end up eating the whole platter. Instead, you could have told yourself you were going to eat in alignment, only consuming foods that elevate your happiness, health, and energy levels. Trust me, you will start to feel more freedom with this approach once you practice it.

You might have to if-you-give-a-mouse-a-cookie the situation because your mindset could very well be *I want it all.* Take it a step further. *Okay, if I buy every single piece of clothing at Vitality, what will my wardrobe look like? Would all that yoga attire be flattering on me? Where would I store all the yoga pants? And how sustainable would that be to buy 900 pairs of pants?* After a while, you'll start to have "oh" moments when you realize you actually *don't* want it all. So what do you want? Practice walking through the clothing racks (or the website pages) literally saying, "yes," "no," "no," "yes," "yes," to whether that piece would or would not be in alignment with you. For now, don't worry about factoring in the price tag or if you are actually going to purchase them or not. We simply want to identify if the thing itself is completely in alignment.

QUESTION 2: IS THE PRICE OF WHAT I AM PURCHASING IN COMPLETE ALIGNMENT WITH ME, MY CURRENT LIFE, AND MY FUTURE GOALS?

This is the same exercise of telling yourself you *can* purchase it, but now factoring in the price. Is this thing I want worth the price that is being offered to me right now? A cookie from the coffee shop down the street might be in alignment with you, but then you see the price is $8. To you, $8 for that cookie is absolutely not in alignment. If the price for something doesn't feel "worth it" to you, it isn't in alignment.

If you're looking at the same cookie and it's $2.50 and totally feels "worth it" to you, then the purchase itself and the price of the purchase are in alignment.

A personal example: Not too long ago, I wanted to get an Iowa Hawkeyes jersey (go hawks) to wear to a basketball game. While shopping around, I found one I liked but then realized the price was $130. I am sure the jersey itself was extremely well made, but I simply wanted a cute jersey to wear to one basketball game and didn't need the highest quality. So to me, the price wasn't in alignment. However, because the jersey was what I wanted but the price wasn't, I looked on Facebook Marketplace and found a used one for $25. Perfect. Sure, it was a little more worn in, but for what I wanted it for, that worked perfectly.

QUESTION 3: IS THE OUTCOME OF THIS PURCHASE IN COMPLETE ALIGNMENT WITH ME, MY CURRENT LIFE, AND MY FUTURE GOALS?

This question is where you connect your spend plan to your alignment and intuition. If you are asking yourself this question, that means the purchase is in alignment with your goals and desires, and the price of it is in alignment, too. Now you need to decide if the outcome of the purchase is in alignment. So first ask yourself, "What is the outcome of the purchase?"

If you've already allocated money for this specific purchase in your spend plan categories, then the outcome is that this purchase will be spending the money you've allocated. If that feels great to you, then mission accomplished! It's getting the alignment stamp of approval and is ready to be purchased.

On the other hand, if this purchase is not something you

have allocated in your spend plan, what would you need to move around in order to make the purchase? Would the outcome of this purchase mean putting less toward your top goal? Is that okay with you? Would the outcome of this purchase be needing to move some allocated money from another category into this category? Is that okay with you? Would you be able to bring in more money this month so you wouldn't need to move anything around to make this purchase? Would you be dipping into your emergency fund? Would this be going on a credit card?

Remember, there is no shame surrounding these questions. You're no longer the eight-year-old in the store with Mommy, who is telling you that you can't have something. You are a grown-ass woman who gets to spend her money as she chooses, and whether you decide to buy the thing or not, you need to practice allowing yourself the freedom to choose.

PRACTICING USING THE BIG 3

Let's look at an example where spending is in complete alignment: Fernanda is a first-grade teacher, and she wants to get a few new outfits for back to school this fall. She goes to Zara to look for a new dress and immediately spots one she is obsessed with. She then practices asking herself the Big 3 (thing, price, outcome).

First, she focuses on the dress alone. *Is the dress I am thinking of purchasing in complete alignment with me, my current life, and my future goals?* she thinks to herself. She knows she wants to curate timeless pieces in her closet that she can rewear, that are incredibly comfortable, and that make her feel confident. The dress in itself is absolutely in alignment with her current and future goals. This step uses her intuition to decide if this is in alignment with who she is (from Chapter 6) and what she wants (from Chapter 7). Is she buying the dress because she loves it or because she is trying to impress someone or follow a fast-fashion trend without it actually being in alignment to her (or to her style, in this example)? She decides step 1 is a "hell yes." On to step 2.

Next, Fernanda focuses on the cost of the dress, which is $98. *Is the price of the dress I am thinking of purchasing in complete alignment with me, my current life, and my future goals?* She asks herself if spending $98 on this dress feels in alignment. Is the dress "worth it" to her at this moment? There can be things we love that are in alignment, but the price is beyond what feels aligned to us right now. This step is important in getting ahead with money, because it is where we link logistics with intuition. For Fernanda, the dress in itself is in alignment, and the price tag also feels in alignment. It feels worth $98 to her. It's a brand she loves, the quality is great, and bonus points because the tag doesn't say "dry clean only." She decides this purchase is again a "hell yes" and moves on to step 3.

Finally, Fernanda asks herself, *Is the outcome of this purchase in complete alignment with me, my current life, and my future goals?* This is the big "aha!" moment right here. The dress itself is in alignment. The dress feels worth $98. However, is the outcome of spending $98 in alignment? This is when she pulls up her planned spending this month. Let's say she allocated $400 for planned shopping. Is the $98 price tag worth it to her to buy the dress and use a portion of the money she'd planned to spend in her shopping category this month? After this purchase, she'd have $302 left to spend in this category. Is that outcome worth it to Fernanda? Hell yeah. She's thrilled to use some of the money she allocated on this dress.

Voilà! This dress is in alignment all around. Fernanda smiles as she grabs it off the rack to take up to the register. She stands in line with no stress or guilt, and the two voices in her head (The Bitch and The Hulk) are stone-cold silent. She's proud she is putting her money toward things that are in alignment, and she knows she gets to enjoy life now while simultaneously putting aside money for her future.

Now, let's look at an example where spending isn't in alignment.

Silvie is a food blogger and new mom and has recently been looking for a sectional for her living room. She sees that there is a sale running this weekend on the sectional she's had her eye on, so she decides to walk through her alignment practice with this potential purchase.

She remembers the Big 3 alignment questions to ask herself:

1. Is what I'm purchasing in alignment?
2. Is the price in alignment?
3. Is the outcome of this purchase in alignment?

Silvie starts with the "thing" in this scenario, aka the couch. Is it in alignment? Hell yes. She's been in love with this sectional for months.

Next, Silvie asks herself if the price of the couch is in alignment (aka how much is the couch, and does she believe that price is worth paying for it). The couch is $2,300 on sale. She has read hundreds of reviews and knows there is a lifetime warranty on the couch, and she knows it's normally $2,900, so she thinks it is definitely worth $2,300.

Lastly, Silvie asks herself if the outcome of purchasing the couch is in alignment. She didn't know there would be a sale on the couch this month, so she did not set aside money for it. The outcome of this purchase would be dipping into her and her husband's conjoined emergency fund. She asks herself and talks to her husband about whether this feels in alignment for them right now. They think over the fact that their current sectional is still totally functional, and that with their almost-toddler running around with food spilling out of her mouth, investing in the new sectional at this moment feels like an unnecessary rush. They feel total freedom to buy it if they choose and know that they could easily move things around to make it work, but the outcome of that purchase doesn't feel completely aligned. They have a good feeling the sectional will go on sale again later in the year (like for Black Friday, for example), and make a note that they want to add "Buy a sectional" to their priority list so next time it feels more like a "hell yes" decision.

The outcome for Silvie was *not* to purchase the couch, but not because she had to restrict or sacrifice what she wanted to hit her goals. She looked at alignment holistically, and the outcome of that purchase wasn't in the highest alignment with her, so she made the confident decision to choose not to purchase it. No restriction. No sacrifice. No guilt. No shame. Only confident decision-making.

Spending in alignment takes time to master, but you can practice this with every single purchase you make, big or small.

The magic of learning how to spend in full alignment is that it simultaneously transforms your entire spend plan and your mindset around spending. It begins to feel easier and easier to spend how you've planned, and you also feel completely free to change your mind and subsequently change and update your spend plan.

BRINGING IT TOGETHER

As you're spending in alignment and practicing the Big 3 (thing, price, outcome), you'll realize more and more how easy it feels to use your spend plan because you allow it to ebb and flow with your life. As time goes on, you want to be constantly updating your spend plan to reflect what alignment looks like in your life at the time. For instance, in Fernanda's example of going back to school and wanting to level up her wardrobe, maybe shopping became a priority that felt more in alignment for her in that particular season of life compared to other times when it is not. The best part is the more you practice spending in alignment, the easier and more fun your spend plan will feel. And more importantly, the more intuitive your spend plan will feel. Have you ever thought you spent a certain amount on shopping in a month, but when you went back to look it was double? The cool part of this process is that when you're setting your goal amount for your spend plan and choosing totals based on alignment, when you go to spend you are so much more aware of how alignment feels throughout the month and while spending. It completely eliminates the feeling of "sticking to a budget" because the ultimate goal is happiness, joy, and the elevation of your current and future life. The more you practice the Big 3 and use it to make decisions on spending and couple that with your spend plan—the more unstoppable and empowered you will feel. This shit gets to be fun.

So much of spending in alignment is leaning into your intuition, shifting your mindset and linking it with your top priorities. But often, there's so many priorities we have that we want to accomplish. So, if you're all ready to hit the ground running, but you're sitting there thinking, *But I have so many goals, Chloe. Which should I be focusing on first?* I'm glad ya asked. We'll figure this out together in the next chapter.

PART 5

Understanding Goals

CHAPTER 14

Your Living Plan

What if you don't make it to retirement?

Harsh way to kick off a chapter, I know. But if you read the author's note and dedication at the beginning of this book, you might remember that this book is dedicated to my mom, who passed away halfway through my writing it. I actually printed out the author's note to show her, and she read it two days before she passed. She was 59 years old.

59 years old is 6 years away from the standard retirement age in the United States.

A lot of finance books will focus on helping you grow your retirement portfolio as big as possible so you can retire when you are 65 years old and enjoy life without work. A lot of finance books teach you how to create the ultimate retirement plan by using restriction and sacrificing your current lifestyle to create the picture-perfect idea of relaxation, fun, and carefree living . . . once you're 65.

But have you ever wondered, *What if I don't make it to 65?*

Don't get me wrong; I *do* want you to have a retirement plan, and this isn't yolo, irresponsible advice on how to live it up with no regard for the future. However, I am going to introduce you to another kind of plan I want you to have in addition to your retirement plan. It's called a living plan. A living plan is your written-out plan of exactly how you want to prioritize your money now, while you're living your life before retirement. Your living plan can include paying off debt, taking a trip, or doing a bucket-list item, but it also gets into the details of what you're focusing on, how much it costs, and when you want to accomplish it. A retirement plan begins the day you slice the goodbye cake at the office farewell party, but a living plan begins today.

Your retirement plan and living plan should complement each other. Combined, they make sure you are elevating your life now *and* later. A plan to enjoy life down the road, but also a plan to enjoy life as you're living it. A plan for you to take the trip after you've retired, but also a plan for you to take the trip now.

If you're feeling a twinge overwhelmed by all the future things in life there are to plan for (paying off debt, saving, buying a house, purchasing a new car, going back to school, paying for a wedding, investing for retirement, etc.), remember this: one of the hardest parts about getting ahead with finances is that there will always be another thing to do, another goal to hit, or another item to pay for. If your entire mindset relies on only feeling accomplished *after* you've hit that goal, you will end up in a perpetual state of stress. Instead, if you look at spending as it relates to your current priorities, in addition to setting goals for the future, you can accomplish both, allowing you to prepare for the future while enjoying life now.

In 2019, I shared a post that started with, "I am going to be a millionaire by 27." My net worth was probably hovering around $75,000 to $100,000 at that time. And if I am being honest, I had absolutely no clue how I was going to do it. I promised myself two things before posting that:

1. I was going to become a millionaire at 27 (before I turned 28).
2. I was never going to do it at the expense of my lifestyle and priorities now.

As I write this, I'm currently 26 years old, I have a year left to hit that goal, and I am on track to do it. And although I love setting big, wild goals and going after them at full speed, the closer and closer I get to my goal, the more that second promise becomes important to me.

Yes, becoming a millionaire at 27 is going to be freaking cool. And yes, let me clarify I haven't done it yet, but I'm calling out my big goal so you can see it in action. As an Enneagram 7, I am a dreamer and a huge goal setter. I have always been this way. I told myself I was going to quit my corporate job, and I did it. I told myself I was going to start my own financial literacy company, and I did it. I told myself I was going to buy my dream lake home, and I did it. I told myself I was going to write a book, and you are reading it. In case you can't tell, I am freaking motivated by big goals. But let me also tell you, I have set plenty that I haven't achieved. And I celebrate that, too, because if I miss a goal in order to stay true to my promise of not sacrificing my life now, I'm still winning. Hitting goals is amazing, but an even bigger priority for me is enjoying the process—which is a very intentional choice.

For example, when it comes to my goal of being a millionaire before I turn 28, there are things I could be doing to hit my goal faster that I am actively choosing not to do. I could be cutting out those "extra" or "unnecessary" expenses like ditching my gym membership and doing burpees from my living room. I could say goodbye to spending $7 on a venti iced decaf vanilla latte with oat milk. I could say no to the vacations and the spontaneous concert tickets when my favorite artist is in town. I could stop buying my friends Vegas bomb shots when we go out, or buying my niece a new onesie every time I see her. I could turn down the trip to Europe, the lake weekend, or the snowboarding excursion. By not doing these things, I could have put all my time and attention into spending as little as possible.

However, if I had turned down all those adventures and opportunities, I might have spent the last three years in a terrible state of mind when it comes to how I look at my money. Maybe my internal dialogue of The Bitch would still be screaming at me, *OMG, you shouldn't spend that or you will never hit my goal of becoming a millionaire* on repeat. I could have had guilt for every matching workout set I bought, or every $14 skinny margarita with Casamigos tequila, or even told myself that every donation to my favorite charity was something I should have waited to do until I hit my goal. I could have looked at every dollar spent as a dollar that wasn't going toward my goal and, therefore, would have spent the last three years filled with guilt and internal judgment. *Ewww.* Just the thought of that makes me cringe.

Why would I want to spend three years sacrificing things I wanted to do or ways I wanted to spend my money to hit a goal with a timeline I randomly made up for myself?

The second goal is important to me because what if I miss my first goal? Let's say I don't hit that millionaire goal and I sacrificed things I cared about on the way. Or maybe I also felt a ton of guilt and shame in any "extra" spending on my way to my millionaire status. Will I care more about the fact that I did not hit a goal that I set? Or will I care more about the fact that I didn't hit that goal *and* I just spent seven years of my twenties missing out on life and being constantly stressed about spending money? On my journey to become a millionaire, I care just as much about my living plan as I do about my big goals and retirement plan.

Maybe your huge goal is to become debt-free or to max out your retirement accounts or to have an emergency fund for the first time ever. Amazing. I love that for you. But what if along your journey it's also important for you to prioritize travel or friends' bachelorette parties or home renovations? That's your living plan. This is the perfect time for you to remember Chapter 7, where we talked about imagining your dream life. You imagined what it would look like, so make sure you are creating a living plan that gets you closer to your dream life, too.

What things are a priority in your life right now?

____

____

____

____

I want you to look at those priorities and number them according to what needs to happen first to last. If you're stuck because it feels like you should have accomplished all of them by yesterday, don't worry; we will talk more about making this list as strategic as possible. However, you are creating a baseline of your priorities right now. Number them from 1 to 4, or however many there are, and order them depending on when you want or need them completed.

For example, let's say you want to pay off credit card debt, but you also want to go on a trip to Italy next summer. Plus, you have a friend's wedding coming up in two months that will require spending money on plane tickets and a hotel. In this case, the wedding would rank before a vacation next summer because it comes first chronologically.

Now let's expand a little more and look more into the future.

What things are a priority in my life in the next 5 to 10 years?

____

____

____

What things are a priority for long-term wealth-building (the next 20+ years)?

____

____

____

Your living plan is going to be your focal point during your financial journey, so I want to ensure you take time crafting it. Why is it so important? Because it's totally and completely unique to you. So often I get asked (by complete strangers on social media), "Chloe, should I pay off my student loans or buy a house?" But it's impossible for me to answer that. *How soon will you be buying this house? Which goal do you care about more right now? How much of a down payment will you need? At what interest rates are your student loans? What's the balance? Do you have an emergency fund?* I could type a whole chapter full of questions I'd need answers to before beginning to respond.

I cannot give you a custom plan, but I can give you a helpful checklist of steps to shape the order in which you tackle your financial goals and accelerate your journey toward wealth. Although everyone's situation looks different, this will help you personalize your living plan and add some structure. Plus, who doesn't love that feeling of being able to check off completed items?

Before I hand you the checklist, I need to give a little disclaimer: as you are reading this guide, it's important to consider that this is based solely on strategic financial gains alone. Your responsibility is to adjust it to be holistic: factoring in your goals, desires, stress levels, mental health, and more. This has to be Deeper Than Money.

For example, let's say you have two debts to pay off: a credit card balance at 25% interest and a personal loan from a friend. Based on how it looks on paper, the checklist below would recommend focusing on the credit card debt first because that's the most efficient approach and saves you money in the form of interest. From a logistics-only perspective, the credit card is "more important" and the personal loan is "less important." However, if the personal loan is causing stress and tension on your friendship, you could absolutely choose to prioritize paying your friend back first. This checklist is for how you are going to allocate your goal bucket (from your spend plan). The money in this bucket will go toward your living plan. We will incorporate some financial strategy alongside your goals and dreams to create your priority list, which will make up your living plan.

The Future Bajillionaire Checklist

- ☐ Build your starter emergency fund.
- ☐ Get your employer retirement match (if applicable).
- ☐ Pay off your highest-interest debt (10% and over) first.

- ☐ Begin or increase retirement investing.
- ☐ Pay off other debt and save for big purchases.
- ☐ Grow your big baller emergency fund.
- ☐ Max out retirement accounts and invest outside of retirement accounts.

Now, let me break down this list.

1. BUILD YOUR STARTER EMERGENCY FUND

We will talk more specifically about how to set up an emergency fund in Chapter 17, but for now, we're talking about a starter emergency fund. This fund is one to three months of core expenses saved for emergencies. By core expenses, I mean all expenses you'd need to pay no matter what. It doesn't have to include discretionary expenses like saving $500 per month for a fun vacation to Paris, or spending $100 per month on random Amazon purchases, because in an emergency (say you lost your job), you'd likely want to be a little more conservative in your spending.

When deciding whether you need one, two, or three months of expenses in your starter emergency fund (I call it your e-fund), consider the risk you'd have if you temporarily lost your income or if your income took a big hit. Depending on your unique situation, your risk might be higher or lower, so we are going to walk you through several factors to see what makes the most sense for you. This flowchart was inspired by the kind you'd read when you were a preteen sneaking away with a *Seventeen* magazine to take the quiz and learn if you were going to get your first kiss that month. Check out the following chart to find out what might be the best amount to save in your starter emergency fund:

How much should you have in your starter emergency fund?

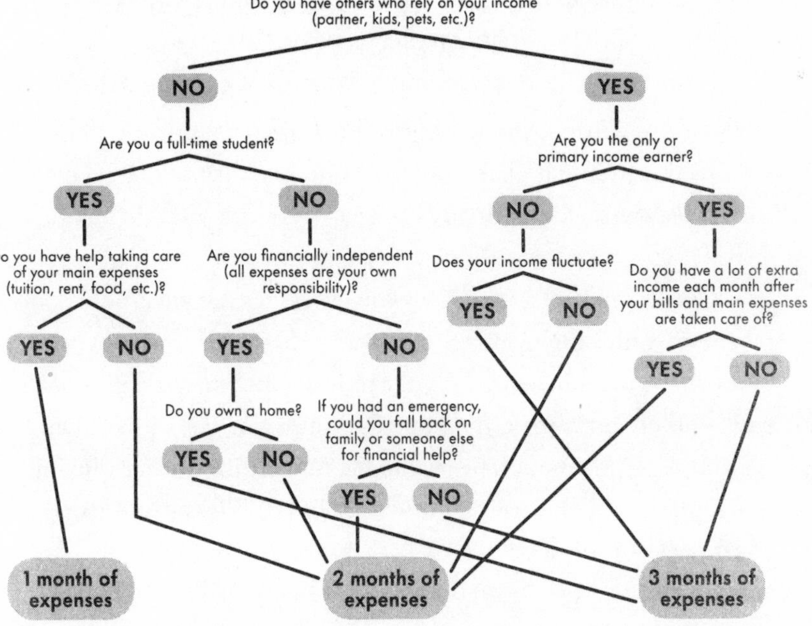

If you are sitting here thinking, *Chloe, I have debt, and you want me to save three months of my expenses first?* I realize it might seem a little backward, but I would much rather you potentially pay a little more in interest on your debt while you're saving for an emergency fund so it's there for you through your debt-paying journey and beyond, providing you with financial security. Plus, if an emergency does come up while you are in the process of building your starter e-fund, you won't have to take on *more* debt, and potentially rocket up your credit card balance, when your goal is to pay it down.

2. GET YOUR EMPLOYER RETIREMENT MATCH (IF APPLICABLE)

A lot of times employers will offer a certain level of contribution into your retirement plan as part of your benefits package. This is a great way to start supporting the goals of future you. If you don't know if you have this, it is super easy to find out. You can send a quick email to HR asking, "Can you clarify for me what our company offers for employer retirement match?" This is money your employer is putting away for your retirement, but often you only receive their portion of the contribution if you are enrolled and are contributing enough to be eligible for the match. Because it is not something you can earn down the road, it's strategic to take advantage of it now.

3. PAY OFF YOUR HIGHEST-INTEREST DEBT (10% AND OVER) FIRST

Now it's time to get down to business on your debt and start tackling high-interest debt, which I consider 10% and over, in order of highest interest to lowest interest. If you have debt that is 7% to 9% interest, that is in the gray area of what I consider high interest; often I will prioritize it as high-interest debt, but there might be a situation like a mortgage at 7%, when you are hoping interest rates will decrease in the next year and you can refinance your home, so you are only "keeping" the 7% interest rate for the short term. However, if you have a car loan at 9%, that can likely fall into the high-interest debt category and could absolutely be worth paying off sooner on the list. The average credit card interest rate for someone with fair credit is more than 25%.[1] Wowza. Tackling high-interest debt like credit cards or personal loans first will help you save a lot of money because you're getting rid of the highest interest first.

Let's start by listing your debt from highest interest rate to lowest. For example:

ACCOUNT	BALANCE	INTEREST RATE
Credit card #1	$1,924	29.99%
Credit card #2	$3,412	23%
Car loan	$9,000	5%
Student loan	$13,233	4%

As you're listing all your debt and creating a plan to tackle it as quickly as possible, I want to let you in on a secret. I have had many clients with high-interest credit card debt successfully call their credit card companies and negotiate their interest rates. I want you to investigate this option as well because it could save you hundreds to thousands of dollars in interest. There will be an exact script for this in Chapter 16.

When you're tackling high-interest debt, another great option to consider is a balance transfer. A balance transfer is taking your balance (for example, an amount of credit card debt you have) and moving it to a new account, most often at a different bank or from a different lender, in order to obtain a lower (or 0% promotional) interest rate. You will end up paying less in total interest because your interest rate is now lower than before. Often, balance transfers can be so appealing because promotional rates are offered. For example, you can look into a 0% annual percentage rate (APR; interest rate including fees, etc.) for a 6- to 12-month balance transfer that you can quickly tackle while your interest is at 0%. Paying off credit card debt that is at 0% interest feels a whole lot easier than paying off credit card debt that is at 27% interest, because the balance isn't growing faster than you can pay it off.

Remember to start by negotiating your credit card interest first. If you don't find success in that, then you can start shopping around for a balance transfer. If you are not sure where to find options for a balance transfer, you can look under "resources" in your Credit Karma account or simply google "best balance transfer promotions" and look through the different options. I also recommend calling the lender and reading the fine print to see what the lender normally wants to see as a credit score before applying. Balance transfers do check your credit, which could ding your credit score. It's important to make sure you are doing all of your research prior to deciding if a balance transfer is the right option for you. Make sure you are okay with an inquiry potentially impacting your credit score as well as making sure you are doing the math on any hidden fees or transfer fees and making sure there is no prepayment penalty for paying the loan off early.

Warning: Getting a balance transfer and then ignoring that debt because it's at a lower rate is not the move here. Only do a balance transfer if you are hella confident that you are going to be able to tackle it and take advantage of the 0% interest rate.

If you choose to go the balance-transfer route, using this strategy can create more room in your budget since you're paying less interest to the bank and keeping more money in your pocket! And that will allow you to be able to focus on other debts—or pay off your balance faster than you were before. Balance transfers can be an incredible tool, but just remember, it won't be at the promo rate forever, so make sure to read the terms and make sure you're making a well-informed decision!

4. BEGIN OR INCREASE RETIREMENT INVESTING

I'll be honest with you. I had written more than 6,000 words about the logistics of investing, from mutual funds to asset allocation, and I cut it from the book. Why? Because it actually was detracting from the main takeaway: You don't have to be an expert on investing to become a millionaire at retirement, to pay off your debt, or to feel financial freedom. You *do*, however, need to know how to use money as a tool to spend, save, and invest in alignment with your goals. My goal is for you to have a baseline understanding of a lot of these concepts and then feel empowered to take the next step of learning about the different retirement options that are available and will be the best for you.

I want you to sit down and start thinking of your own investment goals while remembering the end goal isn't to have as much money as possible in retirement. As a reminder, you cannot take money with you when you leave this earth, and what is the point of having $5 million in your investment accounts when you pass away if you skipped out on every bottomless mimosa brunch with your friends in your 20s because you needed to invest every penny into retirement?

However, the cool thing about money is that, when you die, it can outlive you. Your money can make a massive impact on the people you love and the organizations you care about, even after you're gone. And that is fantastic.

In fact, you'll notice in the Future Bajillionaire checklist you don't see a step in there specific to "giving." When it comes to giving, I feel really strongly about it not being a box you have to check. While I do personally have more standard annual donations, I also make it a point to make the act of giving incredibly personal. I do my best to keep cash in my wallet specifically for giving to someone who I think it could be a blessing to, or buying the groceries of the person behind me in line. I also love giving in a way that's close to home. I love sending my friends a gift card or booking a new flight for them when theirs gets canceled and they are stuck somewhere. I love contributing to local events and charities and GoFundMes used to bless other families. I want to be someone who is always looking for ways to use my money for good, instead of only giving in a standard annual contribution. Giving is so personal, and I want you to think about how you want giving to play a part in your current spending now, because more money doesn't change how you give. It only changes how much.

Back to retirement, the ultimate goal shouldn't be to sacrifice everything now so you can have the biggest possible retirement fund when you're an old granny. There are so many ways you can invest, and if I were to go into detail on all of it, it'd be a whole book in itself. Instead, I am going to encourage you to note that this is the step where you want to set up your retirement plan and direct you to deeperthanmoney.com/book to check out more resources if you're ready to take this step.

5. PAY OFF OTHER DEBT AND SAVE FOR BIG PURCHASES

Next, it's time to start looking at paying off additional debt. At this point, you've already paid off your high-interest debt (go you!), so now, you will work to pay off your additional debt in order of highest interest to lowest interest. If we use our earlier example, we are focusing now on tackling the car loan and student loan with extra payments (what is left over in your spend plan toward your goal amount). Be sure you are still paying all minimum payments on all loans each month, and using your extra to specifically pay off the top priority at a fast rate with additional payments. Even though the car loan is smaller, it has a higher interest rate, so we will focus on paying it off first.

ACCOUNT	AMOUNT	INTEREST RATE
~~Credit card #1~~	~~$1,924~~	~~29.99%~~
~~Credit card #2~~	~~$3,412~~	~~23%~~
Car loan	$9,000	5%
Student loan	$13,233	4%

This is also a great time to start thinking of big purchases you'd like to start saving for, like a new car or a house. One common money myth to call out is that you don't always have to be saving money. I encourage you to have a specific amount in mind (e.g., $15,000 for the down payment on a house or $5,000 for a new car) instead of constantly saving in general. Specifying an amount will allow you to achieve milestones along the way instead of feeling like you're just saving to save.

6. GROW YOUR BIG BALLER EMERGENCY FUND

As you are creating your strategy of paying off debt and focusing on investing, it's also time to consider growing your starter e-fund to become a big baller e-fund. This means increasing the e-fund from one to three months of expenses to six to eight months of expenses. This may sound like a lot, but I promise that the long-term effect of having this type of financial stability from your wealth-protecting money (more on this soon) is unbelievably impactful on your mental health and allows you to turn many emergencies into inconveniences.

7. MAX OUT RETIREMENT ACCOUNTS AND INVEST OUTSIDE OF RETIREMENT ACCOUNTS

One of the most important distinctions when it comes to investing: you can invest *inside* of retirement accounts and you can invest *outside* of retirement accounts. To give you some clarity on which one you should choose first, here's an example:

Think of two clubs next door to each other, Club Piña and Club Colada. They are basically the exact same club, except for a few differences in the types of drinks offered. The big difference is that Club Piña has happy hour from 4 to 8 p.m., when all drinks are half off, *but* it closes at 8 p.m. Club Colada is open from 4 p.m. to 2 a.m. but doesn't offer happy hour specials. If the clubs are right next door to each other and provide the same amount of fun, what's your move if you and your friends are planning to head out for the night around 6 p.m. and stay out 'til midnight?

You likely go to Club Piña first, take advantage of happy hour–priced drinks, and then go over to Club Colada when the first club closes.

Club Piña

Happy hour: 50% off
drinks from 4 to 8 p.m.
Closes at 8 p.m.

Club Colada

Full-price drinks
Closes at 2 a.m.

Club Piña (happy hour prices) = retirement investing
Club Colada (full price) = nonretirement investing

There's your investment strategy.

For long-term investments, investing inside of your retirement accounts, like your 401(k), for example, and getting a tax break on it is a better benefit to you than downloading an investment app and investing outside of your retirement account. However, investing rocks, so if/when you've maxed out retirement accounts or want to do some intermediate-term investing, investing outside of retirement is also great!

IMPLEMENTING THE FUTURE BAJILLIONAIRE CHECKLIST

This might seem like a lot of steps, but I promise this will be fun. We are mapping out where you want your money to go and the life you want to create for yourself. Let's practice what this looks like by going over a common example I see from clients.

Keagan is 27 years old and stressed because she feels like she has a thousand things going on that all require money, and they all basically need to happen right now. She is feeling all over the place. Her short-term goals within the next year are to save for a new car, pay off her two credit cards, attend her friend Hailee's bachelorette party in a couple months, pay off her student loans, max out her Roth IRA, and take a family vacation to Mexico.

Let's structure these short-term goals in a chart where we can lay out the amount and goal completion date:

PRIORITY	AMOUNT	GOAL COMPLETION DATE
Credit card #1	$700	August 1
Hailee's bachelorette party	$400	August 30
Credit card #2	$2,409	October 15
Save for new car	$5,000	February 1
Student loans	$10,381	April 1
Vacation	$750	April 20
Max out Roth IRA	$6,000	August 1

Now it's your turn. Let's lay out your priority list for the next year, combining your priorities from earlier in the chapter with your future bajillionaire checklist to create your living plan:

PRIORITY	AMOUNT	GOAL COMPLETION DATE

Let's say Keagan has $400 per month left over right now after all her bills are paid. This is the leftover (income – expenses) that we found in Chapter 12! See, it's all coming together. In Keagan's example, she is going to put that FULL $400 of (leftover/goal amount) toward priority #1 on the list. Credit card #1 will be paid off in less than two months, and then she is going to set aside the next $400 to use for the bachelorette party. After the bachelorette party, her next priority will be credit card #2. Keep in mind, the beauty of paying down debt is that not only are you getting rid of the balance when you pay it off faster, but you also will free up the money that was going toward those pesky monthly payments, which will allow you to tackle your next goal even sooner!

Short-term goals are important because they have a direct impact on your cash flow, but it's also important to be prepared for more intermediate- and long-term goals as well. As you check off short-term goals, you can add more priorities to your list.

Now, to wrap up the chapter, I want to remind you that it's totally normal and acceptable for your priorities to shift. In fact, I would argue that's the most important part. The practices and habits you're building are meant to last you a lifetime. During the course of your life you'll have many new priorities pop up, as you will likely be moving things around, and that's okay! Creating a living plan is just as important as creating a retirement plan, because you want to be intentional about utilizing your money now, just as you are intentional about planning for your retirement down the road.

CHAPTER 15

Match My Vibe, Elevate It, or GTFO

At 26, I had just gone through some big changes in my life, and I made a promise to myself. The promise was simple:

> I will not let anyone or anything into my life that does not match my vibe or elevate it. If it doesn't meet that criteria, it needs to GTFO.

Now that you are starting to practice finding alignment in your spending choices (and hopefully drawing parallels to areas of your life beyond finances), I want to challenge you to take this concept of alignment a step further. What if it's not just about spending in alignment, but also about spending in a way where every dollar that crosses your path is used to elevate your life?

Remember your money thermostat from Chapter 8? Now I want to introduce you to a similar concept: your alignment thermostat.

Your alignment thermostat, similar to your money ther-

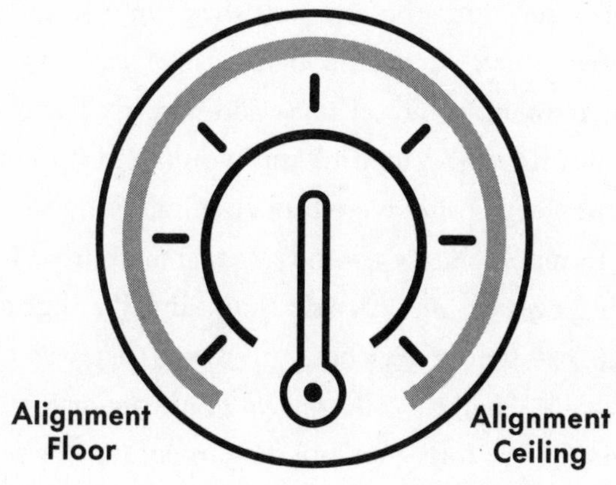

mostat, has a ceiling and a floor that kick into gear when you wander outside of what is in alignment for you.

YOUR ALIGNMENT FLOOR

Your alignment floor is the low point of what feels aligned for you. For me, I could clearly see this in my past life as a low-key hoarder; my alignment floor was pretty low. While shopping, if I found anything cheap or on sale, I would feel obligated to buy it. *It's a good deal, right?* I would drive through suburban streets and spot houses with random stuff at the end of their driveways, and any time I saw that "FREE" sign, you could cue up Shania Twain, because all I was thinking was, *Let's go, girls.* I would end up begging my friends to come with me to haul a broken coffee table, random shelving, and an old vacuum back to my apartment. Let me be crystal clear: I am not dissing or looking down on picking up free things off the side of the road. But I am not a DIY queen, and I wasn't updating these items and using them. I was just obsessed with the fact that they were free (remember idolizing frugality?). I would bring the free items into my cramped apartment (which, I must add, already had a coffee table, shelving unit, and vacuum) and would end up with two of each, and the "new" ones were broken. Grabbing this stuff actually led to so much clutter around my apartment that I struggled with keeping everything organized and tidy. My alignment floor used to mean I would purchase anything that was cheap and made me think, *Ummm, yeah. I might be able to use that.*

Fast-forward to today, and my alignment floor is very different. It has less to do with price; it has to do with true alignment and the Big 3 we went over in Chapter 13. I ask myself these three questions when I make a purchase (or before taking home a free item!):

1. Is the purchase of this item in alignment? (Will it elevate my life?)
2. Is the price of this item in alignment?
3. Is the outcome of this purchase in alignment? (Does it fit in with my goals?)

And although I am always looking to raise my alignment thermostat, full disclosure here: my current alignment floor is a purchase that I may really need, but sometimes I end up accepting something that's not perfect or a "hell yes." In a perfect world, I am working toward every purchase being a "hell yes, best thing ever," but sometimes the perfect product doesn't exist. For example, although I no longer buy things just to buy them, there are times I need something and have an idea of the exact thing I want but cannot find it. Recently, I was redoing my downstairs bathroom sink (and by "I was redoing," I mean my big sister and brother-in-law, who are basically HGTV remodeling stars, were redoing it). The new faucet I was in love with wouldn't fit, and I had to find a backup option. So although my second-choice faucet wasn't screaming "Hell yes!!!" it was a huge step up from before and definitely more than good enough. Those purchases still fall in alignment with me; however, I am always encouraging myself to raise my alignment floor by asking myself, "I believe there is always a 'hell yes' option. How can I find it?" The idea of knowing that a better option for a purchase exists has opened my eyes in so many ways, and I've started to set higher expectations for what is in alignment with me. Now it's your turn.

Describe your alignment floor:

____

What is one thing you'd like to do to elevate your alignment floor?

____

YOUR ALIGNMENT CEILING

Next, you are going to work on elevating your alignment ceiling. Your alignment ceiling is the peak of what you expect for yourself.

Imagine you come home from a long day at work to a Lululemon package outside your front door (ah, **chef's kiss**). You bring the package into the living room, rip off your corporate hot-girl outfit, and start trying on each new piece. Now, here is the decision you need to make: *What kind of energy do I accept?*

Do you keep the clothes that fit *just fine*? Do you keep clothes that are pretty but just not your color? Do you keep clothes that are cute but you don't know when you'd ever wear them? Do you keep clothes that are okay but you feel really frumpy in them? Clothes that are a little too small? Or a little too big?

Have you ever been struck by one of the following thoughts:

Eh, it could probably be cute with the right jeans. >> and you keep it.

Is it cute? I think it's cute. I'll send a pic to my friend to see if I should keep it. >> and you keep it.

Eh, it's already here. I don't want to mess with returning it. >> and you keep it.

It's important to understand where your current alignment is, but what if what you're currently accepting into your life (i.e., what is aligned to you) isn't truly the most elevated vibe possible for you?

Think back to trying on that shirt that's kinda "eh, but could probably be cute." Normally, you'd keep it because it's good enough and it feels somewhat aligned. Now, instead, you go through the alignment process and think, *Nah, not obsessed*, and you immediately return it. Woah. This can take working up to financially as well, in some cases, but remember that something being more in alignment doesn't automatically mean it is more expensive.

What if you genuinely lived by the motto that if it doesn't match your vibe or elevate it, it needs to GTFO?

Your alignment ceiling would raise from "accepting just enough in alignment" to only accepting the absolute best of the best that raises your vibe to the next notch.

Describe your current alignment ceiling:

____

What is one thing you'd like to do to elevate your alignment ceiling?

____

I will tell you this, though: in my experience of increasing my alignment ceiling, fears and doubts do pop up. "What if this is the cutest shirt I will be able to find?" This question comes from a fear of missing out, because maybe it never gets better than this.

I challenge you to choose more for yourself.

This mindset has changed my life when it comes to spending in alignment. If I do not feel like Kim Kardashian's stylist quit her job and decided to come style me instead, it's a no from me, dawg. If my own jaw doesn't drop to the floor and I'm not saying, "Oh my gosh, I am going to wear this every day forever," it does not even get near my closet. And I don't only use this mindset for clothes. You can also use this for home decor, new relationships, friendships, houses/apartments, jobs, cars, and more.

In order to believe that you deserve the things that match or elevate your vibe, you also have to believe that if something *doesn't* match or elevate your vibe, something else will.

Let's take it further than spending money.

If *one person* doesn't match your vibe or elevate it, *someone else* will.

If *one opportunity* doesn't match your vibe or elevate it, *the next opportunity* will.

The freaking cool thing about mastering how to spend in

alignment and spend in a way that elevates your alignment is that you start to understand and trust how you can apply that same philosophy to other areas of your life.

You no longer fear when you don't get the job offer, because you trust there will be a job offer coming that's even better.

You no longer fear rejection from the Hinge date, because if she's not into you, she clearly has shitty taste and that's embarrassing for her. Oops—I meant there will be someone who is a better fit for you who will elevate your life.

Opting into this new belief truly changed my life because when you genuinely believe and expect that you either get the best or better is coming, you continue to attract more things into your life like that, and you set more boundaries around the things that aren't elevating your life.

Whether I see my paycheck hit my account or a dirty ass penny on the ground, I get excited because every cent that comes into my life is used to elevate it (and elevate the lives of those around me). I don't care if you're using money to pay off debt—vibes elevated. I don't care if you're using it to buy the newest workout set—vibes elevated. When the goal is alignment, and you use money as a tool to elevate your life, not only does spending feel fun and easy, but your confidence also increases because every single dollar that comes into your account is a dollar that will be intentionally spent toward creating your dream life.

But now, how do we set boundaries around this newfound energy? Your villain era has entered the chat.

WHAT IS YOUR VILLAIN ERA?

I want you to think of a villain from any cartoon movie. Let's use Ursula from *The Little Mermaid* as an example.

What thoughts come to mind when you think of Ursula? Or any other famous movie villain (Cruella de Vil, Scar, etc.)?

Maybe you think about their traits: selfish, calculating, outcome-focused, powerful, unpredictable, hated, unapologetic. But maybe the most important attribute of a villain is that their primary motivation is to harm others.

Now let's think about some of the attributes of heroes: selfless, courageous, helpful, strong, etc.—all characteristics aimed at the common good.

Sure, heroes are classified as the "good guys" and villains are the "bad guys." But why is it that sometimes the villains become the most intriguing characters? There's something captivating about their personalities.

So what if instead we took the "villain" mentality, but applied it for good? What if we took the captivating parts of their characters and embodied those traits, even if it's just for a short period of our lives?

Interesting thought, right? Let's take a peek at what those "bad guy" traits, reexamined from a "good guy" lens, could look like in your day-to-day life:

- Selfish: Putting your own goals first and prioritizing yourself. Making sure that if something has to give on a busy day, it isn't your own well-being and/or self-care.

- Calculating/outcome-focused: Getting incredibly clear on who you want to become and what goals you want to achieve.
- Powerful: Setting massive boundaries around your time and energy, and enforcing them.
- Unpredictable: Doing what you want, on your own terms, and not trying to fit into the box of what other people want you to be doing. Allowing yourself to change your mind at any time.
- Hated: Allowing yourself to fully be who you are, without caring what other people's opinions or judgments are.
- Unapologetic: You do what you want, when you want, and you don't care how it is perceived.

Notice none of these traits include stealing, lying, or killing Dalmatians. Your inner villain doesn't do evil things; she just has a certain mindset. What if we started claiming the villain mentality and started letting go of some of the "heroic" traits we have tried so hard to maintain? Traits like these:

- Selflessness: Putting everyone else's needs above your own, so you have nothing left to give yourself.
- Helping everyone/people-pleasing: Losing yourself in the effort to please everyone.
- Dropping everything at a moment's notice to help: Having no boundaries, or having some but not enforcing them, and allowing people to walk all over you.

We have been taught our whole lives how to be "good." So

many old-school parenting techniques focused on teaching kids how to obey authority and, therefore, be a "good girl." This mentality can stick with us into our adult lives and trickle into our finances, too.

Dragana Kovacevic, a parent and educator, has some criticism for the saying, "Be a good girl." She explains:

> Not only does it teach your child to conform to problematic societal stereotypes of women and girls, it too teaches the suppression of useful life skills such as speaking up and self-advocacy. Because, let's be honest. Some situations call for constructive social disruption. . . . This comment can also subtly reinforce the dangerous message that they should learn to comply to those who may not have their best interests at heart.[1]

The problem with being taught how to be "good" instead of how to navigate the world is that these ideas of "good" and "right" are subjective. What we should have learned instead was how to listen to intuition or our own desires. When it comes to money, maybe you learned that buying something at full price is "bad" or that avoiding conversations involving money is "good." This learned behavior sticks with us into adulthood, and soon we find ourselves worrying too much because we are afraid of not doing the "right thing" and what people will think of us.

What does a good girl (someone trying to seem good, noble, and likable to everyone) get? A good girl often ends up doing what everyone else wants her to do (in an effort to be likable). But at what cost? When I was so obsessed with being "good" and likable, I was anxious all the time, burned out, feeling like I was going to be judged for everything I did. I was so stressed from my lack of boundaries. I was constantly one menty-b (mental breakdown) away from feeling like I wanted to throw in the towel. A good girl gets burned out from trying to please everyone.

But on the other hand, what does a "bad girl" get? She gets what she wants.

Your villain era doesn't mean being an asshole to everyone or trying to blow up Gotham City. It's about realizing that being taught to be "good" can often be a cage that has us living a life (and spending our money) in a way that other people want us to, instead of living the life (and spending our money) the way we want to.

Focusing on being good often means we are fixating on doing what we think is right in the eyes of others, which leads to perpetual people-pleasing and overvaluing others' opinions.

I want you to think about the five most important people in your life. Write their names down.

1. ______________________
2. ______________________
3. ______________________
4. ______________________
5. ______________________

Now, for each name, I want you to answer the question, "Who does ______ want me to be?" Remember that no one will see it, there is no pressure, and there are no right or wrong answers. Maybe you feel that you need to act in a certain way around some people and differently around others; or maybe it's that you feel the need to hold back your intense personality when around people who may perceive you as being "too much." Freewrite and let your thoughts flow. When we realize who we think people want us to be, it's easier to identify the ways we try to please people and change ourselves to cater to their liking.

Now think of a time in your life when you've gotten pushback or hate from someone for doing or saying something that was unapologetically "you." What immediately comes to my mind is when I wanted to quit my corporate job and go full-time in my business. So many of the people closest to me warned me that it wasn't a good idea and were concerned about what would happen if I didn't succeed. This decision was something that I had internal conflict over because it came down to me making a decision that wasn't viewed as being "right" or "good" in the eyes of so many people in my circle. But for me, it was a decision that not only matched my energy—it elevated the hell out of it.

T-SWIFT ENERGY

If you use social media, I want you to imagine posting something online that's way off base from what you would ever normally share. I want you to think of something that would be so unbelievably vulnerable or opinionated and for which you would likely receive backlash. Or maybe it's something simpler, like posting a selfie or a new job status. A lot of times we make decisions based on other people's opinions and judgments.

But what if you do post it and there is pushback?

What if you do it and there is hate?

What do those negative reactions actually mean about you?

It means people judge you when you aren't living the way they would like you to.

Let me repeat that: they are angry or triggered because you are choosing to live differently than how *they* want you to.

Your dad is upset because you decided not to pursue the career he envisioned for you.

Your best friend is mad because you decided not to take the trip.

Someone online is triggered (and maybe jealous) that you spent your money on a Chanel bag.

I'm sorry . . . are you a fucking Sims character? Their input on your decisions can be considered, but when it comes down to it, you are in control of your own life.

The bottom line: if someone is judging you and hating on you for something that is not harming anyone, it's probably because they want you to live in the boxes they feel most comfortable with and you're scribbling outside those lines.

One example of someone breaking out of those boxes is Taylor Swift. In fact, she wrote an entire *album* about this (cue *Reputation*). Even if you don't follow Taylor Swift's every move, it'd be impossible not to notice the clear rebrand from her America's-sweetheart, country-singing, clean-cut image to pop culture's premiere villain. Finally singing the songs she wants to sing, dating who she wants to date, and dressing how she wants to dress, and, therefore, stepping into a new version of herself. Sure, this transition came at the expense of tabloids, rumors, and hate, but she has only become more successful since.

When I stopped focusing on my reputation of trying to be a "good girl" and believing that other people's judgments meant something about who I was as a person, my life changed and my villain era began. I want you to ask yourself:

Is it more important to live how other people want me to, or is it more important that I live how I *want to?*

That's the bottom line of the villain era: choosing you.

VILLAIN IN TRAINING

Now, let's practice how to implement our villain era in our day-to-day lives by choosing to focus on the ways we can make decisions based on what matches or elevates our lives and no longer just based on how we think others want us to act.

Challenge 1: Let Go of the Fear of People's Judgment

Let's practice how to logistically stop caring about other people's opinions.

1. Open your phone's notepad.
2. Write "Villain in Training" as the title of a new note.
3. Now, for *one* day, go through the day as normal, but every single time you worry about what someone else will think, write it in your note. Examples: Accidentally cut off a car and worried they'll think you're rude. Didn't hear the barista call your name and worried she'll think you're ignoring her. Overanalyzing how your face looks in that one Instagram story you wanted to post.

When you sit back and take note of how often you're aware of other people, it's time to dive into your mindset around this.

Challenge 2: Stepping into the Villain Mindset

Thoughts of fear of others' judgments will still pop up, and when they do we want to support ourselves.

1. After a few days of challenge 1, start to take a step back in those moments as they are happening. Put your hand on your heart and remind yourself that it's safe to no longer try to be the "good girl."
2. Create a "Villain Era" playlist, full of the songs that make you feel like an independent woman ready to rule the world. (Taylor Swift's *Reputation* album is a great place to start.)

When you start supporting yourself and making sure you feel safe in those moments, you can start to feel powerful in those instances as well. Now it's time to set and enforce those villain boundaries.

Challenge 3: Setting Villain Boundaries

Create a list of areas in your life that are currently making you feel drained, depleted, burned out, or overworked.

____

____

____

Examples:

- Always working while on PTO at my job.
- My boyfriend never following through on his household commitments, and my having to nag him to do things.
- That one friend always asking to hang out who drains my energy.

Now, for each line, write *one* boundary that you can enforce with zero guilt, shame, or justification.

- Set your status as OOO (out of office) so it is clear to your team that you will not be reachable. Let your boss know that if they reach out, you will respond on the date you're back. Then follow through and hold yourself to those boundaries you've set.
- Break down the household tasks and decide who is in charge of what so you can function together as a team. Discuss what will need to happen if you notice the basic needs of running your household aren't met.
- Say you are unable to hang out right now when that friend reaches out.

What if they're mad about you setting these boundaries?

You're the villain now. Who cares?

Just kidding—that might take time. Remember that boundaries aren't punishments for the other person; they are ways for you to protect yourself. Anyone else's reaction to your boundary is none of your business. That is for them to work through. If you wait to ensure your boundary is accepted, you are still giving that other person power over you. We set boundaries to protect ourselves, period.

Now, when it comes specifically to applying boundaries and our villain era to our spending, I often notice that as women spend in alignment, even when a purchase feels 100% in alignment with them, they will justify their spending to others as if to validate why they are allowed to spend their own money. Our next challenge is going to change that.

Challenge 4: No Justifying Your Actions or Boundaries

Justifying spending: "Well, I only bought this shirt because it was on sale."

Justifying decisions: "I have to take PTO for a doctor's appointment."

Justifying boundaries: "I'm so sorry I can't go. I have a family thing."

Why do we justify our harmless actions? Why do we justify how we spend our own money?

Because if we aren't spending it in the way "they" want us to, we are failing them.

Let's be okay with failing them.

Let's be okay with not paying attention to people who don't pay our bills.

YOUR VILLAIN MENTALITY WITH MONEY

Now that you're fired up about your new villain mindset and you're on your way to becoming a boundary-setting, unapologetic queen, you might have forgotten that you're reading a book about money. But the cool thing is, your finances are a huge area that can benefit from this newfound attitude.

What are the boundaries around money that you need to set?

- Stop loaning money to friends who never pay you back.
- Stop allowing your partner or roommate to be three months behind on paying their portion of rent.

- Stop accepting invitations to expensive after-work happy hours with coworkers when you are exhausted at the end of the workday and trying to save money.
- Let friends know what their share of the bill is before you put the tab on your card, so you don't end up paying for their share.

How would those boundaries feel if implemented? Like I explained earlier, it's not our first inclination to set boundaries, because it feels like we are screwing over the other person. In reality, this is not the case at all.

Let's look at an example. You and a group of girlfriends go out to brunch. The bottomless mimosas are flowing, and your roommate leans over and says, "Hey. I forgot my wallet. Would you be able to pay for me?" You are already thinking about how she owes you for the NFL tickets you bought last week and her portion of the Wi-Fi bill, and she still hasn't paid you back for the groceries you picked up for her, but now time has passed and you feel awkward bringing it up.

So how do you respond to her? If you allow her to add on to her never-ending tab, not only are you enabling her to not follow through on her financial commitments, but you are also adding stress to your relationship.

Enter villain-era you. You respond, "I love you, so I have to be honest with you. Because you still haven't paid me back for a few other things, it's putting financial stress on me, so I don't feel comfortable adding another thing to that list. I don't ever want money to create any weird energy between us. Could we square up on everything, so we can be on the same page going forward?"

She grabs her phone, opens Venmo, and in the press of a

button, her "debt tab" in your brain has been closed and you feel much less stressed. It's a win-win for both of you. Cheers to that.

VILLAIN ERA WITH HEROIC OUTCOMES

Here's the good news: choosing you, being "selfish," and letting things GTFO that aren't matching or elevating your life can actually turn into one of the most powerful things you can do for others. So often people associate villains with greed: wanting to be rich, to be powerful, and to do evil things. But that's not the vibe in our villain era. We want to be wealthy in order to make an impact.

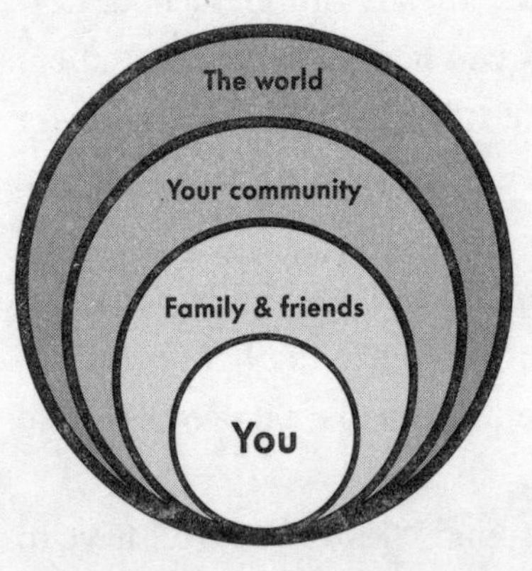

Why do you want to be wealthy?

Imagine you had all the wealth you could dream of. What would it do for you? How would your life change?

Now, what would being massively wealthy do for your family? Your friends? Your community? Your state? The world?

Above is an illustration that shows how you and your wealth are a ripple in the financial ocean of the world! Building your wealth impacts your friends, family, community, and the world. But do you believe you're ready to build this wealth?

BELIEVE YOU'RE WORTHY OF WEALTH

This is not a just-believe-it-and-it-will-happen type of personal development fluff, so don't check out here.

When I was growing up, I genuinely believed that when you graduated high school, the obvious and only next step was to go to college. That's what everyone did, right? That's what the TV shows dramatized. That's what my parents and my sister did. That's what my friends were doing. So I just always expected I would do that, too. And, therefore, I did all the things I knew I needed to in order to go to college, because, well, that's what I saw as the standard.

At the time, I had no clue how privileged I was to have been given that mindset, support, and opportunity. So because I simply thought that my only option was to go to college, I did everything I needed to prepare and then I went.

On the flip side, although no one explicitly said, "Chloe, you will never be a millionaire," I never had any indication that it would even be in the cards for me. No one ever talked about it. No one I knew personally was a millionaire, and the only role models I saw as wealthy were fictional movie characters whose personas were unattainable and, honestly, pretty unrelatable.

If you've never thought to yourself, *I am going to become a millionaire*, that's okay. Likely it has less to do with what could be possible for you and more to do with what you've been taught to expect for yourself. The good news is that you can change both what is possible and what you expect of yourself.

Early on in my business, instead of telling my clients, "I want you to become a millionaire," or calling them "future millionaires," I began calling them "future bajillionaires," as I did with you earlier in the book. Here's why: *bajillionaire* is a made-up word—bajillion isn't a real number. I don't want to tell you that you should become a millionaire when that might not be your goal. I also don't want to tell you to become a millionaire when your goal is to become a multimillionaire or beyond. I want you to choose what that "bajillionaire" status means to you, and I am going to teach you how to figure it out.

But before we nail it down, I want you to first notice any doubts that come up for you when we talk about becoming wealthy. What does your inner mean girl voice (the one who tells you that you're stupid or that those jeans aren't flattering) have to say about you when you imagine becoming a bajillionaire?

Write it down:

____

____

____

____

She's probably got some hot takes on it, but remember, your inner mean girl is only an asshole to you because she wants you to stay in your comfort zone and avoid trying new things that could lead to rejection or failure.

So now that you've taken a second to hear out your inner mean girl and all that she has to say, listen to that voice of truth. That gut feeling. That intuition. That excited dreamer voice. The one who gets giggly thinking about a wild reality where you not only have enough money, but you have more money than you can even decide what to do with. So much overflow that money matters less and what you want to do matters more.

How does it feel to imagine becoming a bajillionaire?

____

____

____

____

You need that voice to be louder than your voice of doubt. I want you to start imagining getting ahead with money and thriving beyond your wildest dreams. You have to actually believe this is possible for you before you can start to implement a strategy to lock in your bajillionaire status. And then when you allow yourself to stop giving a shit about how other people want you to live, you start spending and living by your rules and your rules only. If it doesn't match your vibe, or it doesn't elevate your vibe, then it needs to GTFO.

PART 6

Understanding Boundaries

CHAPTER 16

Getting Alien Probed: Financial Surprises Suck

It was a freezing cold Midwest morning, and I was walking into a 5 a.m. Orangetheory Fitness class. I was fresh out of college, working nine-hour days at my corporate job, and then coming home to put in another three hours working on the side hustle that would become Deeper Than Money. So if you're doing the math, 5 a.m. workouts were the only option.

I was reluctantly making my way over to a treadmill, trying to convince myself I was ready to do sprint intervals for the next 20 minutes of my life.

The treadmill block started, and the *second* I pushed the number on the treadmill up to 10 miles per hour for a sprint, I immediately had this weird shooting pain in what I would call my uterus. Now, this is coming from the girl who didn't know what side of her body her kidneys were on (we have two of those, right?), so I chalked it up to just a weird cramp and went on with my day. Two days later, there was another sprinting portion of class and, like clockwork, the second I hit a serial-killer-is-chasing-me kind of sprint, I felt the shooting pain again. This situation called for a WebMD search, after which I convinced myself I had 10 days to live. I booked an appointment with my gynecologist. Giddyup, cowgirl, it's time to hop in the stirrups. After making some surface-level chitchat about the weather while simultaneously being fingered by my gyno, I was told that everything looked normal. She let me know that she was going to send in some cell samples for testing but also wanted me to come back and get an ultrasound just to ensure everything looked good on that front, too. I'm thinking, *Cool. Sounds easy enough. They'll rub some jelly on my belly, and we will be good to go.*

When the ultrasound appointment rolled around, I honestly hadn't thought much about it because I figured it would be a 10-minute jelly belly rub. I had gotten a call from the office the day before telling me to chug a bunch of water and come with a full bladder. Again, a reminder that I am by no means an anatomy legend, so I assumed that's just a standard thing for pre-jelly-belly appointments. I checked in at the clinic and sat down to look at a few emails and do a quick social media scroll. Jeepers, I was starting to feel hella uncomfortable because I had to pee so badly, but they had told me that a full bladder helps them see what's going on, so I knew I had to suck it up and hold it.

"Miss Chloe?" The nurse came out to call me back.

Aight. Let's do this quick so I can pee and then get back to work.

Nope. Waited another 20 minutes until the ultrasound tech came in. Thank goodness, because I was five minutes away from peeing my pants, and if they were going to push too hard on my belly with the jelly baton thing, I might just eek a little.

"Here's your gown," the tech told me while handing me a cheap cloth hospital getup. "You can leave your bra on if you choose and then just knock when you're ready for me to come back in."

What did this bish just say to me . . . ???

"I'm sorry. I must be mistaken. I thought I was just getting an ultrasound today?" I thought I said it confidently, but when it came out of my mouth, I sounded like a four-year-old begging Mommy for more TV time.

Well, I was 22 years old when I found out that there's also such a thing as a pelvic ultrasound. If you've been fortunate enough to avoid one, let me describe it this way: I imagine it's what being probed by an alien feels like. Don't forget that I also was on the quite literal verge of peeing my pants and then had to proceed to get back in the stirrups. (I was not a happy cowgirl for this unexpected rodeo.) The ultrasound tech whipped out what looked like a baseball bat you'd play dizzy bat with, and I thought to myself, *There is no way she's gonna use that to take pics of my insides.* Like, can I just keep the shooting pain in my uterus at this point? Please and thank you. Yep, the lubed-up dizzy bat was indeed her next move.

Needless to say, I was a little traumatized by the experience, and now before I agree to a new medical appointment, I always ask the doctor, "Can you tell me what that entails?"

I left feeling relieved (emotionally and literally because I did finally get to use the bathroom) to be out of that clinic and to go home. And after that wildly invasive appointment, I thought the discomfort of the experience was over.

Until about four weeks later, when I was hit with a $1,300 bill *after* insurance.

Tears immediately came flooding as I read and reread the three-page bill. This couldn't be real. At the time, I was working diligently to pay off my debt, and it felt like unexpected expenses were always coming up.

This shocking bill felt like a second alien probe.

I procrastinated paying the bill, even though every other day I picked it up off my counter and stared at it, wondering if it would disappear if I ignored it long enough. Each time I saw it I felt anger—this bill left me feeling completely helpless. The procedure itself caught me entirely off guard, but the unexpected bill left me feeling like the whole system was working against me. And although the U.S. medical and insurance systems certainly weren't built with the sole purpose of being anti-Chloe, I want to acknowledge that it certainly has decimated the financial lives of many Americans. In fact, in 2020, more than 17% of people with a credit report had medical debt in collections, and 13% of people had accrued medical debt during the past year but it hadn't gone to collections yet.[1]

In the meantime, although we can't change the entire healthcare system today, we *can* learn how to play the game and win. If we're willing to take that first uncomfortable step into financial conversations, we can decrease situations where we feel helpless and increase situations where we feel empowered and in control of our money.

After a few weeks of staring at the bill, I noticed that it didn't list what I was actually paying for. So I called the clinic, asked for an itemized statement of what I was being charged for, and found two big zingers:

1. The office had billed it as an "elective" procedure instead of a "preventative" procedure. Marking it "preventative" would have allowed my insurance to cover more.
2. They billed me for things I didn't even use. For example, a

wheelchair rental (which did make me cackle because apparently the alien probing can be cause for a wheelchair, and that made me feel like less of a wimp).

I immediately called the billing department and brought up those two problems, thinking, *Well, there's nothing they can do, but I might as well point it out.*

"Oh, whoops. Let me fix this for you," said the billing department lady.

Ummm . . . I am sorry, WHAT?! (I screamed in my head.)

After about four minutes, she took me off hold and said, "Okay, I resubmitted your new bill to insurance as 'preventative' and also took off the itemized things you did not use. You will receive a new bill in the mail. Anything else I can help you with?" In complete shock, I hung up on her.

Later that week, I received a bill for $27.65.

Holy shit. Advocating for myself had rocked my world, and I couldn't tell if the burning I felt inside was frustration that I'd been fooled into thinking I couldn't do anything, or excitement that I'd just received a permission slip to start.

What also blew my mind was how casually the billing department was able to brush off an accidental overcharge of $1,270. When I started to look into it more, I discovered that up to 80% of all medical bills contain errors, and these errors can be costly to you.[2] These types of billing mistakes were found to result in overcharges of up to 26%.[3] That didn't sit right with me, and ever since then, I've been on a mission to stop these errors from going uncontested.

One of the most groundbreaking lessons I learned from this experience is that advocating for yourself is a vital skill to master in your pursuit of financial freedom.

In this one example alone, a six-minute phone call that I almost didn't even make ended up saving me more than $1,270. Advocating for yourself is so important, and negotiation, which we'll discuss next, is one of the biggest—and easiest—ways to do it. But it takes understanding how to actually do it in a way that is in alignment with you and then practicing getting comfortable with it.

LET'S LEARN HOW TO NEGOTIATE

You might be thinking, *But Chloe. If I negotiate, I feel bad because I am stealing from someone else. I feel greedy.* If you've ever thought that to yourself—whether it is about negotiating your starting salary or negotiating your stay on a vacation—let's break it down and see if that's true or not.

Take Bri, for example. Bri is going on a vacation and looking at places to rent for her stay. She finds a gorgeous mountain home for rent, but it's $1,200 for the week—a bit out of her budget for this trip.

Option 1: Bri doesn't book that rental home because it was outside of what she planned on spending. She finds a different place that would feel perfectly in alignment at $1,000 for the week.

Outcome: Bri spent $1,000 and got a place that wasn't her first choice.

Option 2: Bri reaches out to Zach, the owner of the gorgeous rental. Bri tells him she adores his place, but $1,200 is out of her price range, and if he's willing to rent it to her for $1,000 instead, she would be so excited to book. (Tip: Look at their booking calendar. Many hosts want to encourage longer-term rentals, so highlight this as a benefit to them!)

Outcome A: Zach didn't have anyone booking that week, so at this point in time, he was going to be making $0 for that week. Zach gladly accepts Bri's offer and goes from making $0 to $1,000 for the week, and Bri gets her first choice while staying in alignment with her spend plan.

Outcome B: Zach's place is always booked, so he isn't willing to come down on the price because he knows someone else will book it at the $1,200 price point. Zach turns down Bri's offer, and Bri now spends $1,000 booking her second choice so she can stay in alignment with her spending goals.

Notice how the worst possible outcome of option 2 is the same and only outcome of option 1. Bri is far better off negotiating and asking for what she wants, because she may get it, rather than not asking and missing out on the chance. But here is the kicker—what is the best option for Zach (the guy renting out his mountain house)? Option 2 is also better for Zach because he gets the choice of either increasing his revenue from $0 to $1,000 for that week or saying no to Bri's offer and waiting for someone to book at his regular price. If Bri doesn't reach out and try to negotiate, Zach loses the possibility of a renter and could have ended up with $0 in his pocket that week if no one else booked. Bri being willing to negotiate has the potential to massively help not only her but Zach as well.

So what does negotiating look like for you, and what are things you can negotiate?

Honestly, it would probably be easier to name the things that *aren't* negotiable. Now, that doesn't mean I negotiate everywhere and in every situation, but based on my priorities at the time, I negotiate in alignment with my goals. First, I'll tell you my personal negotiating rules and then help you determine what your negotiating rules are as well. The biggest thing to understand is that these rules have changed for me over time and likely will continue to evolve as I change and my priorities change, too. For example, one of the biggest impacts on my finances when first starting my career was negotiating my salary, benefits, and performance-based raises. Now I am the boss of my own business, and there's nobody for me to negotiate my salary with besides myself! I continue to negotiate in other ways that are in alignment in my personal and business life, though. If you're new to negotiation, let's look at where you can start.

CHLOE'S *CURRENT* NEGOTIATION RULES

Rule 1: Get Comfy with Confrontation

Unless you're an Enneagram 8 or a spicy Sagittarius, confrontation might be a bit on the uncomfy side for you. And honestly, confrontation really gets a shitty reputation because of its extremes. Extreme confrontation is walking up to someone at the bar and punching her in the face because she bumped into you earlier . . . yeah, not the move. But avoiding confrontation isn't helpful either. If you are the girl who is terrified to bother anyone, you walk through life trying to shrink yourself and make everyone happy, or you apologize for everything as simple as asking a question, that is also not the move. So in order to get comfy with confrontation, we need to give it a rebrand, a new PR team, and convince everyone (especially you) that it is cool as a cucumber. Respectful confrontation helps you have clear communication on expectations, needs, and desires—all things that help you hit your goals faster.

I can hear it now: "But, Chloe!!! What if they tell me no??"

To that I say, "And what if they do?!" This leads me to our second rule of negotiation: "no" isn't about you. But before we get to that, I first want to give you some tangible ways to add a sprinkle of badass, confident, confrontation-is-your-friend energy into your life.

Here are ways to transform a weak request into a confident (and kind) confrontation:

- At work: "I'm sorry, but can I ask you a question?" >> "Are you available for me to ask a question?"
- In your relationship: "No. I'm fine." >> "It made me feel taken advantage of when you said XYZ."
- With friends: "Sorry to be annoying, but can you Venmo me for dinner?" >> "Happy Monday—going to pay off my credit card today and saw our dinner charges. Your portion was $XX."

These little switches allow you to keep your power and energy instead of apologizing for existing or asking for your money. Start practicing on a smaller scale, and begin getting more of what you want.

Rule 2: No Just Means No

The best skill I ever learned was how not to care what other people think. We talked a lot about that in the previous chapter, but one of my biggest fears around confrontation was the fear that someone telling me no meant something bad about me. When I understood that no means nothing about me, the feedback was purely feedback and nothing more.

Rule 3: Always Be Polite

Negotiating isn't being a dick and shouting at strangers. It's not being a Karen and demanding the manager give you whatever you want. It's about seeing if what you want could be mutually beneficial to the party that is offering it to you. It's about starting conversations with other humans. No need for an Elle Woods you-however-had-time-to-hide-the-gun-didn't-you-Chutney tone. Be kind, but don't be apologetic.

Rule 4: Practice Makes Perfect

Negotiation can be as simple as checking out at Target and asking the cashier, "Did I miss any good deals on the Target app today?" I can't tell you how many times I've said this and an employee has told me, "Here, let me give you a 10% off code we have going on right now." If having a big negotiation conversation makes you nervous, start small with a few questions that can help you save big and work up to bigger forms of negotiating. Here are some low-key ways of practicing negotiation that you can try today:

- Ask if there's a discount for paying in cash. Businesses have to pay processing fees for debit and credit transactions, and sometimes they'll pass those savings on to you if you pay cash.
- Check out company partnership discounts. If you work for a large company, chances are they mentioned in orientation that they have company discounts for phone service, internet, hotels, travel, and more. Reach out to someone in HR to ask how to take advantage of these.

- Ask if there's a discount or bonus for paying in full instead of using a payment plan. (This can be particularly helpful for medical debt and bills.)
- Ask about discounts for joining an email list.
- Check whether current companies you use have referral bonuses. Tell a friend about your gym, dog day care, lawyer, etc., for a bonus or discount.
- Ask whether new discounts can be applied to your current rate. If you pay $30/month for your gym membership and they're running a deal where new members can join for $10/month, ask if they're willing to match that for you.
- Do your homework. A lot of negotiating is simply knowledge. Find other places that have better deals, and use that as leverage.

We also have to talk about the do *nots* of negotiating.

- Don't be rude or demanding, raise your voice, or insult anyone.
- Don't make it all about you ("I really need this," "I deserve this," "You need my business," etc.).
- Don't devalue the product or service you're negotiating ("This really isn't worth the price you're asking").
- Don't try to negotiate price *after* the service has been performed, the goods have been delivered, or you've already verbally committed.
- Don't throw out a random price; it has to make sense. Do your research!
- Don't negotiate goods or services that are extremely exclusive. For example, if you were offered the opportunity

to snag 50-yard-line tickets to the Super Bowl, that wouldn't be the time to try to get a bargain, because someone else will take them at full price. And also, I personally don't negotiate with small businesses for the most part.

- Don't get discouraged! Thank the person for their time, and evaluate your options.

Now let's look at a real-life example of one of my favorite things to negotiate, credit card interest rates, to witness the power of negotiation.

THE FINANCIAL IMPACT OF NEGOTIATING

Have you ever wondered how the minimum payment on your credit card statement is calculated? It's usually a fixed amount, but it ends up being between 1% and 3% of your balance. Paying only the minimum can be tempting, but because of double-digit interest rates, the less you pay now, the more you can end up paying along the way!

Let's imagine you start with a credit card balance of $10,000. It's at a 28% APR, and your minimum payment is $300/month. If you only make the minimum payments, it would take you 66 months (you read that right—more than 5 years!) to pay it off. And along the way, you would have paid just shy of $10,000 in interest alone . . . almost as much as what you initially borrowed in the first place.

Now, if you negotiated your interest rate to 9%, and still only paid the minimum $300/month payment, you would pay it off in 39 months, with only about $1,500 in interest. This change alone would cut the total interest paid by close to $8,500. Or if you found a way to pay more than the minimum payment, say $500/month, you would have it paid off in 22 months, with only $791 in interest! This is more than $9,000 less than if you didn't negotiate!

A starting point to put this strategy in place is figuring out what your credit card interest rate is. And just know, you are not a stupid moron if you *don't* know it. You'd actually fall in the same boat as 21% of Americans who don't know their current interest rate![4] A lot of credit card companies make it difficult for you to find out this info (it's on your statement but can be confusing to find), which really makes it easy to answer the question, "Who benefits when I don't have all the information/education about my finances?" The back of this Laffy Taffy would read: THE HECKIN LENDERS!! Look up your interest rate on your last credit card statement, or call your credit card company and ask.

Naturally, the follow-up question is always, "But Chloe, what do I say?" It's for that exact reason I wrote an entire guide called The Negotiation Playbook that consists of done-for-you, copy-and-paste scripts and emails so you know exactly what to say when negotiating. You can learn more about The Negotiation Playbook at deeperthanmoney.com/negotiation-playbook. Of course, there's a script for negotiating credit card interest rates, and I am going to give you one of the scripts from The Negotiation Playbook now. Here she is in all her glory.

THE NEGOTIATION PLAYBOOK SCRIPT: CREDIT CARD INTEREST RATE

Step 1: Determine Why You Want to Negotiate Your Rate

Understand why you want to negotiate your credit card interest rate. If you pay off your credit card in full every single month (and, therefore, have zero credit card debt), then to be honest, it doesn't really matter what your credit card interest rate is.

Step 2: Compare Offers

Look at other credit card company offers that are better than the one you're currently getting, and research a potential balance transfer (with waived interest and bonus points for no fees). If there is a fee, pull out your phone calculator, because it's time to do some math and see if that fee will be worth it for either 0% or a lowered interest from your other card.

Let's use the example from earlier. The credit card company is making more than $8,000 off you in interest during the life of your loan; they do not want to lose you. You are paying them the big bucks, and they like having you there, which means you have leverage, too.

A balance transfer is other credit card companies, lenders, or banks saying, "Hi! Move your credit card debt over to us. You can pay us less than what you're paying your current bank!" So pretend you are freshly single, back on the streets, and ready to play the field . . . the financial field, that is. With a couple of simple Google searches, you will be able to see what type of alternative offers you'd be able to get. You don't need to get preapproved or actually apply for the offers. You just need to know that they are there. Write down a few of those options:

	COMPANY	PROMO RATE %	LENGTH OF PROMO OFFER	FEES	INTEREST WAIVED OR DEFERRED?
Option 1					
Option 2					
Option 3					
Option 4					

Step 3: Ask to Speak to a Manager

Call your credit card company and immediately ask to speak to a manager. Not in a Karen, rude way. The first person who answers the phone likely is not allowed to change your credit card interest for you. So, you can make a kind request like this:

> *Hi there! Thanks for helping me out today. I am wondering if I could go ahead and be transferred to your manager. I have some higher-level questions, and it will be quicker if I could have a direct conversation with your manager first. Would that be okay?*

Be kind. Be confident. If the person who answers the phone still wants to get some info first, you absolutely can tell them why you are calling, but then, if they are unable to help you, ask again to speak to the manager or supervisor.

Step 4: Advocate for Yourself

Have the following conversation with the manager:

> *Hi, my name is __________________! Your team member who I just briefly spoke to was great, but I wanted to get your direction on a few things, so I appreciate you taking a minute to talk with me. I've been a good customer of [current credit card company] for [number of years], and I make my payments on time. However, my APR is too high. I have lower offers from [competing credit card company A] and [competing credit card company B]. I've had a good experience with you, but I'm considering switching and transferring my balance to a new credit card company because of my APR. Again, I really like this card and would like to stay banking with you, but in order to do that, I would need to have my APR lowered. Is that something you could help me with today?*
>
> Things also to consider:
>
> - If you are unsuccessful, call back again and try speaking to someone else. Don't give up, even if you're told no. If you call back and are able to get the reduced rate on the third try after three hour-long phone calls, saving you $3,000 over the next year, that's $1,000 per hour for your time. It's totally worth it. Don't give up! Keep calling.
> - Decide what lowered APR you would like before you call, but let them give you an offer first on what they can lower it to. After they give you their first offer of a decreased APR, say:

I appreciate you working with me, but that is still significantly higher than what I was looking for. Can you meet me at ___%?

- If possible, start by negotiating 0% APR for 12 months. (Remember that this is only a good option if you are going to tackle your credit card debt in that amount of time, because it will likely jump back up after 12 months.)
- If/when they lower your APR, ask, "Will this take effect today, or are you willing to backdate this?" Sometimes, card companies will backdate it and actually give you a *refund* from past interest. Backdating doesn't happen often, but it is always worth asking for!
- Other things to consider negotiating: your annual credit card fee, penalties, your credit limit, perks, your billing date, etc.

Advocating for yourself truly is powerful, and negotiating is one of the best ways you can make progress when it comes to your finances. The good news for you is that you get to learn this life lesson sitting back, reading this book while relaxing on your couch, on an airplane, or maybe tucked in bed . . . instead of having to defend yourself against an alien-probe experience that forces you into negotiations.

CHAPTER 17

Money Condoms: Protecting Your Wealth

Standing in front of the reception desk at the local mechanic in town, choking back tears, I did what any strong, independent, 16-year-old girl would do: I grabbed my phone and called my dad. My sniffles were the first thing he heard before I could collect myself enough to tell him, "The mechanic said it will cost $200 for my car to be fixed. I don't have that much money!! What am I supposed to do?" The 1991 Chevy truck that my parents had bought for my older sister for $1,000 was now broken, conveniently one month after it was passed down to me on my 16th birthday. Upon getting the keys to the truck, my parents made it clear that because it was now mine, all maintenance, gas, and any other expenses were all my responsibility. At the time of that conversation, I would have absolutely agreed to anything they said in order to get those keys in my hand. It's fair to say I did not plan for or expect that one month later I'd be standing in the mechanic's lobby, where they had my keys and I had a $200 tab to pay if I wanted it fixed.

"Well, I'd probably start by walking home then," my dad responded from the other end of the line.

Now, I'll be honest. As I said in Chapter 2, I grew up in a small town. The mechanic's shop was probably less than two miles away from my parents' house. However, my broke-ass, 16-year-old self could not believe that my dad had so matter-of-factly just told me that.

It was then I learned one of my biggest financial lessons: no one is coming to save you; you are your financial backup plan.

The wild thing is, this newfound information didn't light a fire under my ass to be more frugal or stop spending my money at the mall with my friends. I just started getting scrappier. I found ways to make more money. Yes, my car sat at the shop for a few weeks, but after saying yes to every single babysitting gig I could pick up, I came strutting back to the mechanic to pay the $200 invoice and take my sweet, sweet freedom-on-wheels home with me. From that day forward, I began to live with the mentality that when the shit hit the fan, I would always find a way to figure it out myself, and I wouldn't rely on others to bail me out. And that has stuck with me over the years.

And yes, you read the title of this chapter right: "Money Condoms." You might have heard the slogan, "Don't be silly, protect your willy." Nah. We're putting a financial spin on this: "Don't be a dummy, protect your money." In this chapter, we are going to break down the three different types of money condoms that protect your wealth and ultimately protect you, too:

Money condom 1: Protecting yourself from life
Money condom 2: Protecting yourself from others
Money condom 3: Protecting yourself from bad situations

As we are going through this chapter, you might have thoughts pop up like, *Dang, this is a lot of work and potential worry in order to protect my money. I thought we were not supposed to be obsessed with holding on to money!* A gold star for you. However, although we don't want to obsess over holding on to money, we also need to acknowledge that money is a tool to provide safety, security, and freedom. I never want you to be in a situation where your safety, security, or freedom is at risk, or for you to be in constant fear that your livelihood could disappear if something happened. It can lead to so much anxiety and stress when you're living in fight-or-flight mode around money. Walking through the different money condoms to put on and protect yourself with doesn't mean obsessing over keeping your money; it means the money condom is doing all the protecting for you, so you can sit back, relax, and enjoy the ride.

Okay, let's dive in.

MONEY CONDOM 1: PROTECTING YOURSELF FROM LIFE

The first money condom we want to put on is protecting ourselves from life. Life circumstances pop up and can look like a flat tire after running over a nail, an emergency vet visit for your German Shepherd, or your air-conditioning unit going out on the hottest day in July. Whatever the circumstance, you want to be able to fix what's broken when it breaks. It's important not only to have a plan in place to ensure you can make those purchases but also to have protection in place to keep from having to dip into your wealth-building money in situations like these.

Wealth-building money is money you've set aside with the

specific purpose of building long-term wealth. When you're setting aside money and investing with the purpose of long-term wealth-building, you will likely see short-term fluctuations. Think about the stock market, for example. If you have invested money that is currently in a dip, pulling out that money for an emergency can result in not only loss of that money, but also loss of the potential for it to bounce back and grow in the long term, not to mention potentially having to pay penalties for early withdrawal if it's a retirement account. Even if you wouldn't have early withdrawal fees, dipping into your long-term wealth-building money cuts into the magic of growth in your investment account over time and can hinder your wealth-building money from doing its job: building you some damn wealth.

So if we don't want to touch our wealth-*building* money, then what are we supposed to do in case of an emergency? Enter wealth-*protecting* money. Wealth-protecting money is money you have set aside for a rainy day in an emergency fund that is specifically there if anything comes up. This wealth-protecting money allows you to take care of that expense without needing to dip into your wealth-building money. The first step in creating wealth-protecting money is setting up an emergency fund.

How to Set Up an Emergency Fund

1. Open a high-yield savings account (HYSA). Be sure it is free, has no fees, and is FDIC insured. You can open HYSAs online in less than 10 minutes, and many have no minimum balances. (You can transfer as little as $10!) A HYSA's interest rate is typically significantly higher than a traditional savings account—for example, at the time I'm writing this, you can get 23x the national average interest paid on

a standard checking account—with no additional risk.[1] It's truly a no-brainer first step. Check out deeperthanmoney.com/book for free tutorials in which I walk you through how to set one up.

2. Calculate a rough estimate of a month's worth of expenses. Start with basics: rent/mortgage, food, bills, transport, etc. Round up a little bit, but you don't need to add in a ton of extra spending per month. This would be mostly our skeleton spend plan + adding necessities from non-monthly and calendar expenses (like homeowners' association, or HOA, fees) and necessities from day-to-day spending (like groceries).
3. As we talked about in your Future Bajillionaire Checklist, if you have high-interest debt (anything more than 10%), aim to save one to three months of expenses in your HYSA to set aside for emergencies. If you don't have high-interest debt, work around your other goals to save up to six to eight months of expenses in your HYSA. If your money is sitting in a plain ol' savings account at the bank right now and you have enough to transfer into your HYSA, this is a great move to make. You will likely begin making a significant amount more in interest each month just by changing the type of account your money is in!
4. Set up a beneficiary for your account (and any other account you haven't set it up for). A beneficiary is who your money would go to if you were to pass away. Tough to think about, but it protects your loved ones from having to jump through hoops to get your money.

I know this might seem like a lot, but once you have it, you want this emergency fund to stay there forever, with the hope you never need it. But you always have this backup plan protecting you and your wealth. As your expenses increase, remember to add more into your HYSA to ensure it still reflects either one to three months or six to eight months of expenses.

The next part of protecting yourself from life is a super-sexy topic that might make you feel like you're reading a steamy Colleen Hoover romance novel . . . insurance!! Okay, although insurance might feel like a turnoff to talk about, the nice part is that it's one of those things where the hardest part is setting it up and making sure you have the right type. And the earlier you set it up, the more beneficial it will be. Colton Storla, employee benefits expert, reminds us that "Age is the most important factor that determines how expensive or affordable your policy will be when it comes to life and disability insurance. Some individuals make the mistake of buying it at a later age or after a negative medical event happens, so they are stuck paying a higher premium or being denied coverage."[2] However, it also can be confusing when you're trying to figure out the best type of insurance for you because it's common to be sold more insurance than you actually might need. So let's break down two important types of insurance and how insurance protects your wealth.

What Is Long-Term Disability Insurance (and How Does It Protect You)?

If you got seriously sick, hurt, or disabled (think cancer, disease, blindness, paralysis, etc.), would you still be able to do your current job? If not, how would you make a living? The answer is long-term disability (LTD) insurance. LTD insurance protects you financially if you are unable to work for an extended period due to an accident, illness, or injury.[3] So how do you get it?

Unlike short-term disability insurance (short-term coverage), which can be an employer benefit you may see deducted from your paycheck, oftentimes you obtain LTD coverage based on the amount of income you are currently earning. You will pay a monthly (or annual) premium to maintain this protection. Depending on your level of coverage and policy type, put simply, if you were to have a qualifying disabling event, it usually kicks in after six months (usually after any short-term disability coverage ends) and would replace 40% to 70% of your income by sending you a monthly paycheck.

How to Obtain Long-Term Disability Insurance

1. Shop around (start online), and compare quotes from multiple companies.
2. Once you find a company, they will send you paperwork to apply.
3. They will need to verify your current medical and employment history, so you will likely need to submit paperwork, have an application call, and have a medical exam.
4. If you are approved, they will tell you how much coverage you are eligible for and the terms. If you accept, you will officially begin your policy and begin paying premiums.

What Is Term Life Insurance (and How Does It Protect You)?

Not to be too depressing, but imagine again that you have a long-term disability or illness, like cancer. You are no longer able to work, so you had LTD insurance that was protecting your income; however, your prognosis and life expectancy don't look promising. In this example, assume you are married and have young children who depend on your income. What would happen if you were to pass away? In addition to that being a tragic loss emotionally, the loss of your income could be devastating financially for your family. It could also go the other way, too. What would happen if you had kids and your partner was in a fatal car accident? Would you be able to provide for your family with the loss of his or her income? This is why life insurance is so crucial when you have a situation in which the loss of a life would be a financial catastrophe for those near to you.

Like LTD insurance, life insurance requires that you obtain a policy. There are several types of life insurance, but the one that is the most simple and affordable is term life insurance.[4] You essentially pay premiums in order to guarantee that if something were to happen to you, upon your death, whoever you name as your beneficiary would receive a certain amount of money for a set period of time. For example, a term life policy could be a 20-year term, $500,000 death benefit. If you died in the next 20 years, your listed heir would get $500k, tax-free, to be able to help mitigate the financial loss.

The process to obtain term life insurance is very similar to the one listed previously for LTD insurance, so you can follow those same steps if you want to look into this as an option for you.

What Is a Will (and How Does It Protect You)?

Continuing on from the morbid example above, let's say you get Regina George'd and hit by a bus and you pass away. What would happen to your assets: your bank accounts, your 401(k), your car, your jewelry, and your dogs or your children if you have them? This is where a will comes into play. A will is a legal document that allows you to communicate your wishes of how you want to distribute your assets clearly and precisely (and you also can appoint guardians for minor children).[5] If you don't have a will, the state already has one prewritten for you and will distribute your assets based on their laws. To drive home this concept, you basically get a will either way: the one that old-fart government officials wrote for you, or the one you write yourself. Because let's be honest—how you want your assets handled and how the government wants your assets handled could be drastically different. Therefore, I highly recommend you draft a will, regardless of your marital or financial status.

How to Create a Will

You can always consult an attorney to help you draft a will. However, if you have a simple estate (especially if you don't have minor children), you may be able to use a free online tool and plug in all your information. If you go this route, the key is to ensure it's properly witnessed, verified, and signed. Here's what the process looks like:

1. List all your assets.
2. Decide who will get those assets if you die.
3. Choose guardians for minor children, or if you have pets, choose who will take care of them.
4. Name an executor. This is the person who will be in charge of carrying out the terms of your will. Give that person a heads-up before listing them. It's also helpful to provide them with a copy of your will.
5. Have the document properly witnessed, signed, or notarized if necessary.
6. Continue to update your will as things change in your life.

At the very, very least, you can start today by opening a Google Doc (or even your phone's notepad) and begin to think through some of these things. It can be super weird to talk about, but a will is a way to truly ensure your money creates a legacy even after you're gone. Sit down, think it over, write it up, and then take steps to set it up legally. Then share this document with a loved one and set a calendar appointment to update your information each year.

Money Condom 1 Checklist

- ☐ Set up your emergency fund in a high-yield savings account (HYSA).
- ☐ Set up or look into long-term disability (LTD) insurance.
- ☐ Set up or look into term life insurance.
- ☐ Draft a will (and make plans to set it up officially).

MONEY CONDOM 2: PROTECTING YOURSELF FROM OTHERS

Light your torches and grab your pitchforks because you might not like what I'm about to drop on you in this section. It's important to protect your wealth from others. *Gasp.* This might sound like an anticharity, antigiving, anticommunity type of message, but it isn't. Here's why: protecting your wealth from others isn't about being greedy; it's about giving on your terms and following your boundaries, not giving based on manipulation, guilt, or outside pressure.

"You're treating this like a fucking business deal," an ex once screamed in my face after I took *my* credit card away from him post-breakup. What did he actually mean by that? I protected my assets, and that made him mad. And I know everyone thinks they will never break up, and if they did it would be totally chill (and if you were that couple—kudos). But when it comes to finances, in the worst-case scenario that it isn't a "chill" split, you don't want any gray area. Protecting your assets isn't only for breakups either. Remember when I told you in Chapter 2 that my boyfriend at the time stole $8,000 from me and emptied my entire emergency fund? I wasn't protecting myself *in* the relationship. Protecting yourself and your finances in relationships is vital no matter what the outcome ends up being.

At first, you might think establishing clear boundaries with money (or deciding on them before you have a partner) is a little jaded. Like, where's the romance? But protecting your assets while dating leads to one of two scenarios: 1) you break up and you're hella glad you kept things protected, or 2) you stay together and think, *Okay, cool. That didn't negatively impact anything.* There's no downside to setting clear expectations with money. But there absolutely are downsides to *not* having protection.

If you don't want to only take my word for it, open Spotify and blare Kelsea Ballerini's EP *Rolling Up the Welcome Mat*, where she so beautifully details the heartbreak, betrayal, and hurt of a relationship ending and even vulnerably talks about the impact of her partner taking "half." Protecting yourself matters whether you are a superstar or not, and if you make putting on these money condoms a priority, you have the safety and security even when you or your relationships might be subject to change(s).

Let's take another example, like Marie. Her ex-boyfriend had a terrible credit score, so while they were dating, she let him take out a loan for his car in her name. Then they broke up. Marie's ex was behind on payments and had trashed her credit score. Because he was so behind, the loan company would not remove her name from the loan and transfer it to him. Not a fun situation to be in on top of going through a breakup.

The key thing I want you to understand is that protecting yourself from others doesn't mean they're a bad person or you think you two won't last. It simply means you are protecting yourself—aka what all the baddest bitches do.

So what does protecting yourself tangibly look like? It will look different at every stage of a relationship, and within each stage, these pieces and boundaries will vary for everyone, so go through this section to see what pieces you'd like to implement in your own life. I will also reference dating from a very typical "single >> dating >> engaged >> married" trajectory, but that doesn't mean you need to follow those societal norms whatsoever. I'm only writing it out like this to show the different levels of protection to consider as your relationship progresses. However, it is important to note that marriage is a legally binding contract, so although many people will choose to forgo marriage and instead have long-term partnerships, there are *legal* differences between marriage and a long-term partnership.

Protection While Dating

Here is my motto to live by: combine your love, shared experiences, and maybe some goals, but don't combine finances. I have seen many horror stories of couples who combine finances premarriage, break up, and then have zero (or very minimal) legal ground to recoup their portion of their shared money. And the couples who do have legal ground often don't want to or can't afford to sue their ex. Combining finances before marriage can get wonky.

So what can you do?

If you are in a serious relationship, it's never too early to be open and honest about your income, debt, and expenses. Talk about how money was handled in your life or in your family while you were growing up and how that impacts your beliefs and habits today. If you are cohabitating and have shared expenses or goals, have monthly money dates (make it fun) where you go over what you spent and saved, any big expenses coming up, and how each person is planning to tackle their personal goals (paying off debt, saving, etc.). Even if you're not living together, because money is such an emotional, personal topic, getting it on the table and talking about it can take your relationship to the next level.

If you're not living together, you can talk about if you are both happy with the way you are spending or splitting money right now on dates, dinners, and activities. If you're not, being transparent and honest about these feelings can diminish the potential for any resentment or frustration behind the scenes if one person feels like they are being taken advantage of or are fronting more of the expenses.

If you're at the point where marriage is something you both are on the same page about, talk about what goals you can focus on together while not combining accounts. Create a priority list, and dream about your future together. What kind of house would you want? Do you want kids? Write these things down along with a timeline and estimated costs (you can even add them to your living plan!).

Protection While Engaged

So, you've decided you're ready to spend your life with someone. I am all for money transparency, especially with couples. Without raining on your parade . . . let me say that marriage can be beautiful, but especially with money as a leading factor in divorce in the United States, I want you to have boundaries in place that protect you.

So what can you do?

Have honest conversations with each other. Just like you may go to premarriage counseling for the emotional commitment of marriage, having deeper financial conversations are important as well. What things should you talk about?

- How do you feel about money? Money, it turns out, is *emotional.* Talk about what scares you and what makes you happy when it comes to money.
- Be sure you're both on the same page with debt, saving, spending, and your household expenses.
- Will you combine finances? If so, how?
- Where will you want to live?
- Talk about expectations of spending, saving, giving, investing, and more.

Consider a prenup. A prenup (formally known as a prenuptial agreement) is essentially a contract between two people before they get married. It walks through the property and debt owned by each person, along with each person's rights to that property in the event of death or divorce. I'll start off by saying I do get the argument against prenups. In fact, your homegirl used to be anti-prenups herself. I would think, *It's like I am manifesting a divorce!* But consider this: If you get home insurance, are you manifesting your house to burn down? No. You are protecting yourself so that if the worst-case scenario happens, you know you are covered. Similar to a will, which we talked about earlier, if you choose not to have a prenup, in a worst-case scenario situation of a divorce, the state decides everything in the split for you. You're basically getting a prenup either way: it's either the state's generic choice or one you personally customized and tailored to the both of you. And this is where I highly recommend sitting down with an expert and making sure this is tailored to you and protects you, and that you fully understand all the language in the prenup, too. You can have a generic prenup in place, but if it doesn't protect you, then what's the point? Make sure yours does. We gotta make sure this money condom is on and keeping you fully protected. Why wouldn't you want to choose what happens in a worst-case scenario?

Protection While Married

When you've had all the conversations and are on the same page about each other's financial status and your individual and couple goals, it's time to divvy up the financial labor and the emotional labor. Regardless of who takes the lead on planning out finances or is the more logistical one, it takes two to tango, and it should always be a team effort to manage your joint finances. Now that you're married, you are on the same team, and your finances should be on the same team as well.

So what can you do?

Step 1: Create Your Cash Flow Process Using a Conjoined, Separate, or Hybrid Finance Flow

I love to show couples who have conjoined finances this graphic. When you see an arrow, think of that as the flow of money. First, let's look at Paycheck 1 and Paycheck 2. Whether you both are earning income or just one of you is, this is where you start. If you look to the left, you'll see retirement investing because if

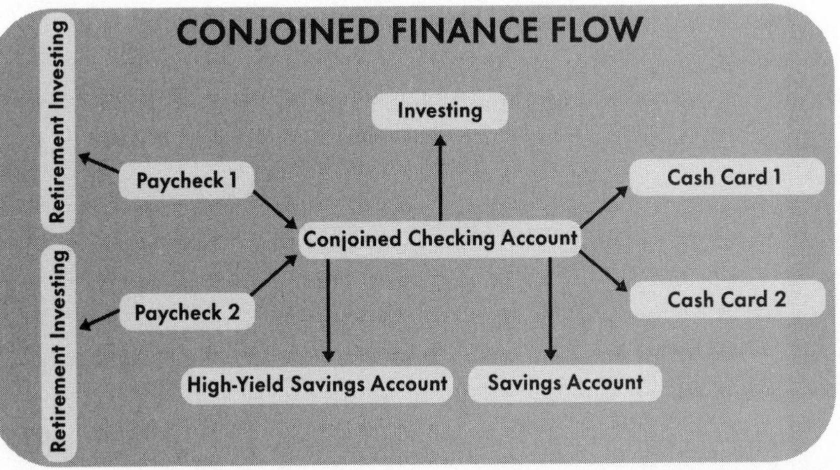

your employer offers an employer-sponsored retirement plan, your contribution will be taken directly from your paycheck (along with taxes, health insurance, and other fun adult things).

With what is left over, you will see arrows directing money toward a joint checking account. This will be the catchall account that pays your joint bills and also directs money toward other accounts, such as investing, a HYSA, and a normal savings account. Investing is there because, for many, investing outside of a retirement account is a priority (think Roth IRAs, a joint taxable brokerage account, etc.). High-yield savings comes into play for your joint emergency fund and for your larger savings goals beyond that. For a regular savings account, I recommend keeping a smaller amount of savings at the ready in case you need immediate access to money. (Money can take a few days to transfer from your HYSA to your checking account if they're not at the same bank.)

Lastly, you'll see card 1 and card 2. This is where your personal spending comes into play! I recommend you decide on an amount to be transferred to these cards each month—and you get to do whatever you want with this money. Want to get your nails done? Perfect. If your partner wants to buy a round of golf? Cool. After all your bills are paid, and saving and investing goals are accomplished, you deserve to have independence and spend that money in ways that bring you an improved quality of life.

This flowchart has proven to be successful for so many of my clients who want to ensure their joint income is being used to accomplish joint goals *and* personal goals.

Another option is using a separate finance flow. Deciding which model fits your relationship is between you two. Again, even with conjoined finances, I recommend having at least a cash card separate, but this model allows for complete separation. Some people prefer it this way, and if that works best for you, that's totally fine.

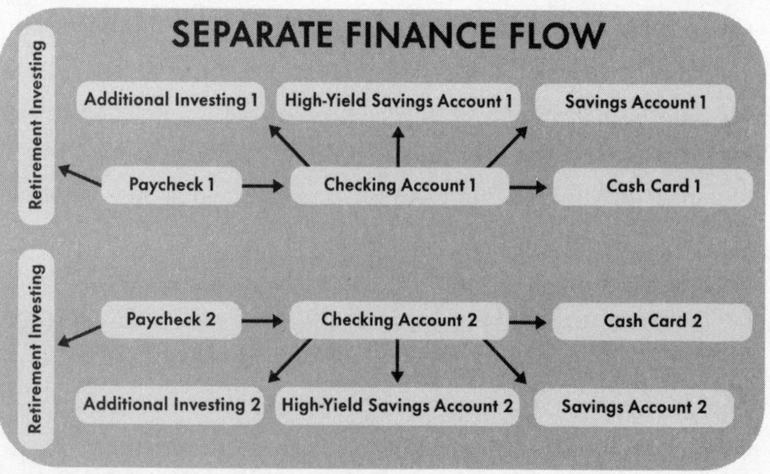

The third model is a hybrid finance flow. The hybrid flow allows you to have some separation but also one or more conjoined accounts. This is nice for big expenses like a mortgage payment, for example, to flow out of the conjoined checking account, but other purchases can stay separate. It can cut back on paying each other back for things by having some sort of conjoined account to pay for purchases you have both agreed on.

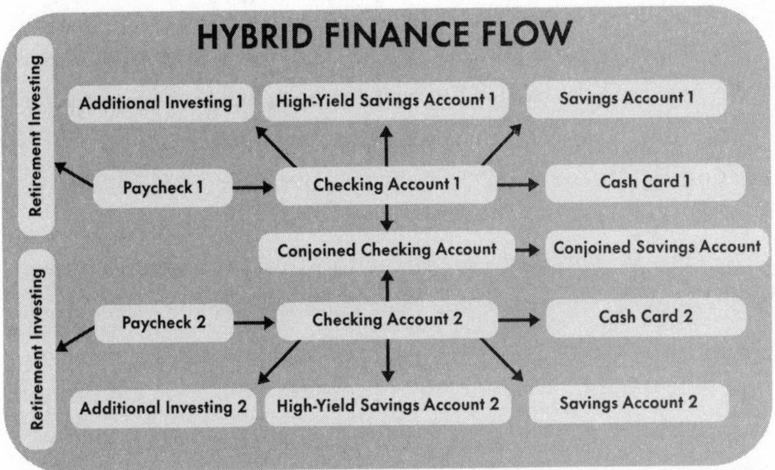

Step 2: Talk About Emotional Labor

Money is only one form of currency and is often the only piece looked at when it comes to division of expenses or finding "fairness" in relationships. How are you splitting expenses, and how are you splitting household work?

This one might be a little controversial, but one issue I often come across is couples automatically splitting expenses 50/50. When it comes to relationships and the workload each party has, it might not be as simple as you think.

We have to look at money as *one* form of currency.

One reason you might not want to split things 50/50 is that statistically (although not always the case), women are significantly more likely to carry a higher percentage of the emotional labor of managing your life/expenses.[6]

What might this uneven distribution of labor look like? Time, energy, and money are all currencies, and if you're in charge of 80% of the physical and emotional labor in your life, like grocery shopping, planning meals, cooking, cleaning, scheduling appointments, planning travel, getting gifts for occasions, etc. . . . who says it's fair for you to be responsible for 50% of the financial commitment, too? Paying for the rent or mortgage is only one piece of running the home, so when talking about how to split the costs of running a household equitably, we have to also talk about how the other parts of running a household factor in.

A 50/50 split has to go beyond just paying for rent; otherwise, one party may become overwhelmed and resentful, and it could add an additional stress on your relationship.

Talk about it. What do you like doing? What are you sick of doing? Maybe you and your partner sit down and have this convo and you realize that you both despise mowing the yard and that it is worth it to you both to pay someone to mow the yard once a month to take that task off both of your plates. (Don't forget about the responsibility of whoever is still in charge of oversight, payment, etc.) When you are deciding how you want to break up tasks, paying for things, and more, you absolutely have to factor in more than just the financials of running your household and lifestyle. You must also factor in who is doing physical and emotional labor as well so you can once again create a holistic view of your finances.

Step 3: Find a Good Check-In Point

Blowing up about this at dinner with your partner and reminding them how they do nothing and you do everything is not the answer, nor is it going to lead to sustainable, loving change in your current dynamic. Instead, reach out to them and say, "Hey, could we sit down and talk about some bigger-picture stuff this week?" That way they're not caught off guard or feeling attacked. Then set up a weekly, biweekly, or at least monthly check-in where you go on a walk or sit down over coffee and talk about how things are going: create your upcoming spend plan, talk about current distribution of all household labor, and make tweaks and changes to make it as equitable as possible.

MONEY CONDOM 3: PROTECTING YOURSELF FROM BAD SITUATIONS

When I ask my clients *why* they stay in a bad environment or crappy situation, they'll often say, "I can't leave." And I'll ask for tangible reasons why. Without fail, one of the top answers is . . . *money.*

"I can't just leave the job."

"I can't just move out of that apartment."

"I can't just break up with him. I have no backup plan."

Money (or lack of money) can keep you paralyzed in a reality that is negatively impacting your mental and/or physical health or in a toxic situation.

At this point, we've talked about setting boundaries and getting certain things set up to protect you financially. But now it's time to take it a step further and ask yourself what you need to do to get to a spot where you can leave toxic environments or bad situations, despite a negative financial impact.

Maybe you're not in a bad situation right now, and I hope you never are. But using these money condoms can stop you from feeling trapped in situations because of your financial circumstances. If you are feeling stuck in a toxic job, relationship, or living situation, it's time to talk about "fuck you" money. "Fuck you" money is having enough money that if you are in a bad situation, you can get out of it, even if it means some negative financial outcomes. For example, when I was 25 years old, I called off a wedding two months before. And despite losing tens of thousands of dollars from a late cancellation, it was one of the best decisions I ever made, because by doing so, I left a manipulative, emotionally abusive relationship. Having "fuck you" money is one of the most powerful assets you can obtain, because it allows you to have the ultimate freedom to leave despite having to take a financial hit. While it may take time to build up that wealth, every move you are making from reading this book is getting you one step closer to being able to use money as a tool to protect your freedom. If you are in a toxic situation, please trust that you can leave it, and take a second to calculate what amount of "fuck you" money it would take to leave.

What is the toxic situation you want to leave?

____

____

What amount of money would you need saved or as income to get out of the situation?

____

____

What other resources could you use to get out of the situation?

____

____

Honorable mention in the "protecting yourself from bad situations" category goes to . . . loaning people money. I will keep my advice quick, easy, and simple: don't loan money to anyone close to you if it would ruin your relationship if they don't pay you back; aka don't loan money you wouldn't be willing to lose. And if you do loan money to someone, create a contract with an interest rate, repayment plan, dates, and two signatures. Make it official. Casual loans between friends can end up ruining your entire friendship.

And when it comes to loaning money, that includes paying for things for others, like saying you'll pay for their plane tickets or help put down their apartment security deposit. Remember, there is a fine line between helping and enabling. Enabling isn't helping. In fact, financial enabling is actually a classified money disorder, according to the *Journal of Financial Therapy*. Financial enabling was defined by Brad Klontz, PhD, as the inability to say no when someone, such as a family member, continues to ask for money. He says, "The enabler [person giving money] believes they are helping, yet the financially dependent individual [person receiving the money] is never taught to be financially responsible."[7] So whether you are loaning or gifting, it's important to ensure you are setting boundaries by outlining the reason for the loan/gift and what is expected on their end in order to avoid enabling the behavior to continue.

Putting on these money condoms might feel like an extra or unnecessary step in the heat of the moment, but taking time to protect your wealth will allow you to always feel safe and secure with money. And that feeling of security is one of the absolute best gifts you can give yourself.

CHAPTER 18

Start Over

I went off hormonal birth control a couple years ago, and it honestly changed my life. In the beginning, though, it was a nightmare. I came off the pill, and my hormones went wild. I was breaking out, constantly feeling bloated and nauseous, moody, and overall miserable. I figured all those reactions made sense as my body adjusted, but a surprising side effect was that my spending felt completely out of control, too.

See, as my hormones (and, therefore, my body and mental state) were out of alignment, my finances were also affected. When it came to spending, at times I felt out of control trying to align my spending to a physical, emotional, and mental state that was in chaos. That intuition we were talking about tapping into earlier? It felt buried. And quite frankly, not being able to feel my intuition was defeating and exhausting. The voices of The Hulk and The Bitch were popping up in my head, fighting for my attention. I felt like I was failing.

However, instead of seeing this as a failure, I wanted to

understand what was going on with my body, so I started investing in courses, programs, and mentors who could help me understand how to find balance holistically in my hormones and body. Then, as a grown-ass woman, I learned for the first time about the four phases of your hormonal cycle, how it worked, and how to balance your hormones naturally.

No, this book is not taking a hard U-turn into women's hormones or trying to convince you to go off hormonal birth control. However, this experience led me to two very big conclusions:

1. You aren't broken.

I was so mad at myself for "failing" at spending in alignment that I overlooked such an important message: my body wasn't broken; it was working to communicate with me. And you are not broken for experiencing times when it's harder to spend in alignment.

You see, the practice of aligned spending lasts your entire life. There is never a point where you will be done spending, because living in a capitalist society requires spending money for our needs to be met. And since spending is an almost daily part of our lives, you simply cannot set the expectation that you will never accidentally spend out of alignment. What you can do instead is stop looking at those times when you spend out of alignment, or fall short of your goal, as a "mess up" or "failure." You aren't messing up—you are living. Living can be messy and confusing, and there likely will be times when your body and life feel out of alignment, making it difficult to find alignment in your spending.

There will be times when it's harder to spend in alignment due to the natural highs and lows of life. We'll all experience grief, sadness, heartbreak, loss, and defeat, but also excitement, joy, hope, and happiness. In these moments, it can be difficult to feel aligned, because you are riding the wave of your emotions instead of experiencing alignment with your body.

There also can be times when your alignment shifts during the month due to natural ebbs and flows of female hormones. The male hormonal cycle is 24 hours, and our entire culture is built upon that hormonal structure (meaning the standard 9-to-5 workday and how we structure our days). However, female hormones are on a 28-day cycle.[1] Consequently, there may be times throughout the month when you feel more likely to spend impulsively, particularly when your hormones drop suddenly. Instead of looking at your body as a failure, take time to understand what is going on internally so you can love your body for communicating with you and even anticipate how you might feel at different phases of your cycle.

If you end up spending out of alignment in these moments of highs, lows, or hormonal changes, it's time to remember my second conclusion:

2. Start over.

There will be times when you won't spend in alignment. There will be times when you feel like you went completely off the rails and "screwed up." Here's your reminder to keep showing up. It might feel easier to say, "Forget it. I messed up. I'll try again next month." But we're working on sustainability here; we're not getting sidetracked by short-term roadblocks or detours.

When there's no guilt or shame surrounding finances, even if you spent out of alignment, you are always able to take a deep breath, come back to your spend plan, and update it going forward. No one is here to yell at you for going over the amount you planned. No one is here to nitpick how you're spending your money. No one is here to judge your spending. Here, in this space, you are safe to return to your spend plan, with new information and experiences, and forge forward. It's safe to change your mind, update your plans, and keep going.

There might be times your old friends The Hulk and The Bitch pop up in your mind. When they do, even if you listen to them and impulsively spend or restrict in the moment, that's okay. The main barrier to getting ahead with money isn't the one-off moment of random impulse spending. In fact, those moments are rites of passage along the way of changing and updating years and years of old beliefs about money. The main barrier in this journey is when we allow shame and guilt to pop up and talk us out of starting over, or tell us to put off starting over. That ends here.

So start over. It's easy to be all in when things are going well, your emergency fund is complete, your bills are on autopay, and your investments are growing. But what happens when you get a surprise hospital bill, you just got invited on a vacation or trip that'll cost more than your rent, and you feel like you're losing control? Instead of having that "screw it" mentality and throwing in the towel on your financial dream life, it's so important to remember you're allowed to reroute, shift, and change your mind. Hell, you're even allowed to feel like you've made massive money "mistakes" and still return to your plan, update it, and keep going.

Spending in alignment matters because it breeds sustainability. Achieving sustainable results and working toward future goals while keeping your lifestyle now, without guilt and shame, will change everything. And often the reason it is so damn hard for us to start over in the first place is that it requires us to face the shame from "failing" in the first place. However, when we ditch shame, we are allowed to start over at any point without the negative self-talk or disappointment in ourselves. We get to constantly restart, update, reroute, and keep going, because shame is no longer welcome here. This will not only give you more freedom with money, it will allow you to enjoy the hell out of the process of building wealth.

As we wrap up our time together in this book, I want you to put your hand on your heart and trust that even if you don't know the exact path of how to reach the destination, your dream life was placed in your heart for a reason. The dream job, the dream partner, the dream family, the dream lifestyle, the dream bank account, or whatever it may be is something you are worthy of. And when those dreams come to fruition, they will impact so many other people than just yourself. You will use money to impact your life, then the lives around you, your community, then our world. Your impact with money is a powerful ripple effect, and while money will always be a factor in the pursuit of those dreams, money no longer comes with stress, guilt, or shame. Going forward, it is a neutral tool only. Going forward, you get to build wealth in a way that matters, knowing that your financial journey truly is Deeper Than Money.

Conclusion

You freaking did it. You've officially read this entire book and are now fully equipped with the strategy and mindset not only to build wealth, but also to enjoy the hell out of it along the way. And although you might feel fully prepared right now, I promise there will be moments when you feel like everything has gone off the rails. There will be times when you catch yourself doubting the process. Maybe life hits you with what feels like a million financial responsibilities at once, and you feel like every time you take one step forward you are knocked two steps back. I can't prevent those feelings, but I can provide words of encouragement for when times feel hard. So here's my final love letter to you in those times:

Take a moment to acknowledge that you have both a new belief in yourself and what's possible for you, and a strategy to make your dreams a reality. But now it's time to keep rolling ahead. As life comes at you, remember that your ultimate goal is to make money matter less. You need to allow your dreams and priorities to take center stage and use money as a way to fuel your goals. Today, I want you to write down something you are going to accomplish:

____

____

____

I want you to think about how unbelievably excited you will be to have accomplished that goal.

I want you to think about telling others about that accomplishment.

I want you to think about what accomplishing that goal would do for your life—apart from the money.

Maybe your goal is to buy a house. Instead of thinking of the equity you could acquire in your portfolio, I want you to ground yourself in thinking about raising a family there, hosting all your friends, drinking your morning coffee on the porch, or growing your career in your home office. Tie that goal to something beyond the money. Let's say your goal is to become debt-free. Okay, amazing. Now look beyond the money. What's there? Freedom. Being able to book the trip at the drop of a hat because you no longer have that monthly student loan payment. Being able to say no to picking up the overtime shift now that your car is paid off, and spending that time with family instead. Think beyond the money. Think Deeper Than Money.

Yes, you might get overwhelmed or feel like you're never going to hit your goals. And on those days, get your comfort snack and your favorite oversize blanket, and cry it out. Vent to someone (bonus points if it's your therapist) and then come back to who the F you are. You are the girl who gets to be wealthy. You are the girl who takes her wealth and does powerful things for herself. Who does powerful things for her family and friends. Who does powerful things for her community. See, as you grow your wealth, you become a drop of rain in a pond creating a ripple effect. You first change your own life and then you start to make an impact on those around you. You have more money to make more of an impact on the causes you care about, and you have the resources to share with those who don't currently know how to get ahead with money. Your financial journey and successes are so much more than money, and both are so much more than you. You getting ahead with money means more good in the world and more people invited to this conversation.

You getting ahead with money matters. You matter. Your dreams matter. And you don't need to use willpower to stick to a budget. Use your priorities. Use excitement. Use alignment. Do it sustainably. Do it with fun. Do it big. Do it your way.

I love you, and I'm here cheering you on.

Chloe Elise

Update: After finishing my manuscript for this book, but before it went off for final publishing, I officially hit my goal of becoming a millionaire at 27 years old.

Acknowledgments

Mom: You are the reason.

Dad: For teaching me it's the journey.

GMO, Dommy, and Pickle: For being my favorite people. I love you.

Keagan, Shaley, Cinnamon, and the entire Deeper Than Money team: For believing in my wild dreams and spending your days bringing them to fruition.

Maria: For dropping everything to help me, and for reminding me that it's never too late to reinvent yourself.

Eric, my agent: For taking a chance on me, signing me, and teaching me how to become an author.

Erin, my mentor: For being no bullshit, advocating for me, and being a powerful force in the finance industry.

Lauren, Ashley, and the PRH team: For taking a chance on

this book and spending so much time in the pages to make it all it is today.

My best friends, who, if you're single in your 20s, truly become your family:

Brenna, Zek, The Council, Katrina and Steven, Mik, Cinn, Hailee, Smalls, Ky and Josh, Riley, Kenz and Matt, Mickey, Silv, Colton, Lathan, Evan and Mileah, Jake, Candace, G, Taylor, and Muggs: For being my village. I am me because I have you.

Polly: For teaching me how to lead with confidence.

Z: For being the most level-headed person I know. You're it.

Whitney, my therapist: For holding space for me and keeping me accountable. I wouldn't have grown into the person I am today without your guidance.

My grandmas and the rest of my family: For supporting me even though this book probably has a few too many f-bombs for your liking.

Rosie and Millie (yes, I'm thanking my dogs, let me live): For sitting beside me through every single word of this book.

Hallie: For making me an aunt and teaching me the importance of leaving a legacy. You should really learn how to read so you can catch up on this book.

To the girl's girls, the ones who carve out paths and say, "Follow me": For believing we all get to rise together—that's power.

My future bajillionaires: For asking for this book, inspiring me constantly, and creating a finance community that is fun as hell.

Notes

Chapter 1: Deeper Than Money

1. Norman B. Anderson et al., *Stress in America: Paying with Our Health*, American Psychological Association, February 4, 2015, 1–23, https://www.apa.org/news/press/releases/stress/2014/stress-report.pdf.

Chapter 3: Ancestral Bullshit

1. "Your Stone Age Brain," Psychology Tools, accessed August 22, 2022, https://www.psychologytools.com/resource/your-stone-age-brain/.
2. Srini Pillay, "How to Deal with Unfamiliar Situations," *Harvard Business Review*, March 13, 2014, https://hbr.org/2014/03/how-to-deal-with-unfamiliar-situations.
3. David Whitebread and Sue Bingham, "Habit Formation and Learning in Young Children," The Money Advice Service, May 2013, https://mascdn.azureedge.net/cms/the-money-advice-service-habit-formation-and-learning-in-young-children-may2013.pdf.
4. Gayani DeSilva, quoted in Claire Gillespie, "What Is Generational Trauma?" *Health*, updated November 14, 2022, https://www.health.com/condition/ptsd/generational-trauma.
5. Brian G. Dias and Kerry J. Ressler, "Parental Olfactory Experience Influences Behavior and Neural Structure in Subsequent Generations,"

Nature Neuroscience 17, no. 1 (2014): 89, https://doi.org/10.1038/nn.3594.

6. Curtis J. Simon, "The Supply Price of Labor during the Great Depression," *The Journal of Economic History* 61, no. 4 (December 2001): 877, http://www.jstor.org/stable/2697910.

Chapter 4: Justin Bieber Is Hot . . . Isn't That the Truth?

1. E. Garcia-Rill, "Reticular Activating System," in *Encyclopedia of Neuroscience*, ed. Larry R. Squire (California: Academic Press, 2009), 137–143.
2. Emily Kwong, "Understanding Unconscious Bias," July 15, 2020, in *Short Wave*, produced by NPR, podcast, MP3 audio, 13:55, https://www.npr.org/transcripts/891140598.

Chapter 5: I'm Behind

1. Amy Summerville, "Is Comparison Really the Thief of Joy?," *Psychology Today*, March 21, 2019, https://www.psychologytoday.com/us/blog/multiple-choice/201903/is-comparison-really-the-thief-joy.

Chapter 6: Main Character Energy

1. "Your Spending Data May Reveal Aspects of Your Personality," Association for Psychological Science, July 17, 2019, https://www.psychologicalscience.org/news/releases/spending-data-personality.html.

Chapter 8: Money Thermostat

1. Nicole Bitette, "Curse of the Lottery: Tragic Stories of Big Jackpot Winners," *New York Daily News*, January 12, 2016, https://www.nydailynews.com/life-style/tragic-stories-lottery-winners-article-1.2492941.

Chapter 9: Shame in the Financial Industry

1. Michelle Fox, "To Combat Financial Illiteracy, Education Needs to Start Early in the Classroom, Advocates Say," CNBC, April 5, 2021, https://www.cnbc.com/2021/04/05/state-of-personal-finance-education-in-the-us.html.
2. Chris Melore, "Are You Financially Literate? Most Parents Wish They Knew More About Money Growing Up," StudyFinds, January 13, 2021,

https://studyfinds.org/financially-literate-most-parents-wish-they-knew-more-about-money-childhood/.

3. "Not All Women Gained the Vote in 1920," PBS, July 6, 2020, https://www.pbs.org/wgbh/americanexperience/features/vote-not-all-women-gained-right-to-vote-in-1920.
4. "Not All Women Gained the Vote in 1920."
5. "Not All Women Gained the Vote in 1920."
6. Ron Sanders, "The History of Women and Money in the United States in Honor of Women's History Month," One Advisory Partners, March 7, 2017, https://www.oneadvisorypartners.com/blog/the-history-of-women-and-money-in-the-united-states-in-honor-of-womens-history-month.
7. Brian Kreiswirth and Anna-Marie Tabor, "What You Need to Know about the Equal Credit Opportunity Act and How It Can Help You: Why It Was Passed and What It Is," Consumer Financial Protection Bureau, October 31, 2016, https://www.consumerfinance.gov/about-us/blog/what-you-need-know-about-equal-credit-opportunity-act-and-how-it-can-help-you-why-it-was-passed-and-what-it.
8. "H.R.5050—100th Congress (1987–1988): Women's Business Ownership Act of 1988," Congress.gov, October 25, 1988, https://www.congress.gov/bill/100th-congress/house-bill/5050.
9. Emily A. Shrider et al., "Income and Poverty in the United States: 2020," United States Census Bureau, September 2021, https://www.census.gov/content/dam/Census/library/publications/2021/demo/p60-273.pdf.
10. Michelle Singletary, "Credit Scores Are Supposed to Be Race-Neutral. That's Impossible," *Washington Post*, October 16, 2020, https://www.washingtonpost.com/business/2020/10/16/how-race-affects-your-credit-score/.
11. Candace Jackson, "What Is Redlining?," *New York Times*, August 17, 2021, https://www.nytimes.com/2021/08/17/realestate/what-is-redlining.html.
12. Jennifer Hasso, "Redlining," Ferris State University, Jim Crow Museum, 2021, https://www.ferris.edu/HTMLS/news/jimcrow/question/2021/february.htm.

Chapter 13: The Holy Grail

1. Christopher Bergland, "Trust Your Gut—There's Nothing Woo-Woo About the Vagus Nerve," *Psychology Today,* September 23, 2016,

https://www.psychologytoday.com/us/blog/the-athletes-way/201609/trust-your-gut-theres-nothing-woo-woo-about-the-vagus-nerve.

2. Katrina Rae Swanson, email message to author, August 1, 2022.

Chapter 14: Your Living Plan

1. Adam McCann, "Average Credit Card Interest Rates," WalletHub, February 23, 2023, https://wallethub.com/edu/cc/average-credit-card-interest-rate/50841.

Chapter 15: Match My Vibe, Elevate It, or GTFO

1. Dragana Kovacevic, "Old School Parenting Advice That We Need to Stop Telling Our Kids," *Slice*, updated October 22, 2020, https://www.slice.ca/old-school-parenting-advice-that-we-need-to-stop-telling-our-kids/.

Chapter 16: Getting Alien Probed: Financial Surprises Suck

1. Krysten Crawford, "America's Medical Debt Is Much Worse Than We Think," Stanford University Institute for Economic Policy Research, July 20, 2021, https://siepr.stanford.edu/news/americas-medical-debt-much-worse-we-think.
2. Kelly Gooch, "Medical Billing Errors Growing, Says Medical Billing Advocates of America," Becker's Hospital Review, April 12, 2016, https://www.beckershospitalreview.com/finance/medical-billing-errors-growing-says-medical-billing-advocates-of-america.html.
3. Richard Eisenberg, "Medical Bills: Even Worse Than You Thought," *Forbes*, October, 8, 2014, https://www.forbes.com/sites/nextavenue/2014/10/08/medical-bills-even-worse-than-you-thought/?sh=5e3c34031e56.
4. Michelle Fox, "40% of Americans with Credit Card Debt Don't Know Their Interest Rate, Survey Shows," CNBC, January 10, 2022, https://www.cnbc.com/2022/01/10/40percent-of-americans-with-credit-card-debt-dont-know-their-interest-rate.html.

Chapter 17: Money Condoms: Protecting Your Wealth

1. "National Rates and Rate Caps," Federal Deposit Insurance Corporation, August 15, 2022, updated March 20, 2023, https://www.fdic.gov/resources/bankers/national-rates/.
2. Colton Storla, text message to author, August 18, 2022.
3. "What's the Difference Between Long Term and Short Term Disability Insurance?," Guardian Life, accessed August 22, 2022, https://www.guardianlife.com/disability-insurance/long-term-vs-short-term.

4. Devon Delfino, "What Is Term Life Insurance?," *U.S. News & World Report*, last reviewed January 11, 2023, https://www.usnews.com/insurance/life-insurance/term-life-insurance.
5. "What Is a Will?," Fidelity, accessed August 22, 2022, https://www.fidelity.com/life-events/estate-planning/will.
6. Kristin Wong, "There's a Stress Gap Between Men and Women. Here's Why It's Important," *New York Times,* November 14, 2018, https://www.nytimes.com/2018/11/14/smarter-living/stress-gap-women-men.html.
7. Bradley T. Klontz et al., "Disordered Money Behaviors: Development of the Klontz Money Behavior Inventory," *Journal of Financial Therapy* 3, no. 1 (June 2012): 21, https://newprairiepress.org/jft/vol3/iss1/2/.

Chapter 18: Start Over

1. "Male Hormone Cycle," Hormonology, accessed August 22, 2022, https://www.myhormonology.com/learn/male-hormone-cycle/.

About the Author

Chloe Elise is the CEO and founder of Deeper Than Money, a global financial literacy company dedicated to empowering and educating people on how to build guilt-free wealth. After paying off more than $36,000 of debt in 18 months, becoming debt-free at 22 years old, she watched her life transform as she learned how to build wealth without giving up her lifestyle. Elise then started on a mission to become a millionaire before she turned 28 years old and officially hit her goal in 2023, becoming a millionaire at 27 years old.

Elise was born and raised in Iowa but now lives in Kansas City, Missouri, with her two pups, Rosie and Millie. She is a financial expert and host of a top finance podcast, and her work has been featured in *The New York Times*, NextAdvisor, *Yahoo! Finance*, and MarketWatch, to name a few. She has worked with thousands of clients around the globe to provide education on debt management, investing, and finances through the Deeper Than Money method—a holistic approach to using money in a way that is emotionally, mentally, and logistically aligned with who we are today and who we want to become. Elise believes that financial education is more than learning how to budget, pay off debt, or save for retirement. It's about the freedom that financial stability can provide and being able to live life to the fullest, feel confident, give generously, and improve the lives of those around us.